SAN PEDRO HUACHUMA

Opening the Pathways of The Heart

JAVIER REGUEIRO

A map for the exploration of consciousness through plant medicine

Dedicated to the People and Land of Peru for their
generosity, wisdom, and kindness.

"If the truth can be told so as to be understood it will be believed."
Terence McKenna

"The truth lies not in one dream but in many dreams."
From *The Arabian Nights*

CONTENTS

PROLOGUE

Dear Reader,

This book is an invitation to explore and reconnect with our inner landscapes with the help of San Pedro, also known in South America as Huachuma. San Pedro (*Echinopsis pachanoi*) is a psychoactive cactus native of the Andes, but more importantly it's an ancestral medicine that has been used for millennia for healing and ceremonial purposes.

As more and more people who are foreign to this part of the world and its history, culture, and traditions are feeling called to engage with this Plant Teacher, it is only natural that we should face different challenges than Andean natives when engaging in this process, and that the medicine we may need and receive as modern people be different. Our psychic and psychological make-up differs radically from that of Andean people, and our needs as modern people differ just as much from the needs of the ancestors and inhabitants of this land. The challenge then is to bridge such cultural gap in ways that honor the wealth of wisdom gathered through centuries of native studies and experimentation, and at the same time address our present day state of emotional disconnection and spiritual confusion, which are at the root of most physical, emotional, and mental diseases.

In order to explore parts of our inner landscapes that may have long been rejected and deserted, and that as a result may feel completely foreign and inaccessible, it is often helpful to draw on the wisdom of those who have explored those regions before us. In my case I entered the world of plant medicine and shamanism already equipped with tools developed by teachers and masters of various spiritual and psychological traditions that proved to be most helpful in further exploring my consciousness and the ways in which it expressed and manifested itself. Furthermore, I have benefitted from the wisdom and knowledge of several plant medicine people and teachers who have shared over the years and in their unique fashion their healing ways and arts with me. Last but not least, it has been my own personal healing journey with San Pedro and the healing process I have facilitated for my clients since 2006 that have taught me the most about my own inner landscape as well as the unique healing properties of this medicine. With all of this experiential knowledge I have written this book and drawn this map with the hope that it may help others benefit as much as possible from engaging with this medicine.

As you will read over and over in these pages, I believe the spiritual and healing paths are not about what we want, but about exploring and facing what we need to embrace and learn as part of our journey. It is for this reason that much of this book is devoted to topics that are often easily overlooked but nonetheless essential to any meaningful exploration of consciousness. Plant medicine is an organic and logical system that teaches us about the wisdom of plant conscious-ness for our own growth and development. The most important part of a plant is the root, the part that is most connected with the densest of elements: Earth. And so we begin in Part II by exploring our own land-scape in its densest manifestations: the physical body and the challenges of this earthly human experience.

Various spiritual paths and doctrines are essentially transcendental: they mire at a different realm, be it Heaven, Nirvana, or other states not bound by phys-icality and conventional physics, as the ultimate goal of human experience. Plant medicine may open the door to expanded viewpoints and realities that make 3-D existence seem laughable, but it will always also bring us back into our bodies, no matter how much we may have resisted that purely physical experience in the past. Such reconnection to our bodies, often brought about through physical purging, is an essential part of this process as much information and wisdom is stored in our very cells and organs.

As modern people we suffer deeply not only from not living in our bodies but also from feeling culturally uprooted by living in societies that have forsaken their own traditions and ancestral connections. The themes connected with ancestral healing will be explored in Part IV.

The deepest of our uprooting though may be the spir-itual disconnection from our divinity, and this discon-nection manifests itself on all levels of our being. We shall therefore continue exploring the ways in which this disconnection manifests on the emotional level in Part III by addressing emotional healing, and the healing of our minds in Part V. The emotional and mental aspects of our lives are the basic modus operandi of our psychological existence, and in today's world they are the levels on which most of us operate in our daily lives. They are also the ways in which we express our spirits, and the way in which our souls continue their journey on this plane of existence. Throughout this book I mention the soul wounds of rejection, abandonment, betrayal, injustice, and humiliation. These wounds are acted out in our psychology and played out most early in our childhood and youth with our imme-diate relations. The healing of these wounds is what I believe we incarnate in this bodies and planet for, and their healing brings about also a reconciling with our families, which are also a basic aspect of our roots in this world. Our families are not only our roots but also the foundation of our being, therefore addressing our relations and healing the wounds we played out with them is a necessary and important step in our spiritual growth. I believe that our bodies, emotions, minds, and relationships are not nuisances to be avoided at all costs through denial, self-mortification, and other spiri-tual practices, but the very vehicles through which we express our innermost essence and eventually realize ourselves as integral parts and expression of Divinity, which is why so many pages are devoted to exploring just such aspects of our being.

Part VI is dedicated to the heart and to the explora-tion of themes related to the infinite space and imma-terial nature of the direction of the Center. The source of all Creation, including ourselves, and the heart of it all are dimensions that defy definition because they are spaces of pure and yet dynamic emptiness: it is the place of the intelligence of all Life. It is not irrational, but it does challenge human understanding and rational logic. In order to embrace and be embraced by such infinite source we seem to have no alternative but relinquish our need to understand it logically, to stop thinking about it, and simply experience and celebrate such infinite well of divine energy, wisdom, and love. The process is not about *gaining* knowledge but about *letting go* of our constructs, our mental boundaries, and limiting beliefs, both individual and collective. It is when we let go of our emotional and mental baggage, when we have the courage to let go of the distorting lenses we unconsciously wear, that ultimate reality is perceived in its full glory, ultimate lovingness, and benevolence.

Part VII addresses the challenges and importance of returning to our daily lives after engaging with San Pedro. Integration is in my opinion the most important part of this process. The culture and spirituality of the people of the Andes have traditionally been earth-based and most pragmatic: until the arrival of Catholicism its focus had always been, so to speak, to bring Heaven down here on Earth rather than seeking Heaven elsewhere. Such attitude of immanence and embodiment has undoubtedly been informed also by centuries of engaging with San Pedro as well as many other plant medicines, which is why plant medicine was systematically demonized by the Catholic Church here in South America as well as anywhere else on the planet. But centuries of spiritual, sexual, and emotional oppression and self-repression have only diminished us as human beings and have created a dysfunctional attitude that affects not only our relationship with ourselves and others, but towards our home planet as well. After exploring our own selves and experiencing the reconnection with our hearts and everything that surrounds us, it is only natural to revisit our earthly existence in the view of such intrinsic connectedness of the Universe, and to explore once again the terrain and environment our roots are in and from which our wellbeing so deeply depends. It is just as important to see how our existence shapes and contributes to Life as a whole: the biggest but also most rewarding challenge of plant medicine is the process of each one of us bringing back to our everyday life the blessings, the expanded awareness, and the openheartedness experienced through this medicine.

It is obvious to those who have engaged in this process that our societies, cultures, and the planet at large have been benefitting enormously from the impact, small and big, of every individual who has engaged in this process. And I feel that the support of this and other Plant Teachers is most important at this time in human history, which is why the final portion of this book is dedicated to raising awareness about the challenges of foreigners and modern people engaging in this process in the 21st century in Appendix I, and to nurturing on an individual and collective level a culture of plant medicine that is safe, responsible, and respectful in Appendix II. I believe that by exercising personal and collective responsibility whenever and wherever we engage with ancestral plant medicines, we will be able to continue benefitting from such an invaluable source of healing and wisdom. As a teacher of mine wisely pointed out to me, it is not information that is power but the *use* of such information.

In this book you will not find any secret formula or esoteric solution to your so-called problems. This is because the spiritual and healing process of plant medicine is one of letting go, including letting go of the need for secret formulas. Someone pointed out to me recently that the spiritual journey is one of subtraction, i.e., of letting go of our constructs, rather than addition. At the end of such journey all that is left is the awareness of our loving essence and our hearts, which is identical to the essence of Creation. In the best of scenarios you may then resonate with this sacred plant's invitation to reconnect with yourself, others, and the entire Universe with a more open heart, renewed enthusiasm, and a greater and deeper appreciation for all Life.

I

BEGINNINGS

Cusco, The spiritual journey, Plant medicine

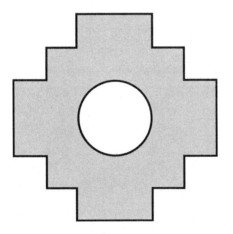

INTRODUCTION

When I decided back in 2005, upon my second visit to Peru, to study Amazonian plant medicine, that decision stemmed primarily from my interest in working with Ayahuasca, a traditional medicinal brew of the Amazon jungle. When later that year I decided to move to the Sacred Valley of the Incas in the province of Cusco, Peru, in order to pursue my work with Ayahuasca, that decision was informed by the realization that my journey, which had begun in the jungle, would also eventually take me to explore the physical and spiritual world of the high mountains that surround the city of Cusco as well.

The country of Peru is magnificently diverse, both in ecosystems and cultures, and my choice of the Sacred Valley happened in November 2005 at the ruins of Moray when I first drank San Pedro by myself. That day I intuited that one of the main reasons the Incas had chosen the Cusco region as the center of their empire was because of the uniqueness of its physical and energetic landscape. The Sacred Valley is a beautiful valley at the eastern edge of the Andes and its main water course, the river Willkamayu, which means "Sacred River" in the Quechua language and has its source in the Altiplano close to Lake Titicaca, runs through the gorges that surround Machu Picchu and eventually arrives in the jungle where it becomes one of the most important emissaries of the great Amazon river. That day in Moray I felt the energy of the jungle sneaking up this river through Machu Picchu and the Sacred Valley, and at the same time I could feel the energy of the glaciers and the crystalline vibration of these high mountains descend and mingle with the rising energies of the jungle in this place where I was sitting and which I decided then and there would be my new home. In that moment it became clear to me that this journey, which had begun in the jungle, would one day take me all the way to the mountain-tops. In a parallel way, the journey that had begun with Ayahuasca would lead me eventually to deeply explore not only the physical and spiritual dimensions of the Andes but also one of its most important medi-cines and sacraments: San Pedro.

In a similar way, when I decided to work for Ayahuasca, which at the time to me meant leading Ayahuasca ceremonies and support those wishing to engage with this medicine for healing and spiritual growth, and later on embarked on the long adven-ture of writing and publishing a book about it[1], I never thought I would be working with San Pedro as intensely and intimately as I do, let alone write another book dedicated this time to this wonderful medicine of the Andes. The idea of writing this book has been growing for a few years now and for a variety of reasons, but most importantly because the more I work with San Pedro, the more unique qualities I've been discovering in this medicine, and the more poignant these qualities seem to me for us in the 21st century.

In this book I will be mentioning and sometimes repeating things I had already written about in my previous book, but this is not just a repackaging of ideas in order to sell books. Once again the main reason for writing a book about plant medicine is the wish to share

---

[1] Regueiro, Javier. *Ayahuasca, Soul Medicine of the Amazon Jungle*. Las Vegas, Lifestyle Entrepreneurs Press, 2017.

my viewpoint and what little wisdom I have gathered in working with this medicine for the last ten years with the hope that this will help you, dear reader, benefit most from the healing qualities, the teachings, and the blessings of this medicine.

My interest in plant medicine has always been about the healing qualities of this process. My approach to San Pedro is not anthropological nor historical, but based on Amazonian plant medicine, and therefore my insights are based on the direct and personal experience I have gathered through my own process with this medicine and that of the many people I have guided in working with it over the years. In this ever-deepening relationship San Pedro has not only opened the doors to my heart but also into the wisdom of this land, teaching me the ways of these mountains and the entire Cosmos, and how to be in harmonious relation with them.

Plant medicine, and shamanism in general, is a deeply subjective and empirical science and art based not on theory but on direct experience and interaction with all aspects of the Cosmos. I'm not writing this book in order to establish some sort of orthodoxy or create a doctrine or dogma, and least of all to find validation for my beliefs and experiences. I'm writing this book simply to *share* my viewpoint, and every sentence in this book should be prefaced with the awareness that everything I say is just my opinion and nothing more. If you find it useful, great. And if you don't resonate with it, then feel free to dismiss it.

The core of this book is about the often conflictive relationship in modern men and women between the mind and the heart. In our times the mind has increasingly become the most dominant aspect of our being, and one of the consequences of such need for dominance is the, in my opinion, ironically laughable and endless quest for all-encompassing theories about everything. It is rather ridiculous that we hold the belief that the pinnacle of our human experience should be the impossible capacity to rationally translate the inexpressible into words and to "scientifically and objectively" explain the Great Mystery of existence.

In the end, or at least this has been my experience so far, the dynamics and patterns of life (both personal and universal) are quite simple and not devoid of logic, but a logic that beautifully transcends the need for the mind to aggrandize itself through complicated abstractions that only lead to often empty intellectualisms and support the idea of an intellectual, philosophical, and spiritual elite that we ought to devote all of our efforts to join as soon as possible and by whatever means necessary.

It is my sincere hope that you will find this book helpful, clarifying, and inspiring for your own journey and life. More so than in my first book I am sharing from my own personal experience and beliefs. This is in many ways my "spiritual coming out" book: growing up as a young gay boy I quickly learned the pros and cons of hiding parts of myself in a closet. As a young adolescent growing up in a Catholic environment I just as quickly became sensitive to dogmas of any kind and I've always preferred a certain vagueness when expressing my spiritual beliefs for fear of sounding like those clergy people I had come to dislike. Many years later, and having let go of all these judgments and projections, and the shame that had kept me silent, I'm ready to come out of my spiritual closet without the fear of sounding like I'm preaching to anybody and I hope that my language clearly reflects my attitude.

The native people of Peru have been experiencing a similar healing in the last thirty years: after centuries of shaming, persecution, and humiliation at the hand of the Spanish Conquistadores, the fierce arm of the Catholic church, and various ways of religious and cultural Inquisition, the people of Peru are now (and this is in particular due to the sincere interest foreigners and tourists increasingly show) reconnecting, honoring, and celebrating their ancestral ways.

The renaissance of ancestral wisdom among more and more people all across the world in the last century has been phenomenal, and the newly found openness to sharing this knowledge and wisdom with other people has tremendously enriched not only tribes, ethnic and religious groups, but our collective consciousness as a whole.

The European scientific revolution of the 17th century sure brought a flattening of the spiritual landscape but also opened the way for a more open-minded exploration of non-Western cultures; in the end it was the progressive desacralization of our world and psyche in the name of progress that has pushed us to the four corners of this Earth looking for ways to reconnect with ourselves and our environment in a once again meaningful way.

It was very much in that spirit and along such a spiritual quest that I first came to Peru in 2004....

Cusco

In October 2004 I headed to Peru with a group of twenty people to go to the jungle outside Pucallpa and drink Ayahuasca for two weeks. This was the midpoint of a yearlong round-the-world trip I had started earlier that spring. I arrived in Peru not knowing what to expect but in definite need of healing as I was still struggling with a painful romantic breakup that had reawakened all my wounds and insecurities. My time in the jungle was most precious in that it allowed me to reconnect with myself as a friend: I was the first one to be surprised when during an Ayahuasca ceremony I realized how deeply I had neglected and resented myself while unsuccessfully looking for love and acceptance outside of myself.

After the jungle I flew to Cusco and went straight to Paz y Luz Guesthouse in Pisac. I had found the listing in my travel guidebook and little did I know I would eventually be living next door to it. A friend who had been to Cusco and Machu Picchu a couple of years earlier had told me about participating in a San Pedro ceremony during his visit to this area and I found myself hoping to find someone with whom to drink this medicine I really knew nothing about. Mountain people seem often more closed and reserved, and an aura of mystery clearly surrounded, at least from an outsider's point of view such as mine at the time, these fabled and powerful Andean shamans and medicine people.

Two weeks later, as I rode the train from Aguas Calientes back to Cusco, the giant cacti along the way renewed my curiosity. At the time there weren't nearly as many people offering San Pedro ceremonies as today, but eventually (and serendipitously) I made the acquaintance of Lesley Myburgh, a South African woman who had been leading San Pedro ceremonies for a while and who ran a lovely guesthouse, Casa de la Gringa, in Cusco, which was a sweet meeting point of adventurous spiritual explorers such as myself. After talking to Lesley for half an hour and feeling comfortable with her loving attitude and energy, I decided to sign up for her next ceremony. The following day we met in the morning and went to a eucalyptus grove not far from the Temple of the Moon outside of Cusco for my first San Pedro ceremony.

Many things happened that day, but the most important one was finding myself sitting inside this ancestral temple carved into a hill and spontaneously opening the poetry book *Love Poems from God*[2] to read out loud the poem by Hafiz, *The Woman I Love*. As I finished reading this poem, a thought arose from deep in my soul which said, "because the man and the woman I love live inside of me, I am marrying thee today." It was thus that I unexpectedly ended up marrying myself. It was November 9, 2004. I know because I wrote this vow in my poetry book and had my ceremony companions sign it as witnesses. I share this with you because in that simple gesture I feel is encapsulated the whole message of San Pedro: an invitation to let go of judgment, heal, and forgive so that we can embrace and embody the loving essence of our true being.

---

[2] Ladinsky, Daniel, trans. *Love Poems from God*. New York, Penguin Compass, 2002.

THE SPIRITUAL JOURNEY

The spiritual journey, and the plant medicine path is one among the many tools available to us all to further such a journey, is a journey home towards ourselves. And nothing else. I say "nothing else" because at the end of this journey we realize that not only are we part of everything, but also that everything is already inside of us, so in order to reconnect with everything outside ourselves beyond the apparent limitations of space and time and without all boundaries created by our minds, all there is to do is embrace all that we are.

Such a journey home was never intended to be a straight line from A to B, but more akin to a multidimensional labyrinth with a unique and ever changing layout for each individual. The classic Western model for such a journey is imagined as an ascending line, whereas my experience has been one of a spiraling—both inwards and outwards, and with peaks and abysses, plateaux, and culs-de-sac. If it's true that the lessons along the way may be identical for all, it is just as true that such lessons will unfold under unique circumstances for each one of us. As in this adventure there are few rules and no ready-made answers, I share my experience not as an example to follow but as an encouragement to others who may find themselves in similar predicaments.

Let's take as an example the experience of loss and grief: such an experience is usually accompanied by feelings of denial, anger, and sadness, fairly common for most human beings. And yet, the same experience of grieving may be the opportunity to learn and remember very different lessons for each individual: for some it may be forgiveness, for others letting go of the fear of dying or abandonment, and for others it may offer a lesson about love and compassion.

The same can be said about physical ailments, which, despite the long list of diagnostic books of both medical and metaphysical natures, are always experienced in a unique way by unique individuals in a very unique place and moment of their lives and soul journey.

As I write this it seems important to express my personal belief about what the purpose of the human experience is about. Since my early years I felt that life was not about paying taxes and the pursuit of a successful and well-paid career. At the age of 13 I read Hermann Hesse's *Siddhartha* and reading that book (and maybe a combination of youthful enthusiasm paired with hormonal outbursts) made me say to myself, "I want to know myself and I want to be happy."

In retrospect I can see that it was pure folly and that I was about to chew on a much bigger morsel than I had expected but then, to paraphrase a quote from Quentin Tarantino's *Kill Bill 1*[3] movie, if I had known it wasn't going to be nearly that easy, I most likely would not have made such a life choice.

That choice, I can see now with ironic clarity, was not a deliberate choice at all but the expression of a choice made on a soul level before this and many previous incarnations. And I believe that deep down we all share that choice, but with different curriculums and with a somewhat misleading idea of what happiness really is.

---

[3] Tarantino, Quentin. *Kill Bill Volume 1*, DVD, Burbank, Buena Vista Home Entertainment, 2004.

The idea of happiness is just that: an idea and an ideal that is most importantly a reflection of who we believe we are, and once again who we believe to be is just an idea, and that idea clearly falls short of the infiniteness of our being. The pursuit of what we call happiness changes with our perception of who we are: in a child it is the feeling of being cared for in the most physiological sense through food and comfort, later on it is about the relational and communitarian aspect of life as we expand the horizon to discover we are not alone but part of a family and a larger and larger community of human beings, and so on and so forth.

In each phase of our lives we pursue what feels important and do our best to fulfill our needs and desires. Such fulfillment we call happiness, but it's really just a temporary satiation that leads us to new needs and desires. Often our development, particularly at the psychological level, stops at some stage where we believe our needs and desires had not been met and we spend many years trying to fulfill them instead of accepting the reality of what happened and didn't happen in the past.

To know oneself will yield different answers and open us to new levels of awareness depending on who or what we believe that "self" to be. From where I stand today I can see that to know myself *is* indeed my source of happiness, that to have discovered the true essence of my being and to be able to honor and celebrate it is happiness in itself. And since that true self is immortal, the resulting happiness is not fleeting but eternal.

The process of knowing oneself through plant medicine is actually one of *remembering* rather than knowing: it is an uncovering and rediscovering of the seeds of wisdom we all carry within ourselves since the beginning of Creation. The main value of any spiritual path lies therefore in its ability to help us reconnect with our own innate wisdom.

I do also believe that self-realization, enlightenment, or whatever name you may think of to describe this longed for state of being and awareness, is not an end in itself: just like death, awakening is not an ending but an opening to a new reality and a deeper awareness of the beauty of Creation within everything and everybody, as well as the reawakening of our natural propensity to support others in embracing that awareness. The vow of the Bodhisattva to deliberately reincarnate in order to support the awakening of all beings is only one of the infinite ways in which all awakened spirits help us in coming home to our true selves. Once I experienced self-realization it was only logical and spontaneous for me to wish the same for others and do whatever I can in order for that to happen because in the end Heaven is truly heavenly when *all of us* are part of it.

I grew up in Europe, a very intellectual place where words and theories are prized above everything else, and spent my high school years reading about spirituality. It was only when at the age of 25 I moved to the United States with its own pragmatic and hands-on attitude that I actually started engaging in spiritual and ritual practices of all sorts. The shift was also one from reading about emotions, beliefs, and spiritual ideas to finally *exploring* and *experiencing* them.

Since my life at the time was a "problem," I was looking for solutions: solutions that would permanently erase such problems from my life and awareness. I see now how pervasive that attitude is and how many people are looking for permanent solutions to their so-called problems. One of the most frequent questions from my clients and friends is "when is this (healing process) ever going to end?" Oftentimes, particularly when we have been doing our best to heal certain core wounds for years and with all sorts of modalities only to find ourselves still having to deal with the same issues over and over again, we start seriously doubting that we will ever see the light at the end of the tunnel.

I have seen that light at the end of my long tunnel. At some point I had the distinct awareness that I had finally received the healing I had come seeking in this lifetime, but that didn't mean that I had stopped living: life is a continuous process of evolution. Even if I had reached, so to speak, some major goal, my life has continued since: I have gotten into more experiences that sometimes asked of me to reconsider my assumptions and beliefs; at other times I have chosen to expand on my life scope, and that has entailed the extension of forgiveness that hadn't been needed prior to that moment, or some healing on a more collective rather than individual level.

What has changed is my attitude, and at some point I did notice a radical shift in my willingness to explore my inner landscape and collective consciousness at large. What used to be perceived as a chore, i.e., looking inside myself whenever an issue or reaction resurfaced in my life, and therefore faced with a frown, became simply an important opportunity for growth and expansion and as a consequence met more and more with enthusiasm rather than discouragement. If it's true that in most cases the closer we get to our core wounds and fears, the stronger the resistances become, it is also true that after dealing with those core issues our lives shift radically from struggle into ease and an increased willingness to be present and alive.

When years later I moved to Peru, I learned from the people of this land how spirituality is not necessarily the abstract experience that I had envisioned thus far but something to *bring* into the world: the awareness of a larger picture is not acquired for its own sake but to actually *inform* in very practical ways our everyday life. It's really about walking our talk, and spending more time walking than just talking.

Concepts like love, self-love, or compassion are totally empty unless practiced, and it is only when embodied that they shine in all their beauty and power. The more I became aware of the importance of embodiment, which I will explore further later in this book, the more I became aware of how my search for spiritual growth had been a thinly disguised escape from *this* life and of how many people are unconsciously doing the same.

Many Eastern and Western philosophies and spiritual practices are often understood and practiced as methods of transcendence, of going beyond this level of reality onto a supposedly higher one. Buddhist enlightenment and Judeo-Christian salvation are often understood as ways to transcend the body and the emotional or more earthly aspects of life on this planet. Spirituality in the Amazon jungle and the Andes is not a search for something beyond this life but a series of practices and disciplines intended to make us more present to ourselves, others, and this life of ours: a life we often can't help but resent and feel overwhelmed by, but that turns out to be the greatest of blessings when embraced wholeheartedly.

So at some point I started exploring the part of myself that time and time again did not want to be here: the one that had been seeking transcendence or oblivion, that had been reluctant to be fully here to the point of even entertaining suicidal thoughts. It was an interesting process that led me to much self-forgiveness and a deeper compassion for other human beings who forget what a privilege and blessing it is to actually be in a body.

There is strong taboo against suicide in our culture and yet we all have had times of such discouragement that we have wished not to be alive, not to have to deal with ourselves, and life in general. A more sophisticated form of escape is often the pursuit of spiritual practices, including plant medicine, with the hope of never having to deal with life again so that we can sit comfortably with our eyes closed and a half smile on our faces. As sophisticated as it may seem, this reminds more of the classic psychoanalytical wish to return to an idealized womb where all of our needs would be met in perpetuity. Such wish is understandable but not, in my opinion, what the pursuit of spirituality and plant medicine are about.

Despite what doomsayers may say about it, the process of Creation is still far from fulfilling its divine purpose and therefore far from ending: the tune the Hindu Lord Shiva has been dancing to for millennia is still far from playing its final notes. What I feel we are being called to do at this time in history and as part of our evolutionary journey is to actually engage more and more with life rather than try escaping from it, and to remember that spirituality as an escape is no longer a lofty pursuit but a distraction. Spiritual practices, as well as the plant medicine path, are not substitutes for life but tools to help us engage with our lives and the life of this planet with more clarity and lightness of being.

Lastly, I would like to quote Claudio Naranjo who wrote that the healing process should only be viewed as supplementary help and not a substitute for self-care[4]. It is illusory, and I am all about the shedding of illusions, to hope and believe that our spiritual lives will culminate in us not having to deal with life just like some magic wand or potion; it is just as illusory to think that someone else, a guru, shaman, or plant medicine person, will one day appear and tell us what to do with our lives so that we don't have to ever make a decision again, and that if things go in undesirable ways there is someone we can blame for our dissatisfaction.

As my teacher, Gabrielle Roth, used to be fond of saying, "...life is a dance, and no one but yourself can dance your own dance."

PLANT MEDICINE

Many books have been written and much talking has been devoted in recent years in regards to traditional plant medicine and the benefits of altered states of consciousness in healing and therapeutic processes. Such investigation started in the West in the late 1800's with the exploration of altered states of consciousness through hypnosis in order to treat people affected by an increasing number of ailments that allopathic medicine and psychiatric care were unable to cure. With this rather revolutionary approach, new methodologies and medications were developed to reproduce schizoid states so that patients could reconnect with those past traumatizing events that had led them to schizophrenia with the hope of healing them.

---

[4] Naranjo, Claudio. *Character and Neurosis*. Nevada City, Gateways Inc., 1994.

16

At the same time psychoanalysis helped expand our view of the human experience with concepts such as the unconscious, archetypes, and so on. It was in particular thanks to the audacity and vision of Carl Gustav Jung that psychoanalysis moved beyond its initial scope of "fixing" people so that they could lead a "normal" bourgeois existence to a modality intended to support people through their psychological and spiritual crisis so that they could re-emerge from them not just functional but whole and reborn.

The article by Gordon Wasson in the May 1957 issue of Life Magazine about his recent discovery and experience of healing ceremonies in southern Mexico that entailed the ritual ingestion of Psilocybin mushrooms sparked a whole wave of young Westerners traveling around the world in search of ancient healing rituals involving the ingestion of mind-altering substances, just like I had done back in 2004. In fact, despite the great availability of both natural and synthetic hallucinogens and entheogens[5] in Western society, many people feel the call to engage with them in a more traditional and ceremonial way rather than recreationally or medically. This is partly because of the desire to reclaim some sense of sacredness, but also because of the increasing awareness of the power of plant medicines and the need to engage with them in as an ideal setting as possible.

Last but not least, it's important to know that the vast majority of people who nowadays feel drawn to this process are not interested in a psychedelic experience but in the beneficial results that we intuit plant medicine may offer us long after the effects of their

---

[5] Entheogens are substances, natural or synthesized, that promote the awareness of our intrinsic divinity.

17

ingestion have faded. I am surprised by the wide variety of people who participate in my retreats, many among whom have never even considered "getting high" or have long left any drug use behind. What drives most people to experience this process is a genuine desire to heal, expand, and grow.

For me plant medicine is essentially a healing process: it's not about trying or ingesting anything but about opening oneself to looking deep inside. I see Plant Teachers such as San Pedro, Ayahuasca, Peyote, etc. as the most easily audible of our brothers and sisters of the plant kingdom on this planet. Their teachings don't differ from the teachings of all other creatures, from quieter plants, from animals, creeks, mountains, and stars. The message I keep hearing is always the same: *come home; let go of your fear, pain, and sense of loneliness and separation so that you can thrive in the love that you are and the abundance of your infinite self as it is expressed and reflected in all of Creation.* It is a simple yet powerful invitation, as scary as it is appealing, and one that more and more people from all walks of life are eager to embrace. As our sense of alienation keeps intensifying and we increasingly continue to destroy this planet, the voice of these ambassadors of the natural kingdoms is being heard by more and more people, positively influencing the human race in beautiful ways.

Unlike politicians and religious people, whose main interest is to disempower people for their own agenda and benefit, plants have no interest in selling us more dogmas and limiting beliefs. There is no need for them to preach because they know that in our core, we *all* share the same truths. Their invitation is then for us to look inside, shed the lies and illusions that keep us small and frightened, and let go of old pains and hurts so that we can stand once again in the holiness and compassionate power of our true being, honoring that light within ourselves and everybody and everything else.

Sounds appealing? It sure is! When I first met my teacher in Amazonian plant medicine, Don Francisco Montes Shuña, I was so seduced by the power and benefit of shamanic diets[6] that I did not stop "dieting" until my physical body was completely shot and beginning to suffer from excessive purging and poor diet. And that was only the beginning: as the Buddhist saying goes, "once we hear of enlightenment, there is nothing else to do but pursue it until we experience it."

I feel it's important to share that plant medicine is not about plants, but about us: it is not an exotic flight into other dimensions but an immersion into the depths and heights of our own being.

Plant medicine is like all other spiritual paths: in this realm there are no magic pills nor shortcuts. Our quest for such magic pills, potions, and the perfectly easy way to get ourselves out of our rut is a remarkably human trait and something we can't altogether avoid but can increasingly become aware of so as not to fall into. The pursuit of effectiveness, a trait of the mind, pervades all aspects of our lives and of course colors the way we engage in spirituality as well. To this attitude pertains our constant search for strategies, models, gurus, and healers that will somehow shorten our journey or make it more palatable. But our hopes are often frustrated by the reality that there aren't and will never be any such shortcuts and that any good

---

[6] A description of the process of shamanic plant diets is in my book on Ayahuasca. Cit.

teacher will sooner or later make us cry with despair and scream with impatience and anger.

Plant medicine as I understand it is not kids' stuff. It will help us make peace with and heal that inner child that most of us carry inside ourselves and that is always ready to have a tantrum, but in order to do that we are asked to start behaving as responsible adults so that we can engage in this powerful process A: without unrealistic expectations, and B: without the impatience that often prevents us from receiving from this process all that it has to offer us.

The awakening process can be terrifying and shocking, something way different from the New Age fantasy of instantly gratifying peace and love, but more akin to Neo's experience after swallowing the red pill in the movie *Matrix*[7]: from the world as we used to know it with all its familiarity and perks we are thrown into an initially unknown territory that doesn't look like anything we had previously imagined and hoped for. Like I told myself the first time I entertained the idea of studying plant medicine in the jungle, "there is no glamour." Awakening is actually a process of letting go of glamour, with glamour in its original meaning as "illusion, something that doesn't really exist." I love that movie sequence because as liberating as the truth may be, it seldom offers the comfortable and familiar bliss of ignorance.

The quick answers and miraculous fixes that most of us can't refrain from hoping for are not only one of the main reasons why certain people fail to find what they are looking for, but they are part of the limited viewpoint we can eventually let go of if we engage in

---

[7] Wachowski Brothers. *The Matrix*. DVD, Burbank, Warner Home Video, 1999.

this process long enough and with the due patience and humility.

I can see the surprise in people and prospective clients' faces when I tell them with all seriousness and conviction that plant medicines are illusory medicines for illusory problems. This statement has them react with the understandable question "then, WHAT am I doing here?" Things get easier when I add that I believe there is nothing to fix, but that there is much to learn and honor from our past and present predicaments. I have realized with time that I need to repeat that statement over and over again: we are not here to fix anything—the real spiritual doctors and medicines are not here to fix or cure us, but to support us in realizing that there is nothing wrong with who we and other people are, and to support us in letting go of anything that may prevent us from being in that awareness.

There are many people, me included, who have read all the right books and will nod in agreement with the statement that we are all perfect just as we are, but to know that on an intellectual level and to actually *experience* and *be* that awareness and truth most of the time is another matter altogether, and a matter in which plant medicine has been more helpful to me personally than any other process and experience.

Of course, this is *my* own view of what this process is apparently all about, and more of a reflection of me, my medicine, and where I am along my journey. And from where I am today and believe myself and the world to be, I perceive everything and everybody to be an emanation and expression of Divine energy, which is why for me this process is primarily an *exploration* of our consciousness and the beliefs held therein.

Physical, emotional, mental, and energetic states are *all* expressions of this consciousness as are our diseases and ailments, our crises and confusion. Everything we express and manifest is for us to listen to and contemplate because therein lies the most accurate reflection of who we are being as a result of the beliefs we hold in our consciousness: our lives and world are a reflection of the beliefs we hold in our consciousness and the exploration of such beliefs within ourselves is the only way I know of bringing significant change within and out ourselves.

Unfortunately we are rarely who we tell ourselves we are: the lies and the limiting beliefs we hold often create a distorted and limited image of whom we are. We are creators who have forgotten about our creative essence, or have rejected it altogether in order to play helpless victims. But whether we embrace this truth about our essentially creative selves or not, we are still creating ourselves and our world nonetheless and who we create ourselves and the world as is simply a reflection of the beliefs, the desires, and the fears we hold in our consciousness. This is why I always view my clients' predicaments, whether physical or non-physical, as expressions of consciousness. Rather than trying to fix these expressions, I invite my clients to explore them all the way to their source in consciousness.

I, as many others, have spent plenty of time and energy trying to fix myself, to improve myself so that I would be someone other than myself. Eventually I discovered that what I was doing was not trying to improve myself but escape from myself and my own pain, wounds, and judgments: escaping was a valuable experience and absolutely the best I could do at the time. What I had been unaware of is that my attempts at healing myself came from the deep belief that there was something terribly wrong with me. Plant medicine, and San Pedro in particular, taught me with time the erroneousness of my thinking and combative attitude towards myself, and gently brought me onto the path of self-acceptance and self-love as part of the greater journey of self-realization.

Eventually, so I believe, everybody is destined for such a journey, and everybody *already* is, each of us in our own unique way. We may embrace it, resist it, dread it, but we can't avoid altogether something that we have not just signed up for but is also our true purpose and destiny. Of course, we still have free will but, I am now certain of it, our free will can only be exercised to postpone as skillfully as we can what is ultimately inevitable.

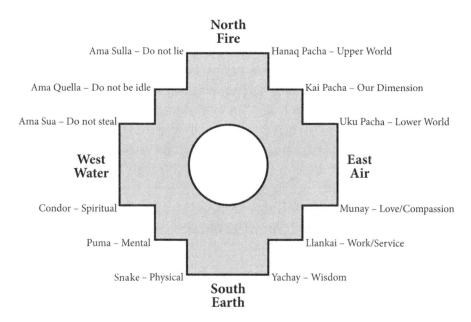

We will take this journey together using the symbol of the Chakana (also known as the Inca or Andean Cross) as a dramatic device. The Chakana is an important symbol of the ancestral cultures of the Andes and is considered the most complete and holy geometric design of the Incas, even though much earlier depictions of the Chakana are present most importantly both at Tiahuanaco in Bolivia[8] and on the third eye of the Lanzón, the sacred stone monolith in the temple of Chavín, Peru.

The stepped cross of the Chakana is made up of an equal-armed cross indicating the cardinal points of the compass and the four elements of Earth, Water, Fire and Air, and a superimposed square. The square is suggested to represent the other two levels of existence. The three levels of existence are *Hana Pacha* (the upper world of Spirit), *Kay Pacha*, (the world of our everyday existence), and *Uku Pacha* (the Underworld). These three levels of existence are also associated with three animal symbols: the Snake for the Underworld, the Puma and the Jaguar for our everyday world, and the Eagle and the Condor for the world of Spirit. These three animals, which are the kings of their respective worlds, represent to me cosmic energies that are characteristic of this planet, but also specific in their representation to this part of the world. The hole through the center of the cross is said to represent Cusco, the center of the Inca Empire, and the Southern Cross constellation, but for me it represents most importantly the void and

---

[8] The Tiahuanaco culture and people are actually believed by many to be where the Incas and their culture first originated. It is no accident that the first Inca and his twin sister are said to have been born of the Sun on the Island of the Sun by Lake Titicaca, which is located only a few miles from the ceremonial center of Tiahuanaco.

unnamable (and therefore indescribable) from which all of Creation originates.

As any ancestral symbol, the Chakana has multiple levels of meaning and understanding. The choice of the Chakana here is totally arbitrary on my part; I confess that my relationship and the way I work with San Pedro is not the result of any specific Huachuma training with coastal or Andean medicine people, nor have I been the recipient of special and esoteric Huachuma initiations. As a matter of fact I can't say that I've ever joined a "traditional" Huachuma ceremony as in what is considered nowadays the traditional way in Peru but is really post-Conquest and heavily influenced by Catholicism and its dualistic view of the struggle between good and evil.

I don't even call nor see myself as a Huachumero or San Pedrero, but as a plant medicine person who leads San Pedro and Ayahuasca ceremonies as part of his healing work: my training in plant medicine is Amazonian at its core and I have simply applied that model in my approach with San Pedro. My San Pedro ceremonies are structured like the Ayahuasca (or any other plant medicine) ceremonies I may lead for myself or others: a simple but solid container is created and ritual aspects of the ceremony are performed only at the beginning and closing because it is understood that the process is really happening between the medicine and the person ingesting it. It is a direct experience, therefore shamanic rather than liturgical and religious. So most of what I write about is really insights I have received through working with this plant over the years.

My perception and understanding of Andean life and culture is also deeply influenced by this medicine as well as by living on this land, walking on it, connecting with the mountains, meeting people, and participating in other people's ceremonies and rituals. Among the most important influences on my life here, I would certainly mention my receiving, from my dear friend and soul sister Diane Dunn, the Munay-Ki Rites back in 2007.

I had met Diane in 2004 when I stayed at her bed and breakfast , Paz y Luz, in Pisac. A year and a half later I asked her to join in her vision to create a healing center that would welcome and honor all spiritual traditions. Two years later I moved into a lot next to Paz y Luz and have worked as the resident plant medicine person of Paz y Luz ever since. I am glad to see that Diane's vision has since grown into a beautiful reality: people from all over the world come to Paz y Luz as individuals or as part of group retreats to engage in a wide variety of spiritual and healing practices, including my plant medicine retreats.

Diane is an initiate in Andean spirituality and for years has been transmitting the Munay-Ki Rites in Pisac and worldwide[9]. When I received those rites from her, my understanding was that this series of initiations were designed for people willing to be stewards of the Earth. Over the years these initiations have been working their magic on me, giving new depth to my relationship with this planet, and so we begin our journey around the Chakana starting with the direction of the South, which is associated with the element of earth[10].

---

[9] Diane Dunn can be contacted at www.DianeDunn.net

[10] In the Andean tradition there is no specific connection between the directions and the elements. The connections you will find here are those that resonate with me the strongest at this point in my life.

II

EARTH

*The South, the Snake, Healing, the Body, and
the Feminine*

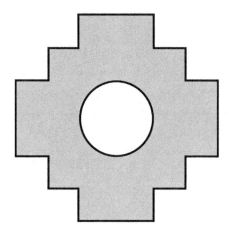

In Part II we shall explore themes connected with the direction of the South, which in the Andean tradition is associated with the Snake and healing. I associate with this direction the element of Earth, which is the densest of all elements and therefore connected with the densest aspect of our being: our physical bodies. Our bodies are the expression of the feminine principle, that energy that brings form to energy, belief, and thought in the same way that the energy of the mother through the umbilical cord supports the growth of the fetus. In the Hindu tradition this energy is personified in the goddess Shakti, whereas in the Andes it finds its most popular expression in Pachamama, Mother Earth.

Some people have suggested that we are not physical beings having a spiritual experience but spiritual beings having a physical experience. I believe that we choose this earthly experience on a soul level for very important and specific reasons, and yet spend a good part of our lives in these physical bodies, tragically and ironically resenting such an experience. The main source of this resistance is the anxiety with which we react to the unknown as oftentimes these higher reasons for choosing to be here elude us. We recurrently ask ourselves "what am I doing here?" and "what is the purpose of my life?" These are important questions that people approaching plant medicines under my guidance hope to receive some clarity about. These questions also create a certain stress related to the fear that one is wasting one's life. To these individuals I offer the reassurance that we are *already* and have *always* been fulfilling such a life purpose: what that purpose is may remain unclear all along but we can be sure that we are fulfilling it.

Even on a more mundane level we have often asked ourselves "Why did I do that? Why did I move to that city, held that job? Or stayed in that relationship for as long as I did?" The often challenging and painful experiences we invite into our lives make us regret and resent our life choices. But the part of us that regrets and resents is just the ego: that tyrannical and grumpy child that, figuratively speaking, doesn't care about nutrition and always expects only ice cream for every meal—the one who is attached to an infantile need for a kind of continuous gratification that is unfortunately unrealistic and becomes more and more unattractive as the years go by.

The first important lesson that this world and this Earth offer us is that *here* everything is in constant flux. The Chinese have been saying for millennia that the only constant in the world is change. As biological beings we are always seeking homeostasis and balance, but our minds have twisted that natural need into a search for a sort of inert stability that would actually lead us to death if truly achieved. Some people come to me looking for balance in their lives and from their attitude I can feel that what they're really seeking is some sort of motionless nirvana away from the reality of this earthly dimension, which is actually a *dynamic* balance in perpetual motion, flowing in harmony with this ever-changing world. This very Earth, even its most solid mountains, is a work in progress and constant evolution, and asks of us to flow and change with it.

Spiritual seeking often turns out to be a thinly disguised attempt to flee from this world: it is often the pursuit of an idealized fantasy outside and away from the here and now. Plant medicine is not a way to escape from this world, but actually a way to dive deep into all the aspects of earthly life and physicality that we may have resisted until the present moment.

Years ago I heard that in pre-Incan times San Pedro used to be ingested in the daytime to connect with the Earth and at night to connect with the stars. As modern people we all suffer (or have suffered) to a degree or another from alienation from this planet we are really part of, so I prefer to lead my San Pedro ceremonies during the day: for me the simple reconnection with this Earth is a profound and healing experience, and one that many people nowadays can benefit from. Traditional plant medicine healing begins on the level of the earth and of the physical body: by taking us back to this planet and into our bodies, Plant Teachers help us coming back to the here and now, and reevaluate our life priorities and choices accordingly.

San Pedro is, as far as I'm concerned, primarily a heart-opener: under its influence we are better able to connect with ourselves and our world through our hearts rather than through our minds. The heart is that part of ourselves that embraces everything; unlike the mind, it doesn't discriminate between good and bad, unpleasant or appealing, positive and negative: it doesn't judge and doesn't choose, but welcomes everything equally. And it can help us tremendously in accepting the resisted experience of earthly life. The sheer physicality of the plant medicine experience is sometimes experienced as a nuisance, but in my opinion it's an invaluable aspect of this process, meant to bring us out of our heads and back into our bodies and on this planet.

As the seat of the principle of connection, the heart is the ultimate healer because healing is simply reconnecting what has been divided, repressed, and rejected. This is why there are countless songs and poems praising the healing qualities of love, the heart's ultimate essence. Reflecting upon this world I've come to the conclusion that the experience we choose by coming here is the experience of separation: separation from the world, from others, but most deeply from ourselves. Modernity has only accentuated the feeling of deep human loneliness and the fear that result from such alienation: people are willing to forego any common sense and join political, spiritual, and religious communities simply to avoid that loneliness and feel like they are a part of something. The English poet John Donne wrote in the 17th century that, "no man is an island." In a society such as ours that is increasingly fragmented we strive for a sense of connection with others and a sense of belonging. This human desire to belong is very deep and beautiful, but in its pursuit we often reject and betray who we are, and often sacrifice our own integrity to the point that by the time we do feel like we belong we no longer know who we are.

For me any community is only as healthy as the individuals that compose it and personal wounds always turn into interpersonal dysfunctions and projections, which is why I invite my clients into a very personal introspection and healing process. It may not seem very effective in terms of numbers and yet any new healthy individual deeply affects the overall wellbeing of the collectivity in the same way that a handful of enlightened beings balance the unconsciousness of the whole human race. This is also why to those well-meaning people who come to me wishing to help humanity I always ask them to start that mission with and within themselves.

The direction of the South is connected with the cosmic energy and symbolism of the snake. The snake is a universal symbol of healing and medicine, and this Earth of ours is for me intrinsically a healing place, best symbolized by the snake. In Peru it is also a symbol of wisdom: the wisdom of the Earth and all of its creatures, mineral, vegetal, animal, and human, too. Healing leads to wisdom and the healing we experience with San Pedro helps us reconnect with our own wisdom and the truth of our hearts. Oftentimes people experience San Pedro as speaking to them in very wise ways. For me the wisdom we perceive to be receiving from San Pedro is a reflection of our own wisdom: if we didn't hold that wisdom already, the messages and insights we seem to receive from this medicine wouldn't make any sense. So, in reality San Pedro reawakens the wisdom and gifts that are *already* within ourselves, and such process of reawakening and the reemergence of wisdom happen through purification, healing, and the consequent letting go.

PURIFICATION

Purification with San Pedro happens on any level where such cleansing may be needed. Just like life, this medicine does not necessarily offer us what we want but what we need, and in the process it may show us aspects of that healing process whose importance and necessity we may not have been aware of. Such purification may happen physically through vomiting, defecating, sudden onset of menstruation, or expectoration.

Vomiting is the result of a cleansing that happens on the level of the abdomen's organs. The abdomen is not only the seat of many repressed emotions but, as the second brain that it really is and connected to the brain by the Vagus nerve, it is often also the storing space of (so to speak) toxic thoughts, beliefs, and resisted memories, so much so that the vomiting may be a release that is not only emotional, but also mental, energetic, or psychological.

Uncontrollable shaking of the vertebral column, the pelvis, and legs is often associated with the release of fear that is lodged deep in the bones and nervous system, or sometimes the release of repressed sexual energy. The shaking of arms and hands is often connected with the opening of the heart and heart meridians so that the energy of the heart can once again flow in and out of the individual.

Understandably, people sometimes complain about the physical discomfort that such cleansing entails and in many cases they try to "fix" that pain with all sorts of stratagems such as stretching, crystals, and so on. We're going to talk about this later but for now I feel it's important to say that in my opinion such strategies are a form of resistance that goes *against* the healing process. We have an innate capacity to go unconscious and numb ourselves when faced with physical pain. It is a form of survival that is incredibly valuable in the moment an accident or traumatic event happens, but that we are not consciously present does not mean that we don't experience those traumas: they are simply relegated to the sub- and unconscious and, when not integrated, they still affect our lives and color the way we perceive ourselves and the world. Our pronounced propensity to self-medicate is a way to once again deal with these uncomfortable and painful physical sensations by repressing them. For me these physical sensations are really just ways for our deeper selves to make us aware that a part of ourselves needs attention in the same way that pain is a way for us to become aware that something is out of alignment in our physical and non-physical bodies. The limitations of modern medicine, with its focus on the suppression of symptoms but inability to actually cure many ailments, should be a lesson to us all in avoiding as much as possible the application of such strategies in our own lives. When physical pain and nausea arise during a ceremony, this is actually the medicine healing us by bringing to our conscious awareness the suffering we have so skillfully repressed.

So often have I asked someone in my ceremonies an hour and a half after the first drink of this medicine whether they feel they have had enough medicine and their reply is "I feel perfectly normal and would like some more medicine," to which I usually reply "how does your stomach feel?" At that point many will complain of some nausea and I have to remind them that that nausea and discomfort are sure signs that the medicine is *already* working, that they would do well to embrace that physical discomfort, and through that feel what may lie below it. Most of these people, when I return to them after a while to see how they are doing, will say that they now feel the medicine and don't need to drink any more.

Since the invitation of San Pedro is to reconnect with ourselves, I invite people to let go of their tricks and actually *feel* what is going on. It is amazing to see how quickly in most cases of nausea such discomfort subsides shortly after the person affected by it takes the time to honor it with their presence and loving attention. Trusting the medicine to take us wherever we need to go and *feel* whatever we need to experience for our greater good and the greater good of all is of paramount importance: by welcoming and embracing all experiences as wholeheartedly as possible we are truly working *with* the medicine rather than against it.

Healing

The author and workshop leader Lise Bourbeau describes in her book *Heal Your Wounds and Know Your True Self*[11] five basic wounds of rejection, abandonment, betrayal, injustice, and humiliation, which most of us hold on a soul level and came to this planet to heal. According to her we choose before incarnating the perfect family, environment, and circumstances that will reawaken such wounds rather than cause them. It is as if our families (often violently) rip the thin bandage over our soul wounds, often in the first few years of our lives, to expose them again so that they can be healed.

I personally find this theory very helpful and empowering as it skips altogether the cause and effect theories of psychological and karmic viewpoints: the suffering we experience is not *caused* by others or by some deed in past lifetimes but the very beginning of a beautiful healing journey we have ourselves chosen with great care and absolute perfection on a soul level before incarnating. This model allows us to easily let go

---

[11] Bourbeau, Lise. *Heal Your Wounds and Find Your True Self.* Saint-Jerome, Editions E.T.C., 2001.

of our belief that we are victims, which is a belief we quickly endorse the moment we resist those uncomfortable experiences we have actually signed up for.

Blaming others, society, or God for our misery is the most popular sport on Earth, and the most disempowering, too. To blame is the easiest way not to take responsibility for our lives and the way we feel, but the blaming game keeps us small and powerless, and this childlike attitude prevents us from truly taking the reins over our lives because as long as we give our power away we are incapable of effectively changing our lives. To explore and integrate this victim identity is a necessary and valuable process for most of us, and in particular for those who have experienced very traumatic and painful events, which they perceived at the time as coming at them from outside themselves and over which they hold the belief that they didn't deserve it or couldn't do anything to avoid it.

One of my most important teachers in this lifetime has been Harry Palmer, the creator of the Avatar© Course, a self-development workshop based on the premise and designed to teach experientially that we are the creators of our own lives. As tedious as it was, I did spend most of the summer of 1995 doing exercises using the Avatar tools to explore my own victim identity. At an Avatar© Master Course in Orlando, Florida, later that year, Harry gave a speech to the 150 participants and was talking about the theme of creating our lives from A to Z. At some point a man in the audience asked whether Harry really thought it had been this man's creation to have a serious accident, which had broken most bones in his body. Harry, with much compassion, simply nodded. And the man walked out of the room in anger with the crutches he still had need for.

I know how sensitive the theme of victimhood can be when people come to me with a history of childhood physical, emotional, or sexual abuse. Children are indeed often taken advantage of by adults and other children *because* they are not yet fully capable of asserting and exercising their boundaries. But the point is that this abuse is an important part of the child's history and that soul's journey, and if the person affected doesn't take responsibility little by little for it, he or she will also remain unable to do anything about it, least of all heal it. The upside of gently taking responsibility for our lives and history is that in so doing we regain the power that is our birthright and start shining again brightly as the stars of our own galaxy instead of feeling like an insignificant satellite at the mercy of other planets. Reclaiming that central place in my own universe has been revolutionary, which is why I invite others to do the same. I deeply believe that we already have all the tools and wisdom to fully step into our power and that the whole of Creation is encouraging us to let go of our victimhood and blaming in order to grow into the powerful and wonderful beings we are destined to become.

The healing journey is such a journey: the wounds of rejection, abandonment, injustice, betrayal, and humiliation are simply symptoms of a belief we hold in our consciousness that keeps us separate from our own inner light and feeling unworthy, undeserving, and scared to embrace our full light and beauty. As challenging, uncomfortable, discouraging, and maddening as it often reveals itself to be, there is no greater and no more rewarding journey than the healing journey that leads us back home into our loving hearts and shining spirits.

LETTING GO

Just like a snake shedding its old skin, I believe the main message of this medicine for us at this time in history is "let go": let go of whatever may have been important (and perhaps even necessary) in the past for our own survival and wellbeing but no longer truly is.

Up until the moment I started engaging with plant medicines I had no idea that letting go was even an option and a possibility available to me as well as everybody else. The importance our society places on history and the need to remember past events are rarely connected with a sincere collective desire to learn from the past so that we don't have to recreate it; most often history feels like a long series of records not only meant to glorify our successes but also the hurt, defeats, and humiliations we may have experienced at the hands of others. Despite the creation after the French Revolution of modern state nations and many transnational organizations such as the U.N. and European Community, we are still easily swayed into a very archaic tribal mentality. It seems to be the duty of the traditional tribe (and that tribe can be of racial, ethnic, political, or religious nature) not to forget and not to forgive those who have trespassed against it. This gives the tribe a sense of identity, often a wounded and victimized identity but an identity nonetheless.

Something very similar happens on an individual level: we tend to hold on to past hurts and resentments with almost a certain pride. It was fascinating and infuriating at the same time to find myself, for no particular reason and without any apparent benefit, repeatedly retelling myself past skirmishes and disappointments years and years after they had happened with the same emotional reaction as if they had happened the day prior. Often people going through a plant medicine healing process—and I am the first one to agree with them—marvel at how much and for how long we are capable of holding on to things and as if our lives depended on it. Our limited sense of self and identity may depend on it but our lives suffer from it: holding on to limited beliefs and judgment keeps us small and frightened, and feelings of rejection, abandonment, betrayal, injustice, and humiliation and their accompanying emotions of anger, sadness, and grief can turn into the kind of toxic matter that is at the source of most diseases.

To discover that I could actually let go of stuff I had held onto for years or lifetimes was revolutionary. To experience the relief and lightness of being after each letting go would always bring a feeling that I was finally doing something very important, beneficial, and long longed for.

Many clients of mine come to me with a genuine and deep desire to let go but often have no idea how to go about it as their "letting go muscle" is completely atrophied. Often all that is needed is simply for the person to give himself or herself *permission* to let go. The truth is that as a species we have become psychically anal-retentive and often letting go is easier said than done but always available to those willing to do and experience whatever is needed to get there.

For instance, it took me nine years of on again/off again personal work with the medicine around the resentment I had felt as a child against my mother and the jealousy against my younger brother, who in my eyes had enjoyed much better care than me. Feelings of injustice and a fear of not being loved and cared for, even if tamed by the age of 40, were far from healed. To top it all off, I would regularly recreate that scenario over and over again with whomever was available, and so each time I would give another go at exploring this theme in ceremony after ceremony.

When in the fall of 2013 I started for the ruins of Choquequirao on a five-day trek with two dear friends I was quite ecstatic and happy that for once I would be drinking San Pedro for the sheer pleasure of doing so at this beautiful site. But, alas, the farther we walked, the stronger the awareness that I was once again playing out my little drama and, with an initial resistance followed by humility, I decided to make this theme part of my intention for my ceremony.

We spent a wonderful day at this archaeological site, blessed by flying condors, the beauty of the place, and for me some powerful insights on the feminine and erotic flavor of this planet. But it wasn't until after dinner and my friends had retired to their tent that my childhood drama came up in a big way: I felt the abandonment, the anger, the loneliness, and the sadness, silently crying in my own tent and probably for the first time simply allowing myself to feel and experience these emotions without resistance and without trying to explain or understand. When it was all over I found myself looking at that old scenario from a much more clear and expanded place rather than through my hurt child's eyes. In that moment I could finally see and appreciate the fact that a mother, my mother included, will take care of the one who needs her most, which in my family's case was my brother. I finally saw the beauty of a mother's love concerned for the thriving of all her children, starting from the weaklings. After receiving this beautiful and powerful lesson on the energy and archetype of the Mother and forgiving my own mother and brother as well as forgiving myself for holding such a grudge against them for so long, it was easy to let go of the pain the medicine had brought up to the surface once again and to let go of the whole story once and for all with deep gratitude for all the gifts and lessons it had offered me.

The completion of this healing process took nine years but at age 47 I was finally free from a shadow that had haunted me all my life and had colored with darkness the way I perceived myself, others, and the world. It was no easy ride and no pleasure cruise, but it was a most rewarding and liberating journey, which I would of course repeat all over again if necessary.

People ask me sometimes if complete healing is actually possible; this question comes up particularly when one starts exploring in earnest a certain theme and realizes how multi-layered and complex the healing process may actually turn out to be. From my personal experience I can honestly say that, yes, the healing process of even the deepest of wounds can come to completion: it is only a matter of time, trust, and patience.

THE BODY

The earth element is connected with the physicality of the earthly experience and most importantly with the physical body and the Feminine, which is the principle of embodiment. Working with San Pedro is a wonderful opportunity to heal our *relation* with our bodies and the Feminine. In the Judeo-Christian

41

tradition and all spiritual and religious traditions that are in essence transcendental, the physical body has often been viewed in opposition to the spirit rather than in relation to it. Moral judgment has declared the body dirty, beastly, and lowly: countless decrees and books have been written to denounce the impurity of the body and further the split between our bodies and our spirits, and spiritual disciplines have been developed to humiliate our bodies and bring them into submission. Not surprisingly, the same can be said about these traditions in regards to their attitude towards women and the Feminine in general.

On my way to Choquequirao I couldn't help noticing once again the beautiful display of Nature's creative energy, and in its beauty and bounty this energy struck me as intrinsically erotic and feminine. I realized then that every mother, before becoming a mother, is first of all a lover, and that Pachamama (Mother Earth in Quechua) is also a playful Lover. I could see that day the uniquely erotic essence of this planet, unlike any other planet in our solar system. And then laughed out loud thinking about the efforts we have made over millennia to resist this erotic energy to the point of developing religions and philosophies that denigrate such energy in every possible way through judgment and demonization. Once again I was made aware of how the deliberate rejection of the Feminine and the alienation from such an important part of our earthly experience seem to be the reason for a large part of our troubles and misery.

I do agree that this physical reality is transient and illusory, and that any attachment to it is cause for suffering: nothing here lasts forever, and yet we are to learn to fully be in the here and now, so to embrace without attachment but wholeheartedly this earthly experience seems to me a very wise choice. The qualities of the Divine Feminine as they manifest on this Earth are far from being negligible and their blessings are most valuable to us all: creativity, tenderness, flexibility, generosity, equanimity, nurturing, pleasure, interrelatedness, beauty, and playfulness can only enrich our lives and spiritual journey rather than be perceived as threats.

I feel very privileged to be on this planet as a conscious human being and be able to appreciate and fully bask in this beauty, and very honored to provide with my San Pedro ceremonies an opportunity for many to reconnect with this planet as well. The rhythms of Nature are much slower than the rhythm of modern man's mind and, unless we are willing to immerse ourselves in the outdoors for long periods of time, Nature's teachings and blessings can elude us. But when we do, Nature invariably showers us with her healing beauty and, since she finally has an attentive audience, puts on the most amazing shows just to delight us and remind us once again of the playfulness of Life.

That we as a species are so resolute in wanting to destroy Nature is troubling not just for the damage to the environment but because in so doing we are unconsciously wanting to destroy those beautiful qualities within ourselves. Luckily for us, we also seem to have a built-in balancing mechanism and the more fiercely feminine energy is repressed and oppressed, the more fiercely she makes her reappearance[12].

---

[12] All Inca ceremonial centers honor both the feminine and the masculine by devoting a temple to *both* the Sun and the Moon as if to remind us that one without the other would be an aberration.

That more and more people since the 60's have been drawn to experiences of ecstatic states through mind-altering substances and other modalities is a sign of how such a balance between the feminine and the masculine is necessary for our health. That such practices have at times been abused at the detriment of certain individuals is only a symptom of how our relationship with the Feminine is still fraught with old misconceptions and judgments. Fortunately for us there are native cultures around the world whose spiritual traditions and connection with Nature are still intimately entwined and at this time in history they are our most precious and valuable teachers. It is no accident that South America (and in particular the area all along the Andes and the neighboring Amazon region) has become such a magnet for people from all over the world in the last thirty years. Peru was never on my list of places to visit and definitely not a place I had thought I would ever call home until 2004 when I went to the Amazon jungle for an Ayahuasca retreat. Both the jungle and the Andean world were completely new landscapes for me, fascinating and yet not ideal in any way as I used to resent mosquitos and cold weather with the same passion. And yet, eleven years later I am still living here. My decision to settle in Peru was first and foremost to be able to conduct my plant medicine work without legal hassles, but also because I intuited that this land and these people had much to teach me, and the most important of these teachings have all been about reconnecting with Nature, the reconnection of the physical with the spiritual, and the beautiful dance of the feminine and masculine energies within and all around.

THE RELATIONSHIP WITH THE BODY

San Pedro invites us to engage with our physical bodies in a different way already during our process with it. People come to me with all sorts of hopes and wishes, but for me the basic goal of this and any other healing process is that we learn and practice love and kindness. That process starts first and foremost with ourselves as I believe that we can truly be kind and loving to others and the planet only to the degree that we are loving and kind to ourselves. A wonderful place to begin this learning process is our physical bodies, from which we are often estranged.

Caringly listening to our bodies and honoring (rather than resenting) their needs is an art that is never too late to learn and practice: our ancestors knew very well that physical health is the most precious of blessings, but in our times the pursuit of success and pleasure has grown into our highest priority and in that pursuit we often reject, abandon, betray, and humiliate our bodies. To make things even worse we compensate for our unmet emotional needs with excessive or unhealthy dietary habits that we know are damaging and unkind. As the body becomes the recipient of our emotional and mental distress, and as we self-medicate our dis-eases with toxic foods and drugs, the body gets heavier and heavier to the point of not being able to process so much any longer and falls sick.

A young woman client of mine used to take heavy painkillers in order to find whatever little peace away from the pressure of her family life and environment to the point of secretly injecting herself with such drugs and causing actual scars on her body. It was the best that she could do but her marriage was falling apart as a consequence. Over the course of many ceremonies much pain came to the surface and a lot of it was from the hurt she had been self-inflicting in her trying to cope with a very stressful predicament. Needless to say, her process required a lot of forgiveness not just to herself but to her physical body as well.

Our bodies are the silent witnesses of our wounding and inner conflicts: they bear the weight of our fears and grievances, and the process with San Pedro can make meaningful progress when we take a compassionate and caring look at the scars these conflicts have left for us to heal. In my own personal process with San Pedro, as I healed my wound of abandonment I learned to care for and nurture my body, and eventually became to myself the attentive and loving mother I felt I hadn't had. I also learned to let go of my bodily shame and not see my body as separate from me but as an integral, however impermanent, part of me. As a result of this shift I could also begin to honor and care for it with love and gratitude.

THEMES AND INTENTIONS RELATED TO THE ELEMENT OF EARTH

Here is a list of important themes connected with the Earth element that would be ideal to explore during a healing process with San Pedro[13]:

- Any resistance to the experience of being in a body

---

[13] The theme of intentions is explored in Appendix I.

46

- Lack of grounding and the sense of not belonging anywhere
- Gender issues and shame
- Sexual issues and sexual shame. Fear of pleasure
- Body shame and the resulting low self-image
- Racial themes
- Survival issues, and fear of aging and dying
- Unresolved issues with our mothers
- Judgments and negative projections of the Feminine

HEALING BY THE WILLKAMAYU RIVER
– SACRED VALLEY OF THE INCAS, PERU –
MARCH 2016

I began the infamous year 2012 with suicidal thoughts and fantasies because of yet another disappointing romantic relationship. On New Year's Eve I joined some friends for a celebration that included the ingestion of San Pedro but I wasn't there to celebrate: I was there to grieve. That night I cancelled all my travels and retreats for the upcoming year and vowed instead to dedicate all my energies to healing my wounded heart for as long as necessary.

Three months later I went by the river near my house and drank San Pedro by myself as part of that healing process. As soon as I settled down in a familiar spot by the river it started to rain and so, with the effects of the medicine already beginning to rise, I made my way through thorny bushes all the way to a cave I had noticed but never visited before.

There the theme quickly shifted from romantic love to Divine Love, one often being a reflection of the other. At some point I connected with my desire for God's love (that was easy) and then fortuitously flipped the coin to look at my resistance to actually receiving and experiencing that love. What I found there was the belief that in order to receive that love I would have to change: perhaps wear a white turban, perhaps never have a temper tantrum ever again. I realized that I held the belief that God's love was somehow conditional and soon realized the fallacy of my belief, which allowed me to let go of it. As soon as I let go of that limiting belief I was flooded with Divine Love, which is really all there is, but that I had kept away from me for lifetimes out of fear, guilt, and shame. In that moment I sat up, opened my eyes, and said to myself "It is done: my healing journey is complete," and with that an experience of full self-realization unfolded: the full realization of myself as part of and no longer apart from Divinity.

I relate this important episode of my life because that moment of profound healing was nothing but a surrendering to my ultimate nature. It was really only the letting go of my own conflicts and resistances that allowed me to fall back and rest in my divinity. I saw then and there how most of the suffering I had created for myself was the result of my own resistance to who I really was. The only solution to that entire struggle was letting go of my inner conflict and surrender once and for all.

In order to get to that place, which is inside all of us, I sure exercised a lot of choice and determination, but it was a choice and determination to simply do whatever necessary in order to meet and embrace all of myself. The experience was as surprising as it was monumental: I had no idea what was in store for me that day and in its simplicity the experience was truly amazing, and it also filled me with hope because if I were able to heal such sense of separation, I knew everybody else could, too.

When I got home later that afternoon everything was exactly the same and yet my own healing and transformation made me experience my familiar life quite differently: there was definitely a sense of elation and expansion but also a serene simplicity I had never known before. And in that simplicity all there was to do was water the garden as usual, just like the Zen monk who goes back to fetch water from the well shortly after reaching enlightenment.

Only a week after that life-changing experience I returned by the river with a friend to test-drive a new batch of San Pedro medicine. I didn't think I had any particular theme to explore that day, but sure enough and before I knew it I found myself holding on to an old judgment against someone. When I finally let go of my resentment and judgment I could see how the Divine Love I had finally reconnected with only a week earlier is really everybody's legacy and destiny. In that moment I was able to own and integrate all my projections about not deserving to receive and be that Love, thus completing the process.

Soon after this, as I was walking by the river, I heard an internal "clunk" and realized that my own wheel of reincarnation had come to a full stop. I was astonished and amazed, and yet I quickly let go of any attachment that it stays motionless forever. I actually had a chuckle and told myself that, even if it started moving again, there was absolutely nothing to fear or worry about: being on the other side of karmic and illusory bonds helped me truly see the thinness of the illusion of separation, not to mention the depth of the much greater reality that contains that illusion. I didn't and don't fear falling back into that illusion because I now know experientially that such illusion is also part, however small and insignificant, of Divine Creation. Pain and suffering are creations and therefore not eternal: as creations they are bound by time and space and destined to pass, and when they are gone only Divine Love and Light remain.

Once I finally connected with and embraced that Love and Light, not only as an experience but also as the very essence of who I am, my seeking came to an end. The last letting go of any spiritual seeker is the letting go of the identity of the seeker through which we experience seeking. Once we find what we were seeking, that identity has fulfilled its purpose and asks to be let go of. Since that final letting go my attitude has shifted from one of constant searching to one of curious and playful exploration: I no longer look for answers as I no longer have any questions, but while I am here I do keep exploring and playing in this field of illusory and temporary creation. I am still fascinated by the many ways different cultures and people have addressed the mysterious process of life and awakening throughout time, and have resolved to do my best to give to others at least as much as I have received. Deeply heartfelt gratitude colors my daily life: what was once experienced as a chore is now a unique blessing and privilege—the privilege of having this unique human life with all of its contradictions and beauty.

A week after all of this, as I was once again taking an afternoon walk up the river, I realized to what extent all my fears had dissipated. Walking on this Earth without the fears that had haunted me all my life allowed me to perceive this planet on a deeper level: for the first time I could see and experience its intrinsic lovingness and nurturing energy. That afternoon I was walking like a puma, confident in my step and in total harmony with the environment. I no longer perceived the mountains and river as large, overwhelming, and possibly dangerous, but as friendly and benevolent: my true and sweet temporary home.

I have been embraced by that love and nurturing energy ever since and no matter where I am. Holding such awareness and the willingness and readiness to be enveloped by this love has made it so that wherever I go Nature is always sweet with me and showers me generously with her blessings and beauty. It was all just a matter of letting go of the (illusory) heavy filter of fear, which is why in my work with San Pedro and Ayahuasca I invite my clients to explore their fears as thoroughly as possible. After that exploration every-thing else is a sweet breeze.

III

WATER

The West, the Puma and the Jaguar, Power, Emotions

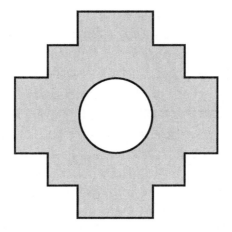

The direction of the West is connected with the element of water. Water is that element that fills every space from the bottom up and therefore represents the depth of the sea of Consciousness: the unconscious, the subconscious, and the emotional aspects of our being. As the surface of the Earth and our own bodies are made of more than 70% water, so is the makeup of our own consciousness: we are a mysterious sea with deep oceans, quiet inland seas, crystalline lagoons, and choppy waters.

San Pedro invites us to dive deep into and explore our inner oceans. It is a blessing that the West is also connected with the cosmic energy and archetypes of the Jaguar and the Puma, which symbolize power, strength, and courage. It is a blessing because it takes a lot of valor and courage to dive deep into our submerged selves and give ourselves the permission to be that open and vulnerable.

When I first drank Ayahuasca, I was well aware that I was not scared of the medicine but of those repressed and hidden parts of myself that the medicine may bring up to my conscious awareness. Even years later, when I first came to Peru to go to the jungle, I was most concerned with what my traveling companions would think of me should my many masks drop all of a sudden and my hidden selves and demons make a grand appearance. Deeply-seated shame was a corollary of my fear of rejection, so much so that it took quite some courage and a feeling that I had reached the end of my rope in order to make that much-needed leap. When I first meet people interested in working with me, they sometimes become apologetic after telling me about their issues and traumas, fearing that I may be burdened with them. But in all honesty all I can see in these people as I am listening to them is their courage, their faith, and their willingness to do anything in order to move through and beyond their present predicament.

In order to reclaim and step into our power we will explore first and foremost the ways with which we disempower ourselves by giving our power away and not taking responsibility for our own experience. And then we will explore the world of our inner waters, of our emotions. Our emotions are an important source of information and wisdom, so much so that embracing our emotions is an amazing way to once again step into our power and embrace the power of our intuition. The theme of emotional armoring will also be addressed because as long as hold on to our old armoring and protection no healing is realistically possible.

POWER, DISEMPOWERMENT, AND VICTIMHOOD

The West, as the direction of the Puma and the Jaguar, which are cosmic energies and archetypes connected with Power, Strength, and Courage, calls us to look into the ways in which we disempower ourselves and often end up portraying ourselves as victims. Throughout this book I talk about taking responsibility for how we feel and the experiences we invite into our lives. But what does it mean to take responsibility? And how do we shift out of victimhood?

When we face an aspect of ourselves we don't like or something painful, our reaction is often resistance: we don't want to experience that which is right in front of us. The reason for such resistance is judgment:

our minds say it is not ok to experience this or that for whatever reason. And yet I believe that all that we invite into our lives is there for a reason and unfortunately our resistance does not make that experience vanish. In the case of emotions our resistance simply drives them deeper into our beings; in the case of life lessons, these are simply postponed until we invite similar circumstances over and over again and we learn through those experiences what we need to learn.

That resistance may be felt at the level of the mind as a judgment such as "I don't like this," and is often a symptom of some deeper resistance on a soul level such as "I have vowed (more often than not in a previous lifetime) never to experience this again because of this and that." The resistance simply postpones indefinitely a valuable learning experience or something to be healed and integrated, which is why what we resist keeps resurfacing into our lives.

The most common way to resist an experience is by blaming others for it. Blaming is a way to decline any responsibility for our lives and therefore is a giving away of our power to whatever and whomever we blame for our experience. There are a lot of talk and endless techniques in shamanic and healing circles about reclaiming our power, and yet I feel that the most disempowering of our attitudes and behaviors is simply blame.

One of my teachers taught me that other people and entities have only the power we give them: no one has any authority and power over us other than the one we offer them, and each time we do so we are left a little more disempowered to the point that we end up feeling like victims. The challenge comes when we experience something that feels imposed upon us by some external agent or somebody else, or in the case of experiences we have in childhood when we are seemingly powerless and unable to say no. From the viewpoint of our physical beings the explanation that we have been overpowered makes perfect sense and we feel entitled to portray ourselves as victims, and our culture sanctions that viewpoint with arguments such as the innate innocence and vulnerability of children. But from a more expanded soul level we can at least entertain the possibility that our lives are *our* lives and not something imposed upon us by some cruel third party. As a last resort we may end up labeling as evil anything that we refuse to experience: our endless fight against evil is simply a resistance to what is.

The first act of self-disempowerment is to claim that our power was taken away from us. In that act we *give* others the power to take our power away. No one can take our power unless we offer it, so to give our power away and then insist that it was taken from us is the first expression of victimhood. To become aware of how we give our power away and then create ourselves as victims is therefore a most important step towards reclaiming our power.

Another way of disempowering ourselves is through the projection of our shadow onto others and the world. Our shadows, those aspects of ourselves that through judgment we have relegated to some dark and hopefully unreachable part of our consciousness, are projected onto other people and the world in general. Projection is a valid way to distance ourselves from ourselves in order to avoid owning and experiencing something we believe is intolerable. Unfortunately, by rejecting parts of ourselves we end up diminished and ever smaller.

In my opinion one of the main reasons we humans feel so overwhelmed by life and so small is because we are really stumbling through life on just one instead of both legs: by rejecting, abandoning, and betraying ourselves we keep amputating ourselves to the point that it's no surprise that we perceive ourselves as stunted victims. It is all of our own doing, and the awareness that it is so is the starting point for shifting out of that powerlessness. That stunting happens on any level: it may be by repressing our erotic and creative energies, by avoiding or not trusting our emotions, or by telling ourselves that we ought to feel, think, and act in ways other than what feels most natural to us in order to avoid rejection or abandonment.

San Pedro has been instrumental for me in accepting *all* of myself wholeheartedly, from my heart, by making me aware of how the judgments against myself were a way to repress and hurt myself. It has made me aware of the deep consequences that holding such judgments had upon me, and has time and time again invited me to let them go and forgive myself for holding such harsh attitude against myself and others. At the end of the road I discovered that there was never anything wrong with whom I am or anybody else is, and that what I had deemed as awful was rather innocent and harmless. It is when we don't question those judgments that our guilt drives us to increasingly hurtful behaviors against ourselves and others.

As *A Course in Miracles*[14] keeps reminding me over and over again, any attack is a call for love: a call for love towards that within ourselves which we believe to be unlovable and is only asking to be loved and embraced. The embracing and integration of our shadow is really the way towards self-empowerment: as we become whole there is no need to assert power and self-assurance, or to rely on crutches to walk through life, but we can simply sit and rest in the power that is the fullness of our being. So, whenever we are invited to experience something that we had previously denied responsibility for, we might do well to entertain the possibility that if that experience is presented to us, such experience is indeed *part* of ourselves and therefore deserves our attention and embrace.

The more we embrace who we are, the less we feel like victims and the more empowered we feel. I always invite my clients to explore their victim identities before anything else if I feel they hold such an attitude towards themselves and life. Otherwise they are so disempowered that any further step is impossible. The exploration and integration of that identity leads the way to true mastery over one's own life and is a precious and important process that I can't recommend highly enough.

It was with much surprise that very recently, the night before entering a solo silent retreat at another healer's own Temple of the Moon, I had a lucid dream that invited me to look at the victim within my feminine side. Considering the amount of work I had already done on this important subject I initially felt rather discouraged

---

[14] *A Course in Miracles*. Wisconsin Dells, A Course in Miracles International, 2007. This text will sometimes be referred to from here onwards as *ACIM*.

and almost didn't show up the next morning. But I did show up and thus began an interesting process of exploring victimhood within my feminine side. It was a challenging experience as I spent the next seven days exploring all the ways in which me, as well as women in general, disempower ourselves by not honoring the power and strength of the Feminine within ourselves, by letting go of the trepidation of fully embracing that power, and by seeing how procrastination, blame, and the expectation that others take care of us are all ways in which we reinforce the belief in our weakness and inferiority.

Every wound contains deep within itself the seed of something very beautiful, usually the awareness that we are exactly the opposite of what our wounded selves tell us we are. So, after a seven-day rollercoaster that ended with a San Pedro ceremony, I found myself embracing my own power, strength, and courage more than ever and seeing myself finally as a master. Not a master like when my teacher calls me "maestro" but most importantly master over my own life.

Another important aspect of reclaiming our power is the healing and integration of past personal abuses of power. One of the main issues for me as I started working as a medicine person was the fear of abusing my position as I had in previous lifetimes. As a result of this lingering fear I took over the years greatest care not to once again fall into the trap of exercising and abusing my power over anybody. Much self-forgiveness was needed in order to make peace with my past and finally realize that my so-called mistakes were just learning experiences *about* the proper use of power. Learning from those experiences eventually allowed me to let go of my fear of abusing my power again in the future, and letting go of that fear opened the way for me to step more trustingly into my power.

I see this process as highly valuable particularly for women who wish to reclaim their own power but hold unhealed memories of being punished for being strong and empowered women in past lives. Usually there is blame against those who have in their opinion unjustly tortured and even burnt them at the stake. In such cases it is often beneficial to explore whatever old fears may resurface when once again wanting to step into one's own power as well as past personal abuses of power, spiritual or sexual.

In my own process I eventually found out that the punishment of exile from the star system where I had been living and had enjoyed great status as a priest and teacher had not been cast against me by a stern jury but had been totally self-inflicted: it had been my own guilt and shame that had sent me into exile—as a punishment as well as an opportunity to make amends and learn about the proper use rather than abuse of power.

ARMORING

As San Pedro invites us to open our heart, it may also point to whatever armoring we may have put up around it. This is a very important part of any healing process, including with San Pedro: to first see and fully understand the purpose of such armoring and to honor—instead of resenting—ourselves for creating such protection.

The present state of not being able to connect with oneself, of emotional numbness, and being stuck in one's head is often the result of a decision in the past *not to feel.* We may have experienced some trauma or even a simple but painful heartbreak and we shut down emotionally, telling ourselves that to feel such pain again would be unbearable.

Even more insidiously, we shut down before we have fully experienced the painful event unfolding in front of us. Shutting down is a valuable defense mechanism and survival strategy, as are all the coping mechanisms we put in place in order to safeguard ourselves from experiencing something we deem too dreadful and painful to embrace. Among those coping mechanisms we have the whole gambit of psychiatric disorders, from schizophrenia, to multiple personality disorder, obsessive compulsive behaviors, all sorts of addictive behaviors, and an infinite list of imaginary creatures and entities (from angelic to demonic) that are meant to safeguard us from re-experiencing any pain by locking that trauma in a tight box so that it disappears from our conscious awareness. Carl Jung went as far as indicating that all therapeutic processes are geared most importantly towards the support and encouragement of traumatized individuals in letting go of these defense mechanisms so that true healing and integration can finally happen[15].

In 2012 I participated in my first Naraya, a four-day native North American ceremony that took place in southern Oregon. This ceremony, also known as "Ghost Dance", was first dreamt of in 1890 as a way to heal the tribe and help it reconnect with its strength and wisdom. One night during the ceremony I suddenly became aware of holding a protective energy, which I perceived as a fierce snake on my chest and

---

[15] In Kalschein, Donald. *The Inner World of Trauma.* London, Routledge, 1998.

that would snap threateningly at anybody who tried to hurt me. I immediately realized that in order to continue my spiritual journey it was time to let go of this precious guardian and attitude that had given me some sense of security over the years, and so I did. A couple of days after the ceremony had closed I went to some hot springs with my friends to rest and relax, and that evening, as I returned to our cottage after my first soak, I suddenly realized how vulnerable I felt in the world without this old protection and for a moment almost claimed it back. Luckily, I could feel how I was just scared and reacting, so instead I reassured myself and offered myself the trust to live on without my old shield.

For most of us the common way to avoid feeling is to seek a safe haven in the tiny tower of our rational mind, from which we can look into our world and try to make sense of it without actually experiencing it. The use of the intellect and any question beginning with "why" are a sign of such resistance to experiencing what we have invited into our lives. Any resistance, however justified, is an attempt to stop the natural flow of the river of existence: we may feel the need to do so from time to time, but we can dam and try to control such flow only for so long. The creation of armoring and defenses can be quite useful in the aftermath of a traumatic experience in the same way that anti-depressants can be valuable when taken for a short while, but they end up having a deadening effect over the long run. Unfortunately, what protects us from ourselves and the world also separates us from ourselves and our environment, and as a result that relatively safe place between our ears eventually becomes a very lonely and fearful one. The heart wants to stay open, and the call to open one's heart again and set it free is what draws many people to the medicine of San Pedro.

Should you then feel that you are holding any such armoring, before any attempt or pretense of letting it go, you would do well to see and appreciate the contract and purpose of such defense mechanism, honor the great value it has had, and ask yourself whether the assumptions and circumstances that led to creating such protection are still valid today, or whether its purpose has already been fulfilled. To complete this process I also invite you to be most honest with yourself and see if you have the courage to stand in this world that naked, vulnerable, and open once again, and willing to feel hurt, betrayed, or loved without any guarantee that you won't suffer again and again.

The speeding up of change in our modern society is widely resisted by most people, and such resistance manifests as a nostalgia for an idealized unchanging world that never really existed: a resistance to change and an anxiety about change. The direction of the West is also the place of the setting sun and of things that come to an end: it teaches us that everything in this dimension comes to pass, but if we muster the courage to allow life to unfold in its cyclical fashion and meet the darkness of night with faith and courage, we can also trust that the sun will be shining again and again when morning comes. As the place where the sun sets, the West is really the direction of death and dying, of mourning and of letting go of what no longer is.

Ever since I moved to Peru and engaged intensely with San Pedro and Ayahuasca my life has been a never-ending succession of deaths, mostly psychological ones. As a result there has been more grieving and mourning than I could have imagined or anticipated. But with each completed grieving came also a lightening up of my being, so I have learnt with time to welcome this process as quickly and thoroughly as possible to the point that I now see my life as a constant death and rebirth. That rebirth is of course impossible unless we let go and allow the old to die and come to pass.

EMOTIONAL HEALING

It is only when we are willing and ready to let go, even if temporarily, of our defenses that the journey into our hearts can continue. In our masculine culture being emotional and vulnerable is frowned upon and we soon learn as we grow up about the societal benefits of repressing our emotions. In my work with San Pedro over the years I have come to the conclusion that emotions don't necessarily need to be understood or explained: they just want to be experienced. Despite our judgments about emotions and displays thereof, we *are* emotional beings and to repress this side of ourselves is an act of rejection and dishonoring.

Emotionality is equated with feminine energy and in our quest to denigrate all aspects of the Feminine we have come to judge and shame anybody who is openly emotional. The latest, I believe unconscious, way to chastise our feelings is the recent labeling on the part of New Age and spiritual seekers of certain emotions such as fear or anger as "negative" and therefore as aspects of ourselves to be repressed or sublimated at any cost. Sadly, spiritual correctness nowadays requires of us that we shut up about our true feelings just like our parents used to tell us, and once again we do as we are told or tell ourselves so as to avoid rejection. We may feel uncomfortable around certain emotions, and therefore we judge them negatively, but all emotions simply *are* and simply ask us to embrace and experience them.

It was a long journey for me until I finally became comfortable with my emotions and feelings. An important shift happened when I attended a weekend workshop with Gabrielle Roth in 1994 in New York titled, *Dance Your Emotions*. I was actually in the midst of one of two bouts of depression I have ever experienced. I had been totally ill at ease with myself for a couple of months until I realized that I was depressed. Depression, I was to finally figure out, is not sadness or anger, but the result of an inability to feel and express those emotions. Once again, ashamed about this less-than-stellar part of myself, I shut down from myself and everybody around me. I was miserable, and yet too ashamed to ask for help.

Being able to dance my emotions unselfconsciously that weekend allowed me to see for the first time their beauty and power: needless to say, it was a liberating experience. After that experience many other processes followed but none have offered me the honesty of heart and the space to explore and experience my emotions as San Pedro.

San Pedro is a wonderful medicine that allows us to finally experience those emotions that for whatever reason we have failed to fully embrace in the past. Experiencing emotions is all that is needed in order for them to be released, and with that we release the dark shadow that repressed emotions casts over our lives and the way we perceive ourselves, others, and the world.

Just like a child who has fallen and hurts, and who will scream and cry freely only to be once again playing with his friends shortly afterwards as if nothing much had happened at all. It's quite amazing and beautiful. Under the effects of San Pedro we rediscover that freedom, which is really the permission we offer ourselves to simply feel. Oftentimes people during ceremonies will be laughing or crying uncontrollably for hours without even knowing what they're laughing or crying about because sometimes the story behind those emotions is so old as to be forgotten, but not the repressed emotions connected with it. I (and many others) can guarantee that there is nothing more rewarding than the release and relief experienced after a good cry or an outburst of repressed anger on San Pedro. And afterwards we are left wondering why in the world we had waited so long for such a simple yet profound release to happen.

FEELING

In our brainy and overly rational culture it feels important to actually share what it is, as far as I'm concerned, to feel. When I did my first Avatar© course in 1994 I had no idea of what feeling actually was. I was so in my head that I couldn't embrace any experience without my head being fully engaged in trying to make sense of it. The experience of having a constant inner dialogue is far from uncommon and one that is often experienced by people drinking plant medicines. When this happens most people simply resent themselves for not being able, as hard as they may try, to shut that dialogue down. For me this is just the medicine bringing out this pattern for us to become aware of it and see how it prevents us from being truly present. Rather than resenting it, I invite people to marvel at it and appreciate it as is without identifying with it.

After years of judging and subsequently trying to control and silence the mind, it can be challenging to begin appreciating it wholeheartedly. Often we don't even know where to begin and how to go about it. We may think that our judgment against our minds is a positive spiritual attitude, whereas judgments are *always* simply actions of our minds and therefore the more we try to silence our mind, the stronger the grip of our mind over us becomes.

Personally, I have learned not to take whatever comes out of my head too seriously for too long. I just let my mind go on, simply witnessing and marveling at it to the point of laughing with it until I ask myself the question, "what are you avoiding *feeling* with so much mental chatter? How do you really *feel* right now?" And then I finally let myself drop deep into my emotional self and feel whatever is there that I was trying to avoid. Finally embracing and honoring those feelings brings inner peace and a natural and effortless silencing of the mind.

Many people who come to me express their wish to shut down their thoughts or kill their minds and egos. I can sure understand such desire but I feel that there is enough killing going on in this world and this wish feels to me more like a resistance than a sincere desire. Unfortunately what we resist, no matter how fiercely, persists. So I have no other option but to invite these people to explore their resistances as expressed in the overactivity of their own minds.

Quite a few Westerners engaged in Buddhist and meditation practices have a limited understanding of such practices and despite their honest intentions they "observe" their thoughts and feelings from the spiritually disguised tower of their minds, once again safely avoiding life by sitting cross-legged in their Zen bubble. I know I'm being a little sarcastic but I'm doing this with love and humor, and humor seems the only way to burst such bubbles.

If I'm not mistaken, the original idea behind "observing" is actually the same as "feeling," which in my experience is to simply but fully be present and embrace our experience and any emotion connected with it. When we are fully present all of our attention is on experiencing: as a result the ego does disappear and with it also dissipate all pretense and all identities, including the one of egolessness. To be fully in the present moment one has to sacrifice and let go of all agendas and beliefs that one *ought to* feel or be a certain way. These beliefs, which color the way of most spiritual seekers who have read and studied too much and felt too little, have little to do with spirituality and meditation but are the legacy of our Western need to perform and accomplish, which insidiously feeds our egos rather than integrating them.

Of course this is all part of the process and there is no shortage of meditators who benefit beautifully from engaging with plant medicines once they are willing to let go of the comfort of their practice as they have known it. I always warn meditators that plant medicine ceremonies are not meditation because of the widespread misunderstanding of what meditation is, and so I dissuade them from holding any meditation posture during our ceremonies together. And yet, in the end the two processes *are* one and the same: an exercise in presence and being that teaches us to be present to ourselves and our worlds all the time.

Another misconception lies between feeling and emoting, which springs from neo-shamanic ideas that confuse dramatic convulsing and other carry-ons with actual feeling. It is true that a little dramatizing and acting up and out can help open the way to a more genuine feeling of emotions, but we are always at risk of falling in love with our performance, thus foregoing true experiencing. Most of us have sat in ceremonies where we could feel that someone's singing, noise, or thrashing around was a performance that was as distracting to us as it was to them. For me San Pedro healing ceremonies are not a fancy ritual nor a performance, but a wonderful opportunity to let go of our perceived need to perform. Performance is a shying away from true essence and sincere expression: it is a way for the ego to disguise itself as spirit. Resisting the temptation to perform is for many the only way to sink deeper into their true feelings and eventually into their true nature. Plant medicine strips us naked from all pretension and formalism so that we can become once again vulnerable and in that vulnerability become honest and truthful.

EMOTIONS

Emotions are feeling states that well up from inside of us spontaneously. Wanting to "control" one's emotions is a desire, luckily often frustrated, to repress and deny a part of ourselves that is simply expressing itself. If such expression is denied, then the corresponding emotion is pushed further down until it eventually manifests through our physical body, more often than not as disease. And physical disease is just a way for us to draw attention to aspects of our being that ask for attention and loving awareness.

Emotions such as fear, anger, and grief, are reactions, i.e., they are expressions of the lower aspects of our consciousness. Using the Hindu terminology we can say that they are an expression of the three lower chakras, which are the energetic centers ruled by the belief that we are separate. The belief of separation causes us to perceive ourselves as small and powerless, and gives rise to the emotion of fear. In reality, grief and anger are also expressions of fear, and ultimately there is either love or fear, with fear being a desperate attempt to deny the universality of Love.

ACIM, which has deeply influenced my own spiritual journey, gently reminds us that even though we like to believe that bargaining is a realistic option, we can only be in either fear or love—where there is fear there is no space for love, and we experience ourselves and creation as love only after all fear has dissipated. ACIM goes a step further and teaches that since fear is an illusion and a creation of our separate minds, love is really all that truly is.

ACIM is a text and workbook that is claimed to be a channeled message from Jesus Christ. My spiritual wanderings started when I left the Catholic Church, which had been my spiritual home until the age of 11. I left the Church the moment I perceived that my budding homosexuality was not welcome there. Over the years I prayed at many temples east and west, and it is ironic that my teacher in Amazonian plant medicine, Don Francisco Montes Shuña, was the one who helped me reconnect with my Christian heritage, and of all places in the middle of the Amazon jungle.

In our first ceremony together I remember my distinct puzzlement and resistance every time Don Francisco would mention Jesus and the Virgin Mary in his icaros[16]. And then, little by little, I relaxed and got to experience these spiritual figures as vibrations—spiritual vibrations that transcend cultural and historical manipulations, and that once again were shining their bright light of Love, Compassion, and Forgiveness upon my path.

I believe the reason that no major spiritual teacher has come to this world since the historical Jesus over 2000 years ago is because as a people we are still learning the all-too-important lessons of love and forgiveness. The teachings of the Christ speak of the opening of the heart and I feel we are still in the process of integrating and moving beyond the lower chakras ruled by fear to fully embrace the joys of love and the heart. That no other teacher of the same stature has shown up on this Earth since Jesus is also because, at least in my own experience, nothing else is really needed once the heart is fully open and its energy informs all of our being and awareness. And I would even go as far as saying that the opening of the higher chakras is simply a deepening and expansion of the heart chakra's blessing and blissful vibration.

Globally we are indeed in the middle of a huge shift in consciousness from the slavery of fear to the freedom of love. It is a beautiful process that is indeed happening right now despite the challenges of shedding our old beliefs of separation, and each one of us is in our own unique way undergoing this shedding and transforma-tion. As the "Message of the Hopi Elders"[17] reminds us,

---

[16] Icaros are traditional healing songs used in Ayahuasca ceremonies and all aspects of Amazonian plant medicine.

[17] Hopi Nation, Oraibi, Arizona.

"There is a river flowing now very fast. It is so great and swift that there are those who will be afraid. They will try to hold on to the shore. They will feel they are being torn apart and will suffer greatly. Know the river has its destination. The elders say we must let go of the shore, push off into the middle of the river, keep our eyes open, and our heads above the water."

This process of shedding our fears and embracing expansion is the very evolution of Universal Consciousness towards the full awareness, honoring, and embracing of the Divinity and Holiness of all of Creation as expression of that same consciousness. This is the fulfillment of Creation, and this is what in my opinion is really happening. What we hear on the news is the dying but stubborn voice of a paradigm that is destined to end but is resistant to such transformation. To resist this shift only adds suffering to a process that is already challenging enough, but like I said at the beginning of this book, we have all the necessary support and encouragement from all of Creation to undergo this process and I have found San Pedro to be a most helpful medicine in opening our hearts.

Fear

If we are to heed the teachings of *ACIM*, then in order to open our hearts all we need to do is let go of fear, and I have written extensively about fear in my book on Ayahuasca, as for me this particular medicine at its most powerful helps us face our deepest fears.

Fear is a reaction and creation of the mind and the separate self. The conscious mind, according to the philosopher and cyberneticist Gregory Bateson

(1904-1980), functions as a filter of awareness that is most importantly concerned with survival issues, and therefore focuses nowadays primarily on safety, sex, money, and power. The mind is the place where experience is remembered for future reference and the resulting conditioning is stored. Memory, whether cellular or conscious, is a most useful but often over-valued tool as all it can offer is a subjective and limited perception of something that is past and therefore probably no longer valid in the present moment. Past data and experiences can be helpful in assessing a situation but they invariably fail to offer an adequate picture of the present moment. Furthermore, our assessment of the present through past experiences prevents us from seeing the situation with fresh eyes and clear sight, often forgetting that those past expe-riences have already taught us much and, as a result, transformed us. Many spiritual traditions have warned us about any part of us that functions on automatic from past assumptions: the path to liberation often involves a process of coming to awareness of these automatic responses and patterns, and their letting go unlocks the way to a new awareness that is no longer limited by the past but open to the infinite potential of the present moment.

Whenever the mind is used as an instrument dedi-cated to survival it then becomes an expression of the ego, that part of ourselves that creates itself as separate from everything and everybody else, and gives us a sense of individuality. We all incur in this process of indi-viduation that has taken millennia for human beings to develop in the very first years of our existence: we start as undifferentiated fetuses in the womb and unaware of anything else outside of ourselves, and grow into fully individuated children and adults. The process of growing up is a process of progressively coming into our own and crystalizing a sense of selfhood and identity. Often we resist that process and long for the ease and comfort of the maternal womb. Such longing is even more acute in Western modern societies where individualism has become the highest of goals and where the most revered of our members can claim to be "somebody," and so there is an unvoiced pressure to become somebody, which is then resisted by a desire to be no one at all, just like a baby before birth.

In mass societies where many people feel insignificant, the pursuit of happiness is really the pursuit of individuality and the fulfillment of ego-centered desires. But it is all a sham because deep down what we want first and foremost is security and a sense of belonging, which in our society can be bought only by conforming. So the present paradox is the creation of falsely unique, but uniquely conforming, individuals. The more individualized, and therefore separate, we become, the more we crave connection and pursue this in relationships and by joining communities. I feel however that the deep loneliness we experience these days stems not only from the breaking down of traditional social structures but most importantly from the split within ourselves as we pursue this ever-fleeting happiness outside of ourselves: we reject, abandon, and betray ourselves in the pursuit of safety and acceptance by adhering to whatever the current social standards may be.

The Judeo-Christian and Eastern/Indian cultures and religions have put great emphasis on the deleterious effects of our desires, often chastising and demonizing them, but I believe that fear is our most tyrannical master and we are its most subservient slaves. Fear is

75

how the ego can keep its stronghold over us, and we feed that fear and the ego by avoiding feeling that which we fear. I jokingly remind my clients that they would most likely pay me much more if I helped them avoid their fears instead of inviting them to face them. The avoidance of what we fear is actually a defense mechanism enacted by the ego in order to keep its supremacy: the fear of facing our fears is a way to keep those fears at bay, whereas in reality what we do is give them even more power while disempowering ourselves with thoughts such as "I can't do it" or "this is way above my capacities and abilities." The first fear to face is then the fear of fear and the self-sabotaging and disempowering beliefs underneath that fear.

The fear of fear is what most people who sign up for plant medicine ceremonies and retreats have to face one way or another in order to engage in this process. Money, time, and other practical matters are only excuses and more truthfully just ways to rationalize this deep resistance, which is as truly paralyzing as it is understandable. As a result of my awareness of this possible predicament I never pressure anybody to participate in my ceremonies and invite my clients to do the same, i.e., never feel obligated to do anything unless they feel somewhat ready to take the next step rather than because of some external or internal pressure to go ahead. In the process of learning to love and honor ourselves it is important to honor sometimes our present inability to move forward: when we embrace that part of us that feels frightened and frozen, one of the best medicines is to offer it our loving patience and understanding.

Fear is to be avoided at all costs in our society, and control is to be exercised under all circumstances in order to avoid the humiliation and danger of exposing ourselves as fearful. At its core the fear of fear is the fear of feeling the profound inner sense of separation and the resulting loneliness and overwhelm. The journey into that dark and cold abyss is only for true heroes: some have stayed at the edge of it and suffered, others have made it through to the other side renewed and reborn.

When I finally took the courage to look at my fear of dying I realized that beneath that fear was actually a fear of living, and when I looked at my fear of failure what I saw was my fear of rejection and abandonment. Looking at my fears allowed me to see the wounds that were at the root of these fears and begin healing them in earnest.

With people who work with me and find themselves paralyzed by their own fear I share the attitude I finally adopted in my life: one day I asked myself whether I wanted to keep on living my life afraid of myself. Since what I had previously feared within myself (mostly because it was unknown and foreign) was after all still *just* me, I figured I would be better off making friends with all of myself instead of wandering within my own being scared of most of its rooms, which I had most likely designed, built, and decorated myself. My decision to marry myself and to be in a loving rather than fearful relationship with myself under the auspices of San Pedro has been the most positively rewarding thing I have ever done: by embracing all of myself I gained the self-confidence I had always wanted, and it was effortless because I was no longer limping through life but comfortably walking on both feet. Looking at our shadows allows us to integrate these parts of ourselves we had hidden away. The resulting wholeness offers us a better picture of who we really are, and in the totality of our own being there is no lack whatsoever.

Fear freezes us. In Dante's Divine Comedy many people in the lower rings of Hell are depicted as trapped in either tree trunks or other contraptions and thus unable to move and live deliberately. Guilt and the fear of punishment and rejection often lead us to retreat to a hidden place where no progress is possible. Many people in ceremony, when in the grips of fear, report the impossibility to move and an experience of being trapped in their bodies. What they are being trapped by is not their physical bodies but their fear and reluctance to surrender and feel the fear that the medicine is inviting them to experience so that they can let it go. In Chinese medicine the emotion of fear is also connected with the sensation of cold and the element of water: when the flow of who we are is frozen by fear, it comes to a halt and the natural movement of life is impeded with disastrous consequences.

It is wise to remember that everything we desire we also resist we equal intensity, and that if we held no resistance against experiencing what we desire, we would manifest our desires effortlessly. In this world of duality every push entails a pull of equal strength, so in the course of our healing process with San Pedro we would do well to explore the resistance part of every wish we bring to the medicine, particularly because most of our resistances are fear-based. For example, a desire to be more open with others may hide a fear of judgment or betrayal. We may desire to have more abundance in our lives but at the same time hold negative judgments about money, or a belief about not deserving such abundance.

Along the same lines it is important to know that we fear what we desire with equal intensity, and that the closer we get to our destination, the stronger the resistance to actually getting there. This is particularly so for anybody on a spiritual path. Any valid spiritual practice has as a goal total liberation: liberation from fears and desires, and the dissolution of the ego that creates and feeds them for its own assertion and survival. The closer we get to such liberation, the stronger the resistance of the ego as it feels increasingly threatened. I used to naively think that things would get easier at some point but it was actually the opposite. What did change though was my willingness to accept and face whatever needed to be faced with increased patience, trust, and faith.

A client summarized this predicament when she shared her experience after her second Ayahuasca ceremony with me. She simply said that, "whenever I was in resistance, I was in hell, and whenever I was in acceptance, I was in heaven."

By the same token it is just as true that every resistance implies also a desire, which means that in the end everything we have in the past resisted and denied responsibility for was also desired on some level. To come to a place of entertaining the possibility that we may have desired to experience something that we felt ambivalent about is an important part of many a healing process. An example would be a desire to explore sexuality paired with strong negative judgments about actually engaging in erotic activities. This ambivalence may express itself in episodes of apparent sexual abuse where the individual can claim that they had no part in it. In this way we can deflect responsibility and deny our own desires.

Anger

Anger is our favorite and uncontrollable reaction when we don't get what we want, what we feel we need, or feel entitled to receive. It is the response of a child unaware of the fact that life always gives us what we need and when we need it, and resistant of the fact that the entire world doesn't revolve exclusively around him or her. That child is always ready to come out and have a tantrum in the hope (rarely fulfilled) that a display of anger will result in receiving what he or she wants.

Anger speaks of an immature self and ego out on the loose, and screaming to claim all possible attention available regardless of the circumstances. That such antics are socially frowned upon makes dealing with our anger all the more challenging.

Anger says that we are not willing to accept things as they are, and even less willing to take responsibility for our own experience. If we are angry the natural tendency is to blame someone or something else for how we feel and that (as explained earlier) is an obstacle to actually dealing with the anger and its real causes.

My own reconnection with the rage, that when it was all done and over I realized I had carried since my earliest childhood, was a long uphill journey as it took me years before I would own my anger completely. Eventually I could see that I had no other option but swallow that bitter morsel, which had by then grown into a full-sized monster. The first big challenge was to *feel* my anger rather than just acting it out: it had been repressed for so many years, and that repression had been reinforced by the internalized social and religious imperative that "it's not nice to harbor such feelings against one's parents." In 2008 I became gravely ill, first with gallstones, and then some mysterious and very painful and debilitating liver disorder. The liver is connected with the emotion of anger and that's often the reason why many people with anger issues resort to alcohol: to help them numb or vent their anger. Unfortunately they also end up dying of liver disorders if the source of that anger is not healed and all one can do is keep drinking in order to find a minimum of release and relief.

I sure didn't want to die of liver failure, even though alcohol had never been my medication of choice, so with patience and humility I engaged in this healing process and started giving myself the permission to be openly angry whenever that emotion arose. After years of self-repression and shame this was a much-needed phase of my healing. It all culminated one night some months later when I exploded with rage in my garden in Pisac: I swear I could be heard on the other side of town but I didn't care and actually screamed out loud my right to be as angry as I was, and to express it as I wished regardless of social niceties. In the throes of it all and underneath that rage I discovered my newly born child self in agony for believing he had been abandoned by his mother. He was utterly scared and confused, and his reaction to that situation was anger. I realized that as a baby I had not been aware of the circumstances that had led my parents to leave me in a nursery for the first year of my life. All that I experienced then was abandonment, injustice, fear, and confusion. It was actually right after birth that my soul wound of abandonment had been ripped wide open and that evening's release of rage was the last step in the healing of that wound.

For a couple of years after that I still let myself be openly angry with others until eventually that phase ran its course and I realized that *my* anger is my own lot and not something I should subject anybody else to. This time the lesson about the futility and danger of public displays of anger came not from social laws of behavior but from my own healed self. I am a fiery person and still have my temper tantrums every now and then but in a much healthier way, and I no longer wait until I burst wildly but can feel and honor that emotion when it is still just a sign of my discontent.

It's not really easy or pleasant for me to write about and share these things; I do not write about it out of vanity but to let others who may be in a similar predicament know that anger, as deeply rooted as it may be, can be let go of. I don't consider myself to be exceptional in any way and firmly believe that if I could do it, so can anybody else.

As with all other emotions and aspects of our being, the most important thing is to give oneself the permission to feel and embrace these feelings, and to let go of any judgment and conflicting belief that may prevent us from doing so. And of course, to offer oneself the patience, encouragement, and humility necessary to see this process through until healing is reached.

Speaking of patience, I would add that impatience is a form of thinly disguised anger that results from unfulfilled expectations. I focus a lot of my work on the formulation of intentions for each ceremony and inform people that if at any point during or after the ceremony they experience frustration or impatience, they can be pretty sure that expectations have made their appearance. That this happens is totally normal, but to want to hold on to expectations is counterproductive, not only because it gives rise to unnecessary anger, but because San Pedro (like Life) doesn't give us necessarily what we want but what we need, whether we like it or not. To accept this is a sign of maturity; to not accept this may be a sign that the person does not yet have the psychological maturity to engage with this or other plant medicines.

Grief and Sadness

Grief is the human response to loss and sadness is one of the emotions related to the experience of loss, so it is no accident that sadness is so pervasive in this impermanent world. The experience of grief is, in human terms, a universal one connected with death and passing. Interestingly, the more aware we become of our finiteness as physical bodies and mental entities, the stronger our resolution to achieve physical immortality has become: we stubbornly keep resisting the most natural of experiences available when incarnating, i.e., dying. Our fear and resistance of death is transferred to all aspects of our lives: the end of a relationship, of any phase of our development, even the breaking down of an object, they all become opportunities to experience loss. Loss is followed by the grieving process, which, when completed, brings us to a place of acceptance of loss and a letting go of that which we have seemingly lost.

When I first came to Peru in 2004 I was still struggling with the difficult end of a ten-year long relationship. It was not long after the initial breakup that I met Pascal, who taught me the importance and necessity of grieving. I had suffered many losses before then but had no clue about the process of grieving, which meant that I had been carrying a lot of un-integrated sadness. When I finally started embracing my grief I realized that loss was an experience I had resisted for many lifetimes and that I was manifesting another opportunity to embrace it. Grieving was the hardest thing I've ever done in this life: it was not easy to embrace my feelings of loss, hurt, resentment, and the emotions of anger and sadness over the following two years, and I wondered often if I would ever see the end of this process or whether I would spend the rest of my days inconsolably sad. But eventually I was able to let go, and when it was all over I saw how the whole process had radically transformed me: for years I had wished to grow into an adult and the full expe-rience of grieving had turned me into the man I had always wanted to become. Up until then I had always just pursued happiness as best as I could, but of course with very mixed results. Surprisingly, embracing fully my grief and the depth of my sadness opened the way to finally experiencing joy with equal wholeheartedness.

From this experience I have learned that when we shut down against feeling a particular emotion we end up completely shutting down throughout the whole emotional spectrum. That shutting down is supported by unconscious fears that if we embrace our anger we may kill someone, or that the well of our sadness is a bottomless pit from which we may never be able to resurface. The truth is that all experiences transform us, so it's not a matter of resurfacing from the same well we leap into, but of allowing ourselves to go deep into our emotions until we eventually come out into another space altogether: embracing experience and letting go not only teach us important and beautiful lessons but also renew us.

As the process of constant renewal implies a letting go and dying experience, then learning to grieve is of paramount importance if we are to embrace renewal and rebirth. Feeling my sadness was the gateway to embracing and beginning to heal my wound of abandonment. For others it may be an opportunity to start exploring their wounds of rejection, injustice, betrayal, or humiliation.

Unfortunately, our modern society's fear of death is rampant to such a degree of collective denial that we no longer have valid rituals and spaces for grieving. It was a true turning point for the Burning Man tribe when in 2000 the first temple on the Playa in the Black Rock desert of Nevada was erected. It had been built to honor people who had committed suicide and children who had died of leukemia, thus including both people who had consciously chosen death and children who were likely destined to die despite their young age. Instantly that temple became a magical place for grieving and honoring our departed ones, thus completing the dying process symbolized by the burning of the Man.

The night following the burning of the Man a large and completely silent crowd gathered around the temple that had been the repository of so much grief, love, and magic to watch it all go aflame. It was a full moon night but with so much wind and dust in the air that we only had the moon to guide us to the temple. After it was set on fire I went as close as I could: my intention was to circle it three times counter-clockwise and three times clockwise to help release all the energy and prayers it had held for many days. As I was silently chanting a prayer to support such release, I unexpectedly fell into a rapture and spent the following three hours praying, meditating, and making offerings to the fire until it was a pile of embers and I was completely covered in ashes mixed with Playa dust.

The organizers immediately saw the importance of creating such a space within the Burning Man gathering that a temple, each one with a different flavor and nuance but always with the same spirit, has been dreamt and built every year since.

Death, just like birth, is the experience that most intimately connects us with the mystery of Life. And when embraced fully it reconnects us with the Sacred, with the mortality of the body and the immortality of love and the spirit. In grieving we discover that the love that connected us to an individual, a time, or a place, never goes away. The grieving process simply helps us deal with the initial sorrow and resistance to things and people passing on to a new expression of their being, as well as the loneliness, confusion, and sadness we feel as a result of that passing.

Many people come to me with unfinished grieving processes and I have found no more supportive medicine or process that beautifully supports grieving than San Pedro. Grieving is the also first process I invite people into whenever necessary because incomplete grieving irrevocably keeps us in the past, prevents us from being in the moment, and is often the biggest hurdle against something or someone new entering our lives.

Letting go of the past is just accepting that what has passed has passed and will not come back in the same way ever again, but will leave a lasting footprint on this planet and live on forever in our memories. To honor and allow our sadness to be and express itself in any way it wishes is a beautiful way to honor the deep bond that connected us to things and people past, and our tears can be a sign of our reluctance to let them go but are also a beautiful expression of our love for them.

Shame and Joy

Shame is a feeling that is the direct consequence of some negative judgment and the resulting guilt, either clearly expressed by the self against itself or, when it's unbearable, projected outside the self and then perceived as coming from others. It is important to be aware that whenever we react to or resist through denial any judgment coming from others, this is a sure sign that that judgment resonates and is identical to a judgment or belief we secretly hold in our consciousness. Fully owning our reaction instead of blaming on is the best way to take responsibility for such judgments and beliefs so that we can explore them and let them go.

When we hold shame about ourselves we hide from the world, thus separating ourselves from it. Our guilt says we no longer have a right to sit at the table with everybody else. We punish ourselves with the hope of assuaging our guilt, but the punishment is a self-inflicted starvation from the ever-flowing bounty of Life's energy.

My own healing journey required repeated visits to the many parts of myself I had hidden from the world because of shame. It turned out that among these were not just aspects that in our society we would easily classify as shameful such as petty thefts or unorthodox sexual fantasies, but also shame about my inner and outer beauty and gifts.

The exploration of shame is of primary importance whenever present, and it is an important gate into whatever beliefs and judgments we hold in our consciousness that may be at the root of such shame. Gender, sexual, body, and racial shame are often explored not just for our own sake, but also for the benefit of all humanity and our collective consciousness.

Joy naturally reemerges once we let go of our guilt and shame by forgiving ourselves wholeheartedly. In so doing, we rejoin the whole of Creation, which is perennial ecstasy and joy. Joy and happiness are not states to be sought outside of ourselves but the natural state of who we are, and they are always available to us whenever we reconnect without judgment with ourselves and the world. That joy is never static but a continuous flowing that beautifully colors and blesses our lives and the lives of others: this is the end state of all healing and the gift I received after years of plant medicine work with San Pedro, Ayahuasca, and the dozen or so plants that I have dieted so far. Spending years vomiting, dieting, and crying was (as challenging as it was) a ridiculously small price of admission into the joyful existence that is my—and everybody else's—birthright.

THE WISDOM OF EMOTIONS

I don't know about you but in my being uncomfortable with my emotions I ended up distrusting and often rejecting them altogether, thus depriving myself of an important source of information and wisdom. As part of that emotional spectrum I would also add all sensations and feelings that are often below the skin and beyond our ability to put into words and explain rationally.

Emotions are not only the expression of old reactions to certain situations, they can also be a valuable input about what we are experiencing or about to experience: they are part of our intuition and truly one of the many ways the unconscious expresses itself. The difference between emotional reactions and the expression of intuition is a difficult one when we resent or judge our emotions, hence the distrusting of precious information. A sense of fear and impending danger may be a playing out of old insecurities, and sometimes it can be an indication that something bad is indeed about to happen. A surge of anger can be an echo of an old unmet need, and sometimes it can point to an important present need. Sadness can be an indication of our reluctance to let go of the past, and sometimes it can be a sincere expression of love and affection. To know the difference between reaction and the genuine expression of our feelings and to follow this expression of our intuition is made difficult and sometimes impossible by our distrust and dismissal of what we feel, like every time our inner judge tells us that we shouldn't feel this or that way.

It is only with time and a positive attitude towards our emotions that we can eventually learn to trust this important part of ourselves, which is most empowering. The emotional opening experienced with the support of San Pedro then becomes the opening of our own intuition as well.

PASCAL'S PROCESS

To illustrate the importance of exploring and embracing repressed emotions during a healing pro-

cess with *San Pedro*, here is the story of someone as it unfolded during his third *San Pedro* retreat with me in 2016.

Pascal arrived in Pisac after a rather difficult time since his last retreat the previous year: I had invited him to make weekly "dates" with himself in order to nurture a more loving and supportive relationship with himself, but following my advice proved to be difficult to implement and was met with resistances and excuses of all sorts until a sudden onset of temporary diabetes made him understand that above anything else he needed to be proactively loving and nurturing to himself. Despite the important shift in attitude, upon his arrival in Pisac Pascal confessed to having been suffering from insomnia as well: his inability to create some financial security for his retirement days and the regrets and remorse about it had been keeping him awake at night for months.

During a walk by the river before his first ceremony we talked about all that until he mentioned the traumatic experience as a boy of not knowing a geometry theorem and having to write that theorem two-thousand-five-hundred times before the next day as a punishment. In the middle of the night his father came to his room, saw him at his desk, asked him what he was doing, and returned to sleep. Forty-seven years later Pascal was still visibly upset because of his father's lack of support, which was not limited to that incident alone but was quite the norm and had left this child feeling completely left to his own devices in a rather abusive school and social environment. The rage, disappointment, and sadness were all still clearly there under his skin, so I invited Pascal to bring this unhealed trauma to his first ceremony, during which he was able to honor, embrace, and let go of these repressed emotions. For me this part of the process seemed like an important gateway as I immediately saw the similarities between Pascal's perceived lack of support from his father in his childhood and his own present inability to create some financial security and support for his old age.

After exploring some debilitating and limiting beliefs about himself in the second ceremony, Pascal went on to explore in the third ceremony his beliefs and relationship with money, which all revealed the extent of deep fears and insecurities related to a chaotic family environment while he was growing up.

Before his fourth and last ceremony Pascal and I had once again a long talk about his intentions for the next day. I had already intuited that it would be important for him to explore his fears of ageing, getting sick, and dying, so I gently stirred our conversation towards these topics and that's when he shared that since his early 20's he had been very afraid of his father's dying. The fear and worry about his father's health and the challenges of old age had only intensified with time and the fact that Pascal had been projecting his own fears onto his father's predicament.

At the beginning of the ceremony the following day I invited Pascal to start the process by going back to the fear of his father's dying as he had experienced it in his 20's. Not before long a much earlier memory came to his awareness: that of his father leaving the family home to go and live with another woman without a proper good-bye and without being able to see him again for the following two months. This story of repeated abandonment and lack of support from his father had been recreated time and time again with Pascal's lack of self-discipline and support to himself.

Becoming aware of this story of abandonment, its dynamics, and repercussions by exploring emotions that had been held in silent check since his childhood allowed Pascal to heal a very important part of his life and finally offer the loving care and support to the child self within him that was still feeling abandoned and in need of that care.

By becoming himself the father he thought he had never had during his childhood, Pascal left Pisac two days later feeling much more confident about his ability to take care of himself. He did confess to feeling at a slight loss because he felt he was to learn how to live all over again from this renewed sense of self. I am very aware that fear of the unknown can make anyone see a gentle hill like an insurmountable mountain, but saw Pascal off with a smile knowing that the first and most challenging step had already been taken.

BOUNDARIES AND PROTECTION

Earlier on we spoke of armoring, and to speak of protection and boundaries, which are closely related to armoring, seems to me very important whenever we speak about shared experiences. Healing ceremonies are among the most intimate experiences we get a chance to share, and sharing such an intimate space brings up all sorts of concerns. Many of these concerns are about the ability of the individual to have their own experience among many other people going through their own process in their own ways.

First of all I would like to share once again my belief that what we sign up for is our own choice and stress the importance of taking responsibility for the consequences of our choices. This means that whenever we choose to join in a ceremony we are also choosing to experience all the unknowns that a ceremony may entail, and so it is most important to remind ourselves and trust that whatever happens is an important part of our healing process. All of it: the good, the bad, the ugly, the distracting, the annoying and so forth.

Even though we always appreciate it when a ceremony unfolds peacefully and beautifully, healing ceremonies are not necessarily pretty affairs by any standards: they can be messy, noisy, and difficult. Even though we hold these ceremonies in ceremonial spaces and temples, since what we drink is after all "medicine," then these ceremonial spaces are really hospitals, and in certain cases they resemble psychiatric wards more than anything else. This is why it is most important that the ceremonial space be a safe space, held with the necessary strength and flexibility, and this is also why I make every participant aware of the fact that in this container we are *all* teachers to one another. That we are teachers to one another can mean that someone may push our buttons to the point of exasperation, anger, or dread. It may mean that someone reflects back to us some part of ourselves we would rather not see but that in the present situation we can't avoid but still do our very best to resist by claiming inside our heads "it's not me, it's *them*!" As someone who rightfully told me on a couple of occasions in the past when I just wouldn't own my judgments and projections, these people "can keep telling themselves that story for as long as they please," meaning that repeating that story, as any attempt at blaming, does unfortunately nothing to help us heal and grow.

If the world is a reflection of us, then the ways we perceive other people are a clear and sharp (to the point of hurting) reflection of our own judgments and beliefs. When we don't take responsibility for our *own* experience of others, then resentment and eventually gossip starts. That there is no shortage of such gossiping in plant medicine circles and spiritual communities is a sign that blame is unfortunately still rampant and unquestioned, often to the detriment of not only the individual but the community at large.

It's important to remind oneself that these circles and medicines are meant to bring out our shadows and that in this shadow play we at times involve others in the game of projection and transference. To look for and expect the perfect community that is all peace and love and no friction whatsoever is not only unrealistic but a sign that we are not willing to look at our own shadow at all. A healthy healing environment is not necessarily a perfect environment but one where these projections and transferences can be owned and explored, and the shadows can be integrated.

This is why in my San Pedro and Ayahuasca ceremonies I don't allow any interaction among the participants for the entire duration of the ceremony, and why before each ceremony I invite people to take responsibility for the reactions that other participants may elicit, rather than acting them out, so that the person we initially wanted to comfort or strangle turns into a precious teacher.

The heart wishes to be open and, particularly in San Pedro ceremonies, the heart is open beyond our capacity to close it, which is a wonderful and welcome experience after so much self-repression and hiding. When in such a predicament, some people fear that some energy or other may enter their being with negative repercussions. These people often show up with an array of not only protective charms, but also cleansing tools and perfumes should they perceive that some "dark" or "negative" energy has entered their space. These people *really* love traditional ceremonies steeped in duality and the belief in a conflictive relationship between dark and light as they reinforce their beliefs that evil is a hard reality and therefore their attempts at protecting themselves are most needed and justified.

Other people mention their apparently innate empathy, which makes them sensitive to everything and everybody around them. Even though I don't doubt the innate empathy of some of these individuals, many who claim such a gift are in my opinion unaware of the true root of their empathy: in many cases I sense that their ability to feel what others are feeling, particularly when that ability is always and compulsively turned on, is not a special gift from being in their hearts but an attitude, often developed in early infancy, in order to feel secure and safe. In many cases this is an ability developed in order to sense danger in a troubled and violent family environment, or a way to sense how people feel in order to help them feel better so that the child feels cared for again. In these cases what has been termed "empathy" is oftentimes a fear-based survival strategy, which is why these people express a fear of being in a healing ceremony with others: their empathy has unconscious reasons and is rooted in fear.

Also, these people are prone to take upon themselves everything that other people feel and experience. Sometimes they wear that propensity with pride and believe that they are healing the world by swallowing everybody else's psychic and emotional garbage, and sometimes they feel the need to protect themselves from others, particularly in ceremony.

I had one such person lately in my ceremonies, and during our first San Pedro ceremony, as soon as I realized that she was unable to hold her space and that she was trying to take on everybody's perceived pain and suffering, I invited her to question the validity of such behavior. It turned out that her belly was hurting and had been in pain most of her life as a result, as far as I was concerned, of her attempts at swallowing everybody else's unhealed energies.

For me this is romanticized old school shamanism that sure has had its value, but I don't personally resonate with it as I feel it's disempowering to others and deeply co-dependent. I say "disempowering and co-dependent" because this attitude of taking on other people's unhealed energies often creates a relation-ship of dependency between healer and patient. I personally prefer to support my clients and encourage them to do the work themselves rather than expect me or anybody else to do it for them.

In the cases of both the fearful and the empathic types, what I really sense is a marked lack of bound-aries. A big part of my journey has been about facing and letting go of fear and letting go of the protective armoring I had put in place since birth and then devel-oped as the years went by. Once the fears started to be integrated there was no logical need to hold on to protections of any kind.

In all honesty I no longer believe in protection: I have spent enough of my time and energy trying to protect myself from the monsters I had created myself.

What I do believe in is the healthy exercise of bound-aries. The shift from protection to healthy boundaries has unfolded as I let go of fear. In this process I was supported and guided by the West African Orisha Exú, also known in the Americas as Eleguá and Legba. Exú is an important energy in the West African pantheon of Ifá spirituality: he is the guardian of the gate, protector of the gate against unwelcome energies and opener of the gate to benevolent spirits. He is the liaison between the world of humans and the supra-human, and in that capacity he is the translator of the sometimes difficult to hear and understand messages coming from the spirit world. As my main Orisha he has been also an important teacher who has taught me that indeed I could exercise healthy boundaries rather than protect myself from any energy or person entering my space and life. That teaching solidified during a San Pedro ceremony when I received the clear message that I no longer needed to be afraid because I had reached the stage of my life where I knew how to exercise such healthy boundaries whenever needed. All of this unfolded as I healed my wounds of abandonment and rejection, which throughout my life made me an easy target of abusive behavior: I was simply too hungry for acceptance and love to be able to say no to any abuse, and would rather betray myself with the hope of receiving some crumbs of love than be alone. It was when I decided I would no longer be an amnesiac beggar but the true master of my own life that I could start being more constructively discerning and make life choices out of love for myself instead of out of fear.

The ability to exercise boundaries is strongly related to our willingness to be in the present moment. Say for instance that I am engaging in some sexual activity with someone I like: it feels good to begin with but at some point I no longer feel comfortable with what I am doing or the person with whom I have been engaging. It may be a strong feeling or a simple gut feeling I am too quick to dismiss. The point is that if I don't honor that feeling and act accordingly by disengaging right away, then I may end up feeling hurt and dishonored. It is easy to blame my partner for such hurt and dishonoring, and this is a recurrent scenario in many cases of sexual abuse, rape, and domestic violence. If we are not present to ourselves and listen to our feelings and emotions, we too often end up feeling hurt, resentful, and regretful. The attempt to deflect responsibility for what happened and how we felt afterwards is a common but highly disempowering one, particularly because there is a part of us that is aware, however secretly and despite any amount of fierce denial, that we always have some responsibility for our lives and experiences.

Such incidents of perceived abuse are unfortunately not uncommon in plant medicine and spiritual circles here in Peru and elsewhere. I see these incidents not as accidents, but as an opportunity for us all to heal our wounds as well as a powerful opportunity to exercise our boundaries and finally have the courage to say "enough, no more." It is good and important to educate ourselves and others so that we live in a respectful and non-objectifying environment, but unrealistic to expect others to behave according to our wishes. Claiming some human rights written at the U.N. or in our countries' constitutions does unfortunately little to actually prevent or stop abuse of any kind from happening. In those cases I believe it is up to us to say no and remove ourselves from the scene of the impending crime, and up to us to listen to our feelings and emotions whenever they arise so that we can act upon them.

As such incidents of abuse, whether physical, sexual, emotional, or mental, do occur in medicine and spiritual circles all the time, I encourage people to always stay present and have the courage to leave any situation we may have signed up for but that, instead of feeling conducive to healing, turns out to be feeding and reinforcing old wounds and judgments.

This is also why I ask people not to call me a shaman as I believe that that the word is overhyped and that people too easily give shamans, medicine people, and spiritual teachers of all persuasions their power and trust only to find their gift of power and trust to be abused and taken advantage of. I always appreciate and honor the trust that clients offer me as they engage in this process under my guidance, but not all practitioners are the same and some are prone to abuse the trust of their patients and students.

Whereas the need for protection originates in fears and insecurities that are fertile ground for fear-inducing beliefs and dangerous experiences[18], boundaries are the expression of self-love and self-care. On an evolutionary level the exercise of boundaries as an expression of self-love is a huge shift: our present civilization and biological make-up have evolved out of deeply-seated fears and our most basic reaction to dangers of any kind has been the flight-or-fight response and the creation of protective strategies.

When we are hurt or fearful, physically or emotionally, we become instantly rigid and protective. By now we know that, as valuable as that response can be, it

---

[18] Not only do we manifest our desires but also our deepest fears.

is also a major hindrance to healing and clarity. As we shift from vibrating on the level of fear, i.e., the three lower chakras, into the vibration of the heart, our relationship with ourselves and the world shifts as well from one of fear to one of love and trust.

In February of 2016 I sprained my ankle really badly. The physiological response was swelling in order to protect the ankle and prevent it from moving: a "no enter and do not disturb" area had been created around the hurt area as a protection and of course I made all the efforts to honor my ankle's need to be left alone in the aftermath of the shock. The only thing I did other than rest was ice the area to allow the swelling to go down, thus bringing in fresh liquids every few hours. Two days after the accident I started massaging the whole area. At first there was a little apprehension, but once I intuited that my body could heal itself with some help and support, I started applying cold and hot packs, and I began massaging the whole area and opening up the channels that had shut down so that the flow of blood and energy could be restored and the body could heal itself thanks to its innate ability to self-repair. It was a repeated offer of support and trust rather than worry. It wasn't *me* healing my ankle but me just fully trusting and allowing my ankle to heal.

In order to restore the natural ability of the body to heal, oftentimes much detoxing and cleansing are called for, but most importantly a shift in consciousness from fear to trust has to happen. The most effective way to be in trust is to let go of fear. Letting go of fear requires a certain degree of vulnerability and that is already an exercise in trust. Once fear is let go of, our natural trust in ourselves and the Universe can resurface and inform our feelings and actions quite effortlessly without any need for protection. Trust in oneself means also trust that no matter what happens we have the ability to exercise our boundaries and say no to unwelcome situations, as well as trust that within ourselves we have all the resources to face whatever challenges life may offer us. Such a shift in consciousness, both on an individual and collective level, and the resulting effects in our daily lives are indeed among the results and blessings of a meaningful opening of the heart.

THE PROSTITUTE

In 2004 my friend Jim Curtan, who had been assisting the author Carolyn Myss in her workshops, offered to work with me using Carolyn's Archetype tarot deck. I was thrown off guard when he told me that among the twelve cards for the reading there were four cards that absolutely needed to be part of the throw. These cards were representations of the archetypes of the Child, Victim, Prostitute, and Saboteur and are all deeply involved in our most pressing challenges related to survival.

The prostitute is that part of ourselves that compromises and sells out in exchange for security, emotional or physical. It is a most widespread archetype in our present culture where we perceive everything and everyone in terms of value, and where we often consciously and unconsciously choose our friends, partners, and work associates according to what we think they have to offer us[19]. We prostitute ourselves each and every time

---

[19] I was made aware of the pervasiveness of such attitude in our culture by reading Fromm, Erich. *The Art of Loving*. New York, HarperCollins Publishers, 2000.

we do something that goes against our truth in order to receive or achieve something; in other words, we betray ourselves in order to appease our fears and insecurities. This happens in all aspects of our lives: in relationships and jobs that we know are not good for us or have long ceased to be nurturing and fulfilling. But we stay on hoping for change or with the hope that our sacrificing our integrity will yield some secret gain, e.g., if I stay in this position long enough I will be rewarded with a promotion and higher salary.

Mind you, we all have made compromises and sacrifices small and big in order to survive or hoping to bring new life into a relationship. This is not what I am referring to: what I am talking about are those instances where our compromises and sacrifices clearly went against our principles and intuition, but we decided to go with it anyway because of fear—fear of being alone, fear of rejection, fear of not being able to survive otherwise, and so on. And such betrayal of our own truth for the sake of appeasing our fears is like a deep stabbing against ourselves.

Perhaps two of the values we hold highest are truth and honesty. We spend our entire lives searching for the truth and hope from others, and most recently from our governments and corporations, that they be truthful, honest, and transparent. But to which degree are we truthful with ourselves? To which degree are we honest with ourselves, honor our feelings and beliefs, and act accordingly?

Most of us have been guilty of secretly prostituting ourselves on more than one occasion. And that's okay because at all moments and in all situations we do the very best that we can, but if we want to live in a world of honesty and integrity, we are the first ones having to start living according to our own truth. This is achieved first and foremost by listening to ourselves and by giving the time and space for our emotions and feelings to be fully honored.

A friend of mine had been keeping a secret from her partner for over a year and that secret was inexorably ruining their relationship. It took much talking, support, and eventually an impending pregnancy for her to finally open up to her partner and share the secret she had been keeping from him. Because she wasn't open, neither could he, and a climate of suspicion and mistrust had eventually grown out of it. Her silence had been her act of prostitution in exchange for not having to confront a difficult situation, but her conscience was troubled and she was most unhappy because she knew she wasn't being honest and she was holding back—because she wasn't in her truth.

If the prostitute archetype speaks of our selling out, our self-betrayal, and our giving our power away to others in order to appease our fears, the exploration of this archetype as we express or have expressed it in the past can bring a lot of forgiveness and healing, and open the way for new ways of being less at the mercy of our fears, more empowered, and in integrity. And of course, our integrity and honesty opens the way for others to also be in their truth.

THEMES AND INTENTIONS RELATED TO THE ELEMENT OF WATER

Here is a list of important themes connected with the Water element that would be ideal to explore during a healing process with San Pedro:

- Emotional and mental armoring
- Unexpressed emotions of any kind
- The Prostitute archetype and ways in which we betray and reject our feelings and emotions
- Perceived needs to protect ourselves or others
- Inability to exercise healthy boundaries in all areas of life
- Unfinished grieving and losses
- Secrets and dishonesty

THE MARRIAGE OF HEAVEN AND EARTH
– *CUSCO TO HUCHUY CUSCO, PERU* –
SEPTEMBER 2014 AND AUGUST 2015

In September of 2014 I hired once again my friend and colleague Miguel Mendiburu[20] to take two friends and myself on a day-trek from Cusco to Huchuy Cusco. Miguel has been a trusted guide whenever I wish to explore new places in this area. His integrity and knowledge make him the ideal guide around these mountains. He specializes in San Pedro walks that are not just walks but a sacred way to receive the healing and wisdom this medicine and these mountains have to offer.

We started our journey above Cusco early in the morning with a ceremonial fire, during which we drank the medicine and offered our prayers and gratitude. As soon as we started our walk I realized I was walking on an ancient pre-Columbian path that felt to me like a snake making its way through valleys and peaks. I saw this path also as a timeline and realized that, as

---

[20] Miguel Mendiburu can be contacted at
www.allpamamajourney.com

invaluable as my previous years' dedication to living in the present moment as much as possible by making peace with and letting go of the past and the uncertainties of the future, this present moment I was inhabiting more fully each day was also part of a bigger process that included both the past and the future. With that awareness I made then and there a commitment to learn as much from ancestral wisdom and do my best to forward that wisdom to future generations.

It turned out that this humble commitment would in the next couple of years, and who knows how else in the future, open new territories, awareness, and projects until then unavailable, and it would also force me to reconsider old priorities and choices. The first repercussion unfolded that same day when I decided that it was time to let go of my boyfriend at the time in order to pursue this new path. It helped greatly to see how little interest I had in continuing to hold on to a romantic relationship that entailed more maintenance than I really liked. I had met Sergeij at a moment in my life of total plenitude when I no longer needed anybody to love or validate me: the experience was exhilarating as for the first time I was in love but not in need, which allowed me to experience at long last the precious gift of free love—love that is free of fear and emotional attachments and expectations.

I had entertained the idea of celibacy in previous years but there was some important healing I still needed to experience in connection with sexuality and intimate relationships. If anything, my previous desire to become celibate had been a subtle way of avoiding those important healings, which often come wrapped up in a whole lot of drama. But that day the path was clear and open, and I chose celibacy in order to engage more deeply in my role as healer and teacher.

When we returned to the same path a year later, I was surprised by the difference in my experience: as a result of my commitment to learn and forward to future generations as much ancestral wisdom as I could, I had this time the whole landscape open up to me to share its teachings in ways until then impossible.

The day before we set out on the walk I had looked Huchuy Cusco up on a guidebook[21] and discovered that the original Quechua name for this small Inca settlement used to be "Kakya Qawani," which means, "From where the lightning can be seen." Lightning was associated in Inca times with Illapa, God of Weather; and as bringer of thunder, lightning, and rain, Illapa truly embodies the masculine principle in the creation game with the Earth. As I walk and ponder about all this, I begin to "see" ancient convoys along this mountain path making their pilgrimage to Huchuy Cusco with servants transporting on a raised platform the Inca and his consort.

As the day progresses I am once again over-whelmed by the Mother essence of this planet Earth and of her unique energy among all planets in this corner of the galaxy: this is a Healing Planet, a place where we come for healing as we are embraced by this cosmic Mother and cared for by her medicines. I can also see the importance of such a planet in the ecology of this galaxy: the unique qualities of this planet are as important to us as they are to all other energies in the planets and star systems around us, both physically and spiritually. The experience for me is most importantly about seeing this planet in all its

---

[21] Box, Ben and Frankham, Steve. *Cusco & the Inca Heartland.* 4th edition. Bath, FootPrint, 2008.

glorious power and uniqueness, and the resolution to do my best to share that awareness.

The walk that day took forever. At some point we seem to be finding ourselves after yet another bend on the path in exactly the same spot as twenty minutes earlier, but eventually we make it to the highest pass and start our gentle descent towards the ruins three hours away. By the time we come close to the canyon that indicates that only an hour's walk is needed to reach the ruins, the sun is already setting and night approaching. Earlier in the day I had asked Miguel about our timing and he answered that there was nothing to worry as we had plenty of drink, food, medicine, and a full moon awaiting us after dark. Sure enough, as we come to the other side of the canyon, the most romantic place I have visited until now in this whole region with its stone path, Inca terraces, and the river running through it, the moon is shining her light on the path ahead of us. Beautiful and magic.

I had realized earlier on in the day that this was a pilgrimage to celebrate the marriage of the Masculine and Feminine as in the marriage of Heaven and Earth, symbolized by the striking of lightning on the earth, announcing the rains that will awaken once again Mother Earth's fertility. August is celebrated here in the Andes as Pachamama's birthday, and it dawned on me that one of the most auspicious times for making such pilgrimage to celebrate and honor the marriage of Heaven and Earth would have been on the first full moon of such month, such as the day we had unconsciously chosen for such trek.

In the return of the rains after the dry season, the people of this land not only rejoiced at the prospect of bountiful harvests but also remembered and celebrated one of the most important principles of creation: the playful and erotic meeting of the Divine Masculine and Feminine.

As we finally sit down for a hearty dinner at the guesthouse near the ruins, I share with Miguel my opinion that the old wisdom is not lost but still quite alive in every rock—the very path we had walked upon still holding the message it was meant to convey when it was first designed centuries ago. But the invaluable information inscribed in these rocks is only available to those who are willing to use it for the benefit of all rather than to those wishing to pillage it for their own personal gain. Ancient civilizations thrived because of their communal vision; therefore ancestral wisdom is only available to those willing to share it for the benefit of the entire community.

IV

FIRE

The North, the Hummingbird, Fire,
Ancestors, Sex

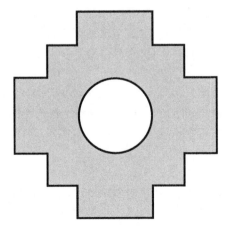

I associate the direction of the North with the element of Fire, and fire is the one element most closely related to humans as the ability to start and use fire is one characteristic that is unique to humans among all other creatures on this planet. The other characteristic is verbal language, and our history of storytelling has unfolded over millennia most often around a fire. This chapter will therefore begin with an exploration of the significance and importance of the stories we create and tell ourselves and others. An important part of these stories is about the wisdom gathered by our ancestors, while the other part is made of the stories we tell ourselves about who we and other people are.

All my life I have been fascinated by our unique passion for stories, in literature, theatre, and movies. The stories we seek and create are powerful reflections of our own lives and inner landscapes: we have a constant need for these stories in order to remind ourselves of who we have been, who we are, and who we can be. Any good story will also remind us of the fictitious and illusory nature of our dramatic experiences and lives: our love for a good story is a reminder that this life of ours is also a story, i.e., an experience designed to convey a message whose meaning we understand as the story unfolds.

For years I had been exploring the viewpoint that we are the creators of our own lives, but it was a radical turning point to see and understand that viewpoint experientially during my first visit to the jungle when, in the throes of both Ayahuasca and one of my most recurrent dramas, I realized that I had not only been the main character of such drama, but had carefully chosen and manifested the supporting characters and the location, that I had written the script, and directed the whole story from A to Z. It was only after that realization and confession that I could begin to understand the important lessons that drama was intended to teach me.

We cannot speak of works of fiction without speaking of critics, and invariably we tend to be our worst and harshest critics. Luckily San Pedro does help us in letting go of such criticism so that we can sit back and watch, appreciate, and learn from our own movies, and by letting go of any blame and victimhood we can also appreciate ourselves as the creators of such movies.

Letting go of the judgment and criticism of our own creations opens the space for learning from those experiences we create or invite into our lives. The stories we create and experience are important learning devices and each of these stories and lessons is an equally important chapter in the unfolding of the true story we have written, which is about waking up to our true divine nature.

Because we do not lack of sense of humor and paradox, the circumstances and themes of our dramas are more often than not diametrically opposed to the beautiful lessons they are meant to teach us. For instance, my story of abandonment was to teach me that I was never and am not ever alone, that divine energies and spirits are always and forever caringly supporting me and everyone else in our journey home, and that I am capable of offering that same care and support to myself and others whenever I choose to.

An example of how a beautiful life lesson is embedded in seemingly tragic circumstances is what happens in the Hindu book the Bhagavad Gita, which is part of the epic the Mahabharata. I was very surprised when I first saw Peter Brooks' movie version of *the Mahabharata*: in the most important scene of this story, which is the episode narrated in the *Bhagavad Gita*, Lord Krishna instead of dissuading the Pandava brothers from entering into a deadly war against their enemies, invites them to go into a bloody conflict, during which he teaches Arjuna, and all of us with him, about the immortality of the spirit. What might have seemed like a senseless bloodshed turns out to be the occasion of important learning and enlightenment.

For me a healing process can be said to be complete only when our wounds have finally taught us the beautiful lessons they were meant to teach us. At the end of such a process we can look back at our stories and see that what we had been telling ourselves about ourselves, others, and the world, were lies or, at the very least, the truth of a very scared and hurt individual.

A powerful aspect of San Pedro and other plant medicines is their ability to make us see our own stories from a wider perspective and a more expanded vision that no longer revolves exclusively around a limited and hurt self. When the old limited viewpoint is finally let go of, then these occurrences become the source of much wisdom, heartfelt compassion, and forgiveness. A client of mine already in his 60s could see with great clarity during a San Pedro ceremony that his mother had been hurting as much as he did when he was a child and she had confronted him with his lies, and that the only reason she had been as strict was not to hurt him, but to teach him an important lesson about life and the importance of honesty.

The final remembering and learning of these beautiful lessons makes the letting go of old traumas and sorrows really easy as we are left only with feelings of gratitude for the gifts received through them.

Sometimes people struggle through long bouts of nausea and wish to be able to purge: in these cases I often advise to ask that which is sitting in their stomach to teach them whatever is still important for them to learn before they can let it go. In my opinion any letting go that isn't accompanied with heartfelt gratitude for the lessons that what we are letting go of has offered us, isn't really the end of the healing process.

Another enlightening experience happens when we realize without judgment that our parents and ancestors carried similar wounds to ours, and that they had been playing out those wounds with whoever was closest to them, often inflicting upon others the same pain they were suffering from. When we are finally willing to let go of blame, we can accept and see our own family members as the empowering reflections that they are, and from owning our own judgment of them we can recover and integrate the parts of ourselves we had until then projected. It is not rare that when I feel that such a process can be beneficial to my clients I even invite them to bring along in spirit to ceremony their fathers or mothers as the great teachers they truly are.

We experience ourselves as who we believe to be, and the stories we tell ourselves and one another are the way to validate and feed those beliefs, which is why I have become aware of the importance of language and choose my words carefully. A way to keep taking responsibility for our experiences is by talking about them in the first person, thus avoiding unnecessary projections and generalizations.

The truth lies not in one dream but in many dreams: we each hold a unique viewpoint, and the total sum of these viewpoints *is* our collective truth (or collective illusion depending on the case). The willingness to question the present validity of our stories and assumptions feels to me like the most important requisite of anyone wanting to engage with San Pedro. San Pedro helps us learn from our own history the lessons we haven't yet learned and invites us to let go of those stories that no longer serve us.

As we let go of those stories a last important challenge may arise: the self, whose identity depends on the stories it tells itself, may get scared and we may end up asking ourselves "well, if I am not this story, then who am I?" Such fear is normal as we easily fear the unknown, and people sometimes need the reassurance that to be in a space of no longer knowing who they are is okay. To allow oneself to experience such an unknown may be difficult, but it creates the space for a deeper truth of our identity to resurface from the vastness of our silent and expanded self.

I had a memorable incident while I was healing my wound of betrayal where at some point it became clear to me that if I wished to heal that wound I had to let go of the "resentful" and "executioner" identities that had been important corollaries of my stories of betrayal. These identities were such an integral part of who I had thought I was that letting go of them was not that easy or instantaneous, but eventually I saw the necessity of it and sacrificed them, meaning that I wholeheartedly offered them to the Earth with gratitude for everything that these identities had allowed me to experience and learn, thus making them sacred.

It is always a delicate moment in my San Pedro ceremonies when someone lets go of an important story only to get scared by the emptiness and sense of confused unknowing they feel as a result of that letting go. With that letting go also a sense of who we are is sacrificed and, since who we tell ourselves to be is intimately connected with the stories that we tell ourselves, we literally no longer know who we are. In these cases I always remind people that it's really okay to be in a place of confusion and unknowing, and that to embrace the awareness that we don't know is the beginning of true wisdom.

Years ago a young man, who had been working at a healing retreat center and was sincerely dedicated to making this world a better place, came to me for a series of ceremonies. Before going back home to the U.S. he confessed to me that he had come here looking for answers and confirmations, but he was leaving knowing less than when he had arrived. As confused as he was I couldn't help but congratulate him for going from a place of relative and limited knowledge to a place of deeper wisdom.

ANCESTORS

In the pre-Columbian cultures of Peru, in South America, in Mexico, and in North and Central America, the North is the place beyond life: this is where Life both originates and returns to.

As the preferred symbolic place of the Divine, it is also the place where some people believe we go after death to rejoin the Divine and our Divine Source, thus making it the preferred direction to honor our ancestors—from spiritual teachers long departed to ascended masters, Buddhas and Bodhisattvas, star beings, and our own ancestors and deceased family members.

Under the effects of San Pedro it is not unusual to be able to connect with these energies and receive from their wisdom and support. In the case of our own ancestors we can also feel the unhealed pain that we may have inherited from them, as everything that is not healed and integrated keeps being passed down from generation to generation. It is very important to remain aware that that ancestral pain is not just theirs, but necessarily resonates with our own wounds, and that we choose our ancestry and tribes precisely *because* they carry the same unhealed themes.

So, to say "it's not me, but what I've been carrying is *their* lot," and leave it at that, in my opinion kind of misses the point. I prefer to invite people to call in spirit the presence of living or long deceased relatives and return to them, with the same love and loyalty that had made them carry it, whatever pain back to their original owners, trusting that they will know what to do with it in their own way and time. I recommend this process because I believe that to carry someone else's pain, despite the nobility of such a gesture, first of all is not our duty and secondly it doesn't serve these other people to be deprived of an important opportunity for healing and growth.

Another important part of this process is to become aware of the possible secret reasons and agendas that may have influenced our decision to carry someone else's pain or grief. In many cases there was in child-hood or adolescence a desire to alleviate the pain of someone close. In the case for instance of an important loss in the family a child often takes on the unexpressed grief of the parents hoping that the parents will once again be present and caring to the child. This is why a therapist friend of mine will always see the parent first when they bring a child to her practice: more often than not it is not the child but the parent who needs healing, and the child's dis-ease is just a symptom of whatever pain the parent hasn't embraced.

When all of that is complete, I then invite my clients to see what their ancestors' predicament may mirror to them about themselves, and begin healing it, thus completing the process.

The same can be said and done when we connect with unhealed aspects of collective consciousness, such as when during a ceremony someone feels the overwhelming pain of all the suffering of all women throughout history, or the pain and guilt for our disrespectful behavior towards the Earth.

Another important aspect of the work with our ancestors is the healing of any dissociation from our family roots we may hold. This is often due to judgments and prejudices against family members or the clan altogether, or some sort of ethnic or cultural shame. As our ancestors are somehow a part of ourselves, such dissociation results in a diminishing of whom we are. In our ancestry, whether by genetic or spiritual heritage, we have a wealth of wisdom and strength even among the most dysfunctional of clans: reconnecting with our ancestry and letting go of our previous judgments not only opens the way for much healing but also allows us to see and embrace the often overlooked power, strength, and wisdom of our clans and benefit from them.

FIRE

The element of Fire is that which burns away all that is no longer useful and releases it: Fire is the symbol of transformation and transmutation. For me it represents the burning away of illusions so that we can see clearly into the beauty of the Divine within ourselves and in all aspects of Creation.

In 2006, one year after beginning my apprenticeship and work with plant medicines, I went to Burning Man for the last time, and this time primarily to express my gratitude to a place and gathering that over the previous ten years had been teaching me most important life lessons about surrender, play, community, and Nature.

The night of the burning of the Man, when I finally sat by what remained of the fire, the spirit of Burning Man spoke to me one last time with her wisdom and said "Javier, this fire in front of you is the same as the medicines you have agreed to work for. It's a powerful fire that burns away the past so that we can see the beauty of the eternal now with clarity and an open heart and mind. As you can see, its flames are scorching hot and frightful, so as you walk your people through this burning fire, do it as kindly and lovingly as possible."

I relate this episode not only to remind myself of that precious piece of advice, but also to extend it to anybody interested in experiencing this process: plant medicine is not the easy ride some would hope it to be. But as challenging and meaningful as any spiritual path, it is equally rewarding when approached with humility and patience.

Fire is the revered element of Death and Rebirth by excellence: its power to bring new life is intimately tied with its ability to burn down everything that is no longer useful so that its ashes become the best possible ground for new life. Fire speaks to us of the cyclical nature of this Universe, from the smallest of bacteria to the largest of stars, continually dying and evolving into something new. And San Pedro is one of those teachers that, as lovingly as possible, reminds us of not only the necessity but also the value of such death and rebirth. The dying we may experience with San Pedro is symbolic and the result of a purification of the densest bodies so that the light of the spirit can shine brightly once again.

SEX

The Fire of the North in both its life-bringing and destructive aspects, speaks to us of sex and sexuality. The human process of creating fire is in itself a highly graphic depiction of sex and arousal. It is no strange coincidence that thunder, the most common atmospheric cause of fires, is connected in Peruvian cosmology with the cosmic serpent Sachamama, the snake that together with the serpent of the waters, Yakumama, brings life to this planet through rain. It is a cosmic copulation that is a celebration of the marriage of Heaven and Earth.

Sex is a wonderful thing. Seduction, beauty, and lovemaking are the main modus operandi of Life on this planet. It is a constant and a joyous activity for most creatures on Earth, with the notable exception of us human beings. We have turned sexuality into such an ordeal that nowadays even menstruation and childbirth, not to mention sex itself, are often faced with dread. With our evolution as a species we have invested sexuality with all sorts of meanings and values, and have projected onto the sexual arena all sorts of judgments and agendas that have little to do with the simple enjoyment of sexual pleasure.

Sexual pleasure is a most feminine experience: it asks of us to slow down, be present, and yield to our most physically pleasurable experience. It is also deeply feminine in that it requires a willingness to be vulnerable

119

and intimate. When engaged in with another person it asks that we join with that person in ways that are unique and very profound. This is most scary for men because in that union we have to sacrifice our own individuality and egos. It was a woman psychoanalyst, Sabine Spielrein (and no one but a woman could have figured this out), who first explained the deep connection between Eros and Thanatos. I had tried really hard for years to understand what psychoanalysts meant by equating erotic energy with death, Eros and Thanatos. It wasn't until I watched A Dangerous Method[22] and read the book that inspired it[23] that I started to understand the reasoning behind that equation.

Sabine Spielrein offered the insight that in order to enjoy the sexual act we need to forego our individuality and that the orgasm is the quickest way to enter that oceanic state of consciousness, which is essentially feminine and that mystics have been familiar with for thousands of years. Because civilization, as we have understood and pursued since recorded history and most strongly in modern times, is about the preeminence of masculine values of efficient productivity and the sublimation of sexual energies, the need to repress and sublimate those energies has only increased with our need for increased productivity and social conformity. Now please allow me to point out that all of this, while claiming to have been put in motion for the sake and in the name of civilization, is really a strategy to create and perpetuate a *certain* kind of civilization. The flavor of our present civilization is not in harmony but in opposition to Nature: it is a masculine energy that

---

[22] Cronenberg, David. *A Dangerous Method*. DVD, Culver City, Sony Pictures Classics, 2011.

[23] Kerr, John. *A Most Dangerous Method*. New York, Vintage Books, 1997.

creates itself as an opponent to feminine energy rather than complementary to it; and because it is competitive against feminine energy, which it perceives as a threat on many levels, it does everything possible to demonize and repress it.

Human masculine energy, as it has been expressed in the last few thousand years, is most violent to the point that we are the only species I know of that consistently and deliberately kills large numbers of its own population. We are not a violent species but have turned into one because we feel that violence is the most effective way to assert our power and superiority. But when I look under the bloody lining all I can see is that all the displays of brute force are attempts to mask our fears and insecurities. The biggest fear for the ego is the unknown and rather than getting to know and befriend that unknown, our most common reaction is to squash it. It happens among different ethnicities, political and religious groups, and even in our relationship with Nature. Our fears are what create our enemies, and if there is no one to project those fears onto, then we create them out of thin air. Broadcast news is an endless record of such attempts and the devastating consequences of our conflictive attitude towards others and the world.

I mention all of this not as a tirade and judgment against the patriarchy and whatnot, but because by looking at our world we can see a better picture of our own inner landscape. Even health and spirituality are informed with this conflictive attitude: we engage in wars against cancer and a long list of other diseases, and we engage in wars of good vs. evil, shadow vs. light, and ego against everything else. San Pedro, with its ability to make us feel more and think less, gently

121

brings us to a new paradigm beyond the either/or of masculine energy and into the comprehensiveness of a more feminine nature. It is a process towards wholeness and re-union so that the spark of these two energies coming together can further the unfolding of Creation.

When I first came to the Cusco area I visited the ruins of Moray, which are believed to have been a large-scale agricultural laboratory where vegetable species were developed for different climates. What I did see and was deeply moved by that day was how pre-Columbian cultures here in Peru had developed technologies that were not against but in harmony with Nature. And seeing that harmonious merging on a such a large scale inspired me to hold such an attitude with my own inner landscape.

In the same way that thunder is revered as an expression of Illapa, the male principle that comes from the sky in order to mate with the feminine Earth, Pachamama, it can be easily said that all pre-Columbian ceremonial spaces were designed by the ancestors of this land to remind us that there is no feminine without the masculine and vice versa: all the temples were built to celebrate the very nature and working of Creation in ways that could be understood or perceived by all members of their society. On a microcosmic level this is about the meeting and mating of these energies within ourselves, and under more contemporary circumstances it is about the meeting of the mind and the heart. Sigmund Freud cunningly remarked how our brains have become our biggest sexual organ. As a result, our sexuality has become increasingly masculine and goal-oriented, to the point that our contemporary Western tantric practices are most importantly geared towards the reconnection between our sexual organs and our hearts, as my teacher Joseph Kramer[24] taught me back in 1992.

The important shift in consciousness of the 60's was spurred in great part by the sexual revolution and women's emancipation that came with the availability of modern contraceptives. That sudden sexual freedom has pointed out over and over again to how deeply sexual (self)repression has run in Western societies and the importance to heal and celebrate our erotic energies. Erotic energy is not only the source of our ability to procreate but one of the many manifestations of our divine creative energy. Despite what religious and social authorities may have been telling us for centuries, I believe that when our erotic energy is healed and allowed to flow and express itself joyfully and playfully, it can only contribute in positive ways to our human earthly experience and our spiritual journey.

NEEDS AND DESIRES

In May of 2016 I took a group of nine people to work with my teacher in Iquitos for three weeks. During that time I had some interesting talks with a couple of participants about sexuality, sexual needs, and desires. Our talks brought to light for me our widespread reluctance, some sort of thinly disguised prudishness and shame, to openly express and share our sexual needs. Two months later, as I was reading Marshall B. Rosenberg's brilliant book, *Nonviolent Communi-*

---

[24] For more information, visit: Joseph Kramer's *Heartful Erotic Touch*: www.eroticmassage.com and *Heartful Erotic Practice*: www.orgasmicyoga.com.

cation[25], I came across a passage about our cultural assumption that needs are negative and destructive, and how the expression of our needs is often judged and reprimanded. This same statement could be referring to our desires just as well. Our unease in regards to our needs and desires end up driving them into a nebulous limbo, from which they can't help but eventually resurface, but in often distorted ways.

I bring this up because San Pedro, just like Life itself, does not necessarily give us what we want but most importantly what we need, hence the importance of reconnecting not only with our desires but also our needs, and to explore and let go of any belief that prevents us from openly expressing such needs. Our difficulty in expressing our needs and desires often first arises with the onset of sexuality, whether in childhood or adolescence. The budding of erotic feelings and urges denotes a major change not only in our physiology but also in our psyche: it is the time when we are no longer the children we used to be, but don't yet know who we are becoming. It is often a very confusing stage of our development and made even more so by the silence that surrounds sexuality, which brings many of us to deal with it by ourselves and without any support.

The same silence and reluctance to express our sexual needs and desires often extends to our emotions and thoughts later in life. To take the time to connect with our needs before each ceremony and expressing them to the medicine in the form of an intention (while letting go of any expectation) is a wonderfully empowering process that reestablishes the legitimacy of our

---

[25] Rosenberg, Michael B. *Nonviolent Communication*. Encinitas, PuddleDancer Press, 2015.

needs. And it's a powerful practice that teaches us how to express our needs and desires in all areas of our lives, including sexuality.

Unconsciously we spend most of our lives desperately trying to fulfill old unmet needs. And we transfer old unfulfilled desires onto present situations. A classic example is when we unconsciously ask of our partners to give us the love we felt we didn't receive from our parents. In many cases this is an attempt to change a past that cannot be changed, and therefore rarely effective. Some schools of therapy and neo-shamanism recommend processes by which the individual engages in a dialogue with this old self and finally fulfills those unmet needs. As valid as this process may be, I prefer to invite people to first of all honor these old selves and allowing them to fully express their anger, frustration, or sadness. This process usually is all that is needed in order for these old selves to find peace and release, and be integrated. Many of our present desires are just an expression of old unmet needs, so exploring and releasing those parts of ourselves that are still attached to the fulfilling of old unmet needs is a good way to let go of those desires that are not rooted in the present but keep us unconsciously in the past.

Many religions and spiritual processes have warned us for a long time about the dangers of pursuing our desires, in particular desires connected with sexuality, food, etc., often denigrating some of our most natural tendencies and appetites. The judgments around sexuality, for instance, have created a strong resistance and guilt whenever we pursue and engage in eroticism. I believe that such warnings are not against sexuality, food, or other earthly pleasures per se: the warning comes from the awareness that often such pursuits are ways to feed the ego, thus taking us further into a spiral of dissatisfaction that in its most extreme cases turns into addictions of all sorts rather than liberation. I feel it is therefore important to explore the *nature* and *reasons* of our desires as much as our needs, and to contemplate our conscious and unconscious *attitude* towards them. Just like in plant medicine where plants can be just as easily good medicines or poisons depending on our attitude as we engage with them, the pursuit of eroticism and other physical and mundane pleasures can either loosen and break or strengthen the chains of our egos.

RECEIVING

Our prayers are always answered even though they are seldom answered in the way and timing we had hoped. Unfortunately, we can bark our prayers as loudly as we can but if there is no space within us to receive that which we ask for, we are just wasting our time and breath. As much as we say we want this or that, it is often very difficult, challenging, or downright impossible for us to truly receive what we long for. It is therefore very important as part of any healing process to explore whatever may prevent us from receiving the very healing we seek.

The inability or reluctance to receive is often a symptom of our unease around our needs and desires, and just as often it points to feelings and beliefs of unworthiness and not deserving. The life we experience is a gift from the moment of conception until our last breath. The most basic things, such as air, water, and food, are gifts offered to us with generosity by the Universe. And yet we have created a whole value system whereby we feel we need to deserve (in our culture that deserving is often in the form of monetary wealth) in order to receive. Because of our self-judgment and limiting beliefs most of us are in a state of constant self-imposed semi-starvation. An example of that is the way we breathe: most of us go through life breathing less than we ought to, even when air is free and available to us all.

To open oneself up to receiving from the Universe and receiving from our own selves are two aspects of the same journey. The gifts are infinite, even when they are clouded by our own beliefs of scarcity and inad-equacy, and are patiently waiting for us to receive them. Luckily, we don't have to become someone else or improve ourselves in order to deserve and receive those gifts: all that is required of us is an exploration and integration of whatever beliefs may prevent us from simply receiving.

In the depiction of the Buddhist hell, as part of the Wheel of Illusory Existence, there is a section of just such beings with long thin necks and bloated stomachs: these are beings unable to receive no matter how hard they try to ingest anything and are therefore destined to remain dissatisfied and hungry.

It was a sad moment when I realized to which extent I had gone through life as an insecure beggar, begging for crumbs of love and acceptance, often hungry and desolate. San Pedro was instrumental in helping me let go of those beliefs that kept me from sitting at the world's table and being able to fully digest and enjoy Life's banquet. In 2008 I started getting seriously ill in what turned out to be a very important healing process. Two months after the initial symptoms I was at a dinner party at someone's house and in the

middle of it I went out in the veranda to have a ciga-
rette by myself. As I was smoking I looked at a big San
Pedro cactus nearby and before I knew it I heard it say
to me "I am not here only for your clients, but for you
as well." In the following days I came to realize that
the previous years of offering healing ceremonies had
been a way to teach myself that I could receive as
much as my clients, and that I could also allow myself
to be as vulnerable as everybody else. So I stopped all
work and devoted myself to my own healing. It was a
long process that entailed becoming so weak physically that I eventually let go of all my resistances. In
the end I not only managed to make myself available
to receiving an important emotional healing, but also
learnt about the importance of receiving and of being
generous with myself.

SEX AND SAN PEDRO

One of the most frequent and passionate questions
I have received from people is about the taboo
against sexual activity, including masturbation, connected with the use of plant medicines. Why is it that
people are asked to forego sex before, during, and
after ceremonies?

I personally expect that abstinence for periods that
may vary from three days to two weeks depending on
the person and the process people wish to engage in
under my guidance for two important reasons. The first
and most important one is the awareness that we tend
to play out in the sexual arena many of our neuroses
and wounds. The plant medicine process is one that
ideally helps us *heal* these neuroses, so in order to

allow for the healing to unfold we would do ourselves a big favor by not feeding them. Abstinence, from sex and certain foods, alcohol and drugs, helps us not only become aware of our attachments, but more importantly helps us reconnect with those uncomfortable feelings and emotions that we may have suppressed by indulging our appetites. Abstinence from the ways we self-medicate is the beginning of the undoing of denial and repression: it lifts the strong defensive lid over our true feelings so that the medicines can work with us. The use of antidepressants is another such defense mechanism that needs to be sacrificed in order to engage in this process: antidepressants are really just masking deeply uncomfortable predicaments and to drink San Pedro while on antidepressants is like receiving a massage through such thick blankets that we may wonder if we are being massaged at all.

Even though I have heard of one woman engaging with excellent results while still on antidpressants, I personally do not allow anybody in my retreats while they are on such medications, and depending on the daily dosage and time of treatment I expect my prospective clients to wean themselves off anywhere between two weeks and two months before their first ceremony. It is not just a matter of physical health due to the chemical interaction of medications and San Pedro, which can be seriously damaging and possibly even lethal, but also an important sign that the person is taking this process with the due respect, humility, and determination. I believe that if someone cannot adhere to such requirements then they are not ready for the experience ahead: they either lack the motivation or the psychological maturity to be able to face whatever may come ahead in the process.

Of course, weaning ourselves off antidepressants, drugs, or alcohol is not an easy experience but I am always surprised by how many people have successfully given them up never to use them again once they decided to seriously engage with plant medicines and heal themselves. I always recommend that such weaning be supervised by a doctor, and make people aware that during such period many repressed emotions may start reemerging, so it is most important that the individual, apart from being monitored by a doctor, puts in place a loving support system of friends and family that is aware of the process.

Our abstinence is part of what we offer to the medicine in exchange for what we hope to receive from it, and it is an important offering because in so doing we open up to the medicine *and* we easily avoid one of the worst scenarios that are unfortunately as damaging as they are common in medicine and spiritual circles: sexual and power abuse, projections and transferences between the plant medicine person and their clients, and among participants as well.

I always warn my clients against falling in love or having sex with the ceremony leader or other people during and right after a plant medicine process: at best, these relationships are often delusional and short-lived, but cause of long-term confusion as is the case when we wake up with a stranger we are not particularly attracted to in the morning but to whom we have promised eternal love the night before while under the influence of drugs or alcohol. At worst, they are most damaging because instead of healing some important issues, we discover that we have sunk deeper into them and in a more confusing manner than ever. This may be helpful and perhaps a necessary step in our healing process as it may help us connect with our inner saboteur and finally hit bottom so that we can start heading in the direction of true healing. As painful as it may be, hitting bottom is one of the most empowering things that can happen to us: once we get to the end of our rope and have explored and acted out our dysfunctional patterns as thoroughly as possible and seen their futility and damage, we have no other choice but do things differently, and change is one of the requisites and the beginning of healing.

If I hadn't been in such pain in 2004 I doubt I would have made the Ayahuasca retreat center I visited in the jungle part of my travel itinerary. I am also not sure that in the following years my resolution to face and heal parts of myself would have been as strong had not my pain become unbearable and had not my own drama become a cul-de-sac that had lost all appeal and attractiveness. I am grateful to have eventually reached that sort of desperation that pushed me beyond my comfort zone and into the wild, scary, and unknown world of plant medicines. Unfortunately, the comforts and crutches we surround ourselves with, as important and often necessary as they may be in the short run, often tend to dull and kill our inner fire.

On a collective scale we can either despair from our present predicament as a species on this planet, or we can rejoice for it as an opportunity for change. The failure of our aggressive attitude towards Nature and ourselves can be taken as a sign that this is a time to learn from this experience and take a new approach towards Life in general: these times are indeed ripe for transformation and a new rekindling of our inner fire, our courage, and faith.

Another reason for the required abstinence from sex is that the healing process requires not only all of our attention, but also all of our energy, including physical and sexual. Healing often happens on levels of our being that require quite a bit of energy and a lot of rest, even more so when engaging with San Pedro, whose effects are quite long and can leave even the fittest among us rather exhausted at times.

Last but not least, the adherence to certain restrictions as dictated by one tradition or another is one of the many ways with which we show our respect for those traditions and the only way for us to drink not only from the wisdom of San Pedro, but also access the incredible amount of wisdom gathered by all the people that have engaged with this medicine within that tradition.

Required abstinence of any kind will bring up a rebellious and often sabotaging ego: the natural reaction of an ego on the loose is to simply oppose anything that is perceived as a limitation, particularly when the abstinence is from anything that feeds the same ego. A funny example of that is how much time us Westerners spend while under a strict shamanic diet speaking about foods that are not only unavailable but forbidden as part of the diet process. In order to enter the world of spirit we have to forego the temptations of the ego, and the adherence to certain restrictions is, at least with plant medicines, a necessary practice if we intend to follow that path and reach our destination quickly and safely.

CLEANSING THE DOORS OF PERCEPTION

Like the fire that burns our illusions, San Pedro has the ability to open our eyes, our minds, and hearts to a more expanded view and a more accurate picture of who we are and what the world truly is. As fire turns various seemingly opaque elements into transparent glass, San Pedro can help us cleanse the often-distorted lenses through which we perceive and experience the world and ourselves.

The first step is by actually becoming aware of our projections: we do so by acknowledging that our ideas and judgments of others and the world are more often than not a reflection of ourselves rather than an objective viewpoint. As we take responsibility and let go of these projections, we can see others for whom they are. And once we let go of the projected judgments we can honor and accept others as they are.

I cannot stress enough the possibility that our perception of the world and other people is just a projection, no matter how popular and pervasive that projection may be. A common scenario during San Pedro ceremonies is the projection onto this planet of our hurt and pain. Nobody will deny that we have damaged this Earth dramatically over the last century, but the Earth, and this is *my* perception and reality, keeps on giving with the same generosity. Draughts and floods are not the expression of anger or resentment, or some kind of punishment from this planet for what we have done and keep on doing—this is a very archaic viewpoint that says more about our collective guilt than about the Earth itself. But it's easier for us to project our feelings and say things like "Mother Earth is very angry" or "She is very hurt" rather than taking responsibility for our feelings and acknowledging our emotions. When invited to see if these ideas and feelings somehow reflect some familiar parts of ourselves, then people can let go of this or other projections and move much deeper into their healing process. Owning our projections is not only healing but makes the space for clearer vision and perception.

People who engage in this process often ask me when they are going to see the fabled visions that they have heard or read about. I remind them that every person has a distinct journey to experience, and as part of that journey they may or may not experience any visions. I also remind them that in these fantastical accounts the authors often skip the less-than-stellar parts of their journey when they were confused or despairing.

San Pedro is not a psychedelic substance that we imbibe in order to see fun and colorful images for a few hours—for that we would do better to resort to movies and fun fairs. San Pedro is a medicine that may offer us visions, but is primarily devoted to helping us heal and let go of our limited viewpoints, and that can happen with or without any visions. The visions we may experience are the result of an expanded consciousness *and* a willingness and readiness to see beyond our present viewpoint, and not the result of our *desire* to see extraordinary things or experience extraordinary phenomena. Individuals seeking such thrills are sooner or later put in their place by this seemingly innocuous plant: San Pedro is not a recreational substance and those who approach it with that attitude not only fail to see its full power but also end up experiencing for

themselves in often unpleasant ways the erroneousness of their judgment and behavior.

Personally, the more I engage with this medicine
the more respectful I become of it. It is not uncommon
for people, and even medicine people, to develop a
casual approach with this medicine once they believe
they have become familiar with it, and even stop
adhering to dietary and sexual restrictions. They think
they know enough or even better than anybody else
and start breaking common sense rules, mixing and
matching as they please. I concede that I am a slow
learner but my experience, with this medicine as with
the world at large, is that the more I know the less I
actually know, and as a result the more humble and
respectful I become.

Only recently during a personal San Pedro
ceremony did I realize that the thought "I know" is one
of the most limiting and insidious beliefs we may hold
in our consciousness. When that thought is entertained
and fed by the ego, it gives rise to an arrogant attitude
and delusional state that can be very dangerous. I
personally prefer the Socratic wisdom of "I know that
I know nothing." Within that humble place I find that
there is space for true growth and expansion. This is
not to say that we ought to keep our heads low all
the time: there are times when true wisdom resurfaces,
and to honor that wisdom is important, as it is important
to make sure that that awareness doesn't turn into
another ego-centered trip.

When people hear about plant medicines and
psychedelics they often think of visions and hallucinations. Hallucinations, by definition, are things we
perceive that are not really there, such as seeing a
door in the hallway and lowering our heads so that

we can go through such door when there is no actual door to go through and we crash our heads against the wall instead. Visions are the result of being able to see *deeper* into reality and beyond mere sensory perception, like in the case of seeing a door in our own inner landscape that leads to a forgotten place within ourselves.

It is not always easy to know whether under the effects of this or other medicines we are hallucinating or having visions. My rule of thumb is to never take any vision at face value and to entertain the possibility that what I am seeing may mean something other than what I am first lead or would like to believe. It is important to remind ourselves that we are essentially symbolic beings, and altered states of consciousness may open us to the language of the unconscious, which is symbolic in essence. Symbols imply something more than their obvious and immediate meaning, which is why I advise my clients not to take the images they receive in ceremony as necessarily literal as often their true meaning reveals itself only with time. Many symbols are universal and part of our collective consciousness, and yet their meaning is unique to the individual in their particular and present predicament, so their interpretation should not be automatic as in out of a manual but in relation to each unique indi-vidual, e.g., the same door may mean that the path is temporarily obstructed for someone or an invitation to explore new dimensions for someone else.

The visions and intuitions we experience under the effects of San Pedro can be expressions of our desires as much as our fears. Visions of the future where we see ourselves happily married with children may be an expression of our desires. For me visions of the future are only one among infinite possibilities as I believe that the future is completely up for grabs rather than fixed forever: as possibilities they still require for us to step into them and take the necessary actions in order to make them a reality. As a possibility they may be inspiring, but they are still just one among infinite scenarios and therefore any degree of attachment can result in suffering and disappointment. Many people I have encountered hold such disappointment because what they saw or heard in a ceremony never came to be despite their momentary certainty that what they saw was true and sure to happen. A minimum of detachment is in these cases a valuable way to avoid such disappointment.

Visions that are not literal but an expression of our fears are just as important. The vision of a dear person on their deathbed is in most cases just an opportunity for us to connect with our fears of death or may point to some unfinished business that the imagined impending death may help us finally deal with. In both the case of fears and desires the most important thing to embrace are the feelings and possible reactions to such visions, just like in our lives the more important thing is not that we are finally driving the car of our dreams but the feeling of satisfaction and happiness that driving that car elicits in us. Events and experiences, people and objects are not as relevant as our *reactions*, emotional and otherwise, to them, and for me the same is true in regards to our visions.

Our perceptions under the effects of mind-altering substances is *still* just a perception—a perception that is subjective and relative to our present state and level of consciousness in the same way that a familiar landscape is perceived differently according to our moods, age, or state of mind.

A woman shared with me her visions during an Ayahuasca ceremony that depicted some higher dimension and involved some intricate pyramid of supernatural light and colors, which she interpreted to be some kind of heaven. After she described it to me I reminded her that what she saw was her perception of such heaven and not necessarily an accurate and objective image of Heaven, which is probably beyond our ability to see as a place or object but is most likely just a state of consciousness. I didn't say this to dismiss the veracity and validity of her vision, but simply to put it into perspective. So many people will enthusiastically say after a ceremony how they were shown the fabric of the Universe and so on, and end up believing that what they experienced was the absolute and sacrosanct truth just like the prophets of old. For me there are very few absolute truths in this Universe and one of them is that the truth is not carved in stone so that we can hit other people with it until they agree with us.

For me the truth is not something to discover but something that resurfaces from deep inside ourselves as our consciousness expands and can hold greater degrees of awareness. This is what plant medicines help us do by cleansing us in various ways. Like I wrote in my book on Ayahuasca, my experience in the jungle as I began my shamanic apprenticeship while dieting the Datura plant (*Brugmansia*) was that the plant I was dieting was initially only preparing my being on many levels, cleansing and polishing me like a crystal, so that I could safely hold greater degrees of awareness later in the diet. And from the preparation of my own cauldron so to speak, little by little started emerging the wisdom I had been looking for outside myself all my life.

At times, through the ingestion of this or other substances or through some spiritual initiation of some sort, we can be catapulted onto levels of awareness that, as much as we may crave them, we are not quite yet ready to experience and sustain, which is why after a while that awareness dissipates and we find ourselves pretty much where we began. This is an all-too-common scenario for many spiritual seekers who go from ceremony to workshop, from jungle retreat to meditation ashram: they feel great for a while and then it's as if nothing had happened at all. And in order to feel the same kind of expansion they have to go back and do some more, like an addict always looking for the next fix. The reason for such occurrences is twofold. First is the naïve assumption or secret wish that we are going to feel the same kind of elation forever, when in reality if we were to do so we would fry our nervous system within days. The high we may experience under the effects of medicines or during a workshop is temporary and just a metaphor for a deeper high that is not sensory but in consciousness. It opens our eyes and teaches us about the magic of our lives *as is*: I personally no longer need to resort to anything anymore in order to experience such magic, and it's a quiet experience rather than a necessarily euphoric one. The second reason is that for as long as we hold heavy energies in our being, we will always end up on that lower vibratory state no matter how high we may have been for a few hours or days. It is a simple law of consciousness and unfortunately not one subject to discussion.

As maddening as it can be at times of impatience and frustration, I admire the natural cleansing and purifying process offered by plant medicines: it often starts with cleansing our bodies of toxins and then moves upwards to our emotions and thoughts in a specific way so that our shift into higher levels of consciousness can be permanent rather than fleeting. It's true that sometimes an apparently sudden leap in consciousness can result in a permanent shift. This is often called by many "grace." But in my opinion it is simply the result of lifetimes of spiritual pursuit: there are countless entities that support us in our journey, but there are no freebies and in the end we get only what we are willing to give, no more and no less.

The visions that San Pedro most importantly offers us are not visual but internal. They may express themselves visually but not necessarily so. I personally never look for visions and even less so for cool visuals, but explore my inner landscape even before the medicine takes effect by exploring the themes of my intentions right away. Even though I don't dismiss such visions should they occur, I find images with my eyes open or closed a bit of a distraction unless they elicit a strong reaction such as a recurring vision I had every time I drank San Pedro a few years back. In those visions I could see my inner physical body as membranes, organs, tissues, and mucus, and my reaction was always one of mixed disgust. With time I explored my reaction, which had to do with my unease and judgments at my being in a human form. Needless to say, once I let go of those judgments those visions stopped.

Not everybody reacts to San Pedro in a visual way and that's not an indication of anything in particular, and it's definitely not a judgment on the character of the individual: so many people I have encountered hold some judgments against themselves for never having had visions either with San Pedro or Ayahuasca. They assume that something is wrong with them or that they are simply not spiritual enough, thus actually expressing some hidden expectation or low self-esteem that the process is bringing to their awareness more than anything else. When our reactions to the fact that we have no visions are embraced, explored, and healed, then the fact that one can or can't see any vision becomes completely irrelevant.

The purpose of cleansing the doors of our perception is not to experience extraordinary visions and images, but to see ourselves and our lives with greater clarity. We all seek and pray for clarity so that we can align our actions accordingly, and yet have often developed a habit of softening the edges of our vision and sacrificed our integrity to the point of ending with an altogether blurred image of ourselves, our lives, and the world. Denial, inner bargaining, and procrastination are ways with which we soften and cloud our vision so that the naked truth doesn't strike us as too sharp, too vivid, or too blunt. Many of my clients over the years have called my brand of clarity "tough love." Clarity, as an expression of Light, is always also an expression of Love—it's Love that seeks only the truth of its own essence. But whenever necessary, that Love may shed all sugar coating and cut like a knife through the multiple veils of our lies and illusions in order to fully shine once again.

There is something incredibly beautiful and profound about those moments of clarity that the experience with San Pedro affords us. It is not about the ability to see solutions to old problems, or a clearer vision of our life purpose and future, but for me more significantly, the ability to honor our true feelings and to be honest with ourselves. That kind of honesty may point to old anger and resentments, but it also often unveils deep sentiments of love, affection, and sincere compassion towards ourselves and others, e.g., when a long-held resentment towards a parent or friend has prevented us from feeling the deep love we feel towards them and we finally get to honor and embrace that love under the effects of San Pedro. To embrace and feel at long last the depth of those feelings and emotions reminds us of the bright and warm light of our spirits which we sometimes forget about. This is unmistakably the sweetest of coming homes: a return to the loving-ness of our hearts.

THE POWER OF SMALL THINGS

To close this chapter, I would like to share one of the many stories in Andean lore about the humming-bird, the animal that in more recent times has been connected with the direction of the North...

A long time ago, a wild fire that was threatening the survival of all living creatures on Earth broke out. All the animals gathered to discuss the situation and find a solution to this impeding disaster. As they were talking, someone finally noticed a tiny hummingbird flying back and forth between the fire and a nearby creek, carrying a single drop of water to the fire each time. When asked what he was doing, the humming-bird replied simply: I am doing what I can.

I love this story because it tells of the power and beauty of even the smallest of acts. We can feel easily overwhelmed by the challenges of existence and equally discouraged at times by how stubborn certain aspects of ourselves turn out to be in the course of our healing process. And yet, even the tiniest of actions, rather than endless talking about it, does make a difference and is deeply empowering. The healing process lasts as long as necessary and along that journey it is most important that we pace ourselves and take good care of ourselves. The process teaches us to live with love, kindness, patience, and generosity with ourselves, and we can start practicing those beautiful lessons from the very start as best as we can and in the smallest of ways.

THEMES AND INTENTIONS RELATED TO THE ELEMENT OF FIRE

Here is a list of important themes connected with the Fire element that would be ideal to explore during a healing process with San Pedro:

- Passion and lack thereof, i.e., depression and apathy
- Appetites and addictions, or crutches of any kind
- Needs and desires
- Sexuality
- Our relationship with our own and the opposite sex
- The relationship between our sexual organs, our hearts, and our minds
- Ancestral, tribal, and racial healing

REMEMBERING OUR DIVINE ANCESTRY
— ISLAND OF THE SUN, BOLIVIA —
SEPTEMBER 2015

It was only a couple of weeks after returning to Hu-chuy Cusco in 2015 that my student and assistant at the time and I went to the Island of the Sun on the Bolivian side of Lake Titicaca for another pilgrimage. I had not been there in a few years and it was high time to pay a visit to this island that is sacred to all people of the Andes. It was by the sacred Puma Rock on the north side of the island that I had prayed years before and had asked the cosmic Puma for the power, strength, and courage to make my vision of a healing center in Pisac a reality.

We stayed at a guesthouse on the edge of the community in the south of the island where most of the tourist infrastructure is, and two days after our arrival we set out early in the morning after drinking San Pedro for a walk all the way to the north side and back.

When we had first arrived by boat on the south side, with its beautiful rock path climbing steeply and surrounded by streams of fresh water, I understood this docking place to be the beginning of an ancient pilgrimage route that would of course begin with the purification through water in order to visit the sacred Puma Rock at the other end of the island. Our purification would continue two days later with the support of San Pedro as we walked all morning along a dirt path and blessed with a unique landscape, surrounded by the waters of Lake Titicaca at 3810 meters of altitude, the glaciers surrounding it, and a stunningly clear blue sky.

As I walked and connected with the possible meanings inscribed in this sacred site[26], I remembered the ancient myth, according to which the first Inca and his twin sister were born of the Sun and first stepped on this Earth in a place I believe to be the Puma Rock or close by. In ancient times the Inca (or the ruling King elsewhere) was not perceived as different from the commoners but was the individual upon whom regular people could project their own highest selves. As I keep walking, the messages in the myth of this extraterrestrial birth of the first Inca and his sister begin to mean and remind me of our divine ancestry: our birthplace is not the Earth nor the physical, but the heavenly and spiritual.

Our spiritual source and roots are symbolized by the Sun and the Sky: what better place to reconnect with such source than on the Island of the Sun, so high up that the sun is closer than ever, and where the stars at night sparkle with a special brightness through the rarified atmosphere! This is a place where one can't help but look up: the whole place was carefully chosen to keep reminding us time and time again about our spiritual essence. As I walk I keep drinking in this simple yet powerful teaching until all my being is fully imbued with it and I can only marvel in gratitude that people thousands of years ago saw the importance of inscribing in nature, stone, and myth such a fundamental truth about who we are.

Sacred Architecture, just like Sacred Plant Teachers such as San Pedro, is so called when its purpose is to help us reconnect with the sacred within and without

---

[26] The Island of the Sun was never a common dwelling place but a sacred ground.

ourselves. Our ability to receive these sacred teachings depends most importantly on our readiness to receive and the reasons for our wishing to learn. Such readiness depends on our level of physical, emotional, mental, and spiritual purification. And when the ego's agenda is finally out of the way, then and only then can we receive ancestral teachings, which we can then share with our entire community.

I had been to the Puma Rock many times in the past but never before had I approached it with as much reverence as that day. Once we got there we made our prayers with coca leaves and settled on the back and below the rock, in a familiar place facing the lake and the Bolivian peaks. This time I realized that if there is any one prayer for courage in our times, that that prayer ought to be for the courage to walk in our truth: such is the challenge of living in a culture where we can too easily come up with reasons and excuses to betray such truth and ourselves with it.

It turned out that in the following months I would be invited again and again to see and honor my truth: it was a challenging process that required changes that were not easy to make and often charged with doubt and guilt. Surrendering to the naked truth of our hearts can be brutal: not only does it require unflinching honesty but also the strength and courage to act upon it. Prayer can be so tricky as what we pray for always comes to be, but hardly ever in the shape and timing we had wished. It is an art to formulate our prayers and surrender to whatever may unfold in the answering of those prayers. In most cases we find ourselves having to bite into morsels much bigger than we are willing to chew on. Our entire lives are the answer to the prayers made on the level of soul before we incarnate, and

146

yet we cannot help but complain about the ways our prayers are being answered and fulfilled, which is why the lesson of surrender offered by San Pedro is not limited to the ceremony space but extends in its practice to our lives and to the way we surrender to our feelings, emotions, and truths.

On our way back to the south side later that afternoon I am once again struck by the mythical energy of this island, a place where myths were born and where the symbols inscribed in its layout and rocks are still alive today. A friend I had met in the jungle years earlier once shared with me the teaching that whenever we wish to learn how to grow it is best to observe plants as plants excel in it. When we wish to learn how to move in this world we then observe and learn from animals. And when we wish to learn from the past we connect with rocks and mountains as they have been here longer than anybody else and therefore carry the oldest of memories.

I walk on this dirt path created thousands of years ago and I feel the power of the prayers of those who have ceremoniously walked this same path before. And in that moment I realize that we are the answer of our ancestors' prayers and that our own prayers will continue to bless our descendants long after our death.

That night after a warm dinner, all there is left to do is sit outside our cottage and look at the stars above us. Lake Titicaca is famous for its extraterrestrial activity and maybe we can spot a spacecraft or two, but my attention finally shifts from looking for something I cannot see to looking at what is right in front of my eyes: a Universe so vast and beautiful, and my present home, school, and temple.

V

AIR

The East, the Eagle and the Condor,
Breathing, the Mind, and the Masculine

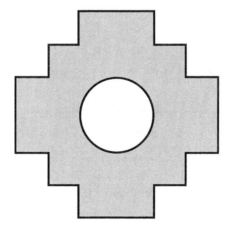

associate the direction of the East with the element of Air and the world of mind and thought. The exploration of our minds, rather than their dismissal, is a very important part of healing. It is through our minds that we create our worlds through perception colored by judgment and through beliefs. A deeper awareness of how our minds work and shape our experience of the world is essential if we wish to open our hearts. We shall also explore the theme of surrender and the challenges of letting go of our heads so that we can drop deeper into our hearts.

Interestingly, the direction of the East is diametrically opposite the West and the world of emotions. In modern times many people seem to suffer the consequences of their ongoing struggle between what they feel and what they think. My teacher Gabriel Roth used to say that we are in a state of permanent dyslexia: we feel something, think something else, and still act in a third different way that is neither in alignment with our feelings nor thoughts, but the expression of the ambivalence and confusion our struggle creates. That struggle often also results in an inability to put into words how we feel and express our feeling genuinely.

The more we glorify the mind, the more tyrannical it has become, and in so doing we have become slaves of our minds rather than their masters. Descartes' words, "I think therefore I am" have led us to believe that our thinking mind is more truly our "self" than our bodies, feelings, and spirits combined. The mind is a masculine energy that creates hierarchies, always seeking supremacy instead of seeing itself as part of a whole, and will keep on asserting such supremacy for as long as we identify with it and feed its thinly-disguised insecurities. Since the scientific revolution of the 17th century we have come to see ourselves as the sum of our thoughts, and scientific conventional thinking tells us that such thoughts are the workings of our brains, which *control* all of our biological life-sustaining functions.

Whenever in my San Pedro ceremonies I see someone afraid of letting go even for a short while of their thinking because they somehow believe their ability to survive depends on their ability to stay in control and think rationally, I remind them that our bodies are perfectly capable of functioning while we are asleep and there are infinite biological, neurological, and chemical processes within our bodies going on at all times over which we exercise no conscious control ever. As "Homo Erectus," we seem to have bought a little too literally into the fact that our brain is the highest placed organ of our bodies. This is in my opinion just a secularized version of the artificial split and hierarchy that were created when we started believing that body and spirit were two separate and separable entities, and gave greater importance to the spirit. In such duality, and all dualities are creations of the mind, we can see this evolution in perspective as the subtle but relentless strategy of the mind. We have created a hierarchy within our own selves: most spiritual and religious doctrines view the spirit above the physical body, and in secular and mainstream science the mind has taken the same dominant role over the body. We can see the disadvantages and the pernicious repercussions of such an attitude, and yet we are reluctant to let it go because upholding such dualities and hierarchies allow us to feel good about ourselves: putting ourselves above others, morally, economically, or otherwise, is an easy way to deal with our own insecurities and make sure we come out on top, even if we have to find that victory in the smallest of ponds. The Darwinian theory of evolution, which is to this day still just a theory, has been distorted and turned into a religion that justifies any abuse of force in order to assure the survival of the fittest, i.e., of the most powerful, indeed a very male-oriented attitude. In reality, Darwin's theory is always quoted in an incomplete way: survival of the fittest was defined by Darwin not by strength, but by the *ability to adapt to change*, which is a yielding and feminine quality that implies elasticity, an indispensable quality for all creatures (both animal and plant alike) to be able to thrive on this water planet.

The rational mind is by definition rigid and struggles with change. It fears change and deals with it by creating possible future scenarios based on past experiences and events. This has allowed for enormous technological advances, but in the same breath fails to *align* itself with the processes of Life, from smallest to largest, which are in constant flux. The way to deal with such change so far has been to want to exercise increasing control over the environment at a great cost to a biosphere that needs change in order to thrive. This is the globalized manifestation of a mentality that through culture, politics, religion, and philosophy, has judged women and the Feminine (and by extension, the physical and emotional parts of our beings, as well as Nature at large) as inferior and in need of subjugation or repression. It has been an interesting and by all means important phase of our evolution, and a necessary way to experience individuality and all aspects of the rational mind, but we do suffer now more than ever on an individual, social, and global level from the excessive glorification of the mind and the limited goal-oriented ways with which it approaches Life.

JUDGMENTS AND FORGIVENESS

Under the influence of San Pedro we are better able to connect with ourselves and our worlds through our hearts rather than our minds. In so doing, we can not only experience emotions long held in check but also experience ourselves and our lives without the rigid lens of our judgments, which is how the mind operates on a psychological level. Most of the people I have met over the years who wished to work with San Pedro have expressed a sincere desire to open and live more from their hearts, but very few were aware that such opening to love entails first and foremost a letting go (and therefore exploration) of their judgments and the repressive patterns of their own thinking. The exploration of those judgments includes also our judgments of others, onto whom we gladly project the judgments against those aspects of ourselves we are least proud of.

Our hearts want to be open because love is our nature. We are love and to love is the natural expression of our essence. Love is not an emotion nor an abstraction but the energy of our true identity. And as any energy it needs to flow freely. Free expression of love *is* the fulfillment of that energy and of our ultimate nature. Judgments are the expression of beliefs we hold in our consciousness that in one way or another say that we don't deserve to be that love and the loving creatures we actually are.

There was no need for Adam and Eve to be expelled from the biblical Garden of Eden: it was their own guilt, the natural consequence of negative judgment, that made them go into exile. In the Judeo-Christian tradition we have projected our inner judge onto the figure of a stern God, which is often internalized once again in modern man as the Super-ego. Growing up Catholic I spent the first 28 years of my life in the grips of fear of divine judgment and the awful consequence of eternal punishment. Guilt and shame colored the deepest layers of my inner landscape and rejecting Catholic dogma did little to relieve me of my guilt. What did finally help me let go of my guilt was the heartfelt extension of forgiveness to others and myself. What was most helpful in deepening that practice of forgiveness was my work with San Pedro, the medicine that helped me let go of judgment and open my heart, and A Course in Miracles, which is all about the teaching and practice of forgiveness.

Over the years I have come to understand that forgiveness is not only the best and sweetest of medicines, but also the only remedy against judgment. When I invited a client to explore and *feel* her judgments in ceremony, at some point she found herself in a courtroom and felt, to her great surprise, how deeply her judgments and the judgments of others had hurt her and how palpable that pain was. That is because judgments are really attacks on the self that holds guilt, and that judgment is perceived as the necessary punishment and cause of enough suffering to relieve the self of such guilt. But only forgiveness can heal judgment, and that's why people who feel guilty can punish themselves to no end and without ever finding solace. Our jails are in their best sense not a

154

punishment, but a place to feel contrition and to find forgiveness for one's actions.

Forgiveness can be extended when we let go of our judgments, finally see that we are here to learn, and that our past "sins" and misdeeds were really just learning experiences. True forgiveness arises when we let go of our judgments and realize that what we had labeled as wrong or hurtful was no big deal at all.

Our Super-ego is that part of ourselves that internalizes all sorts of tribal and social projected expectations. The rigidity of moral laws is the expression of the rigidity of the mind, which always creates unmanageable goals and unrealistic ideas of perfection in order to feed our beliefs of inadequacy. The price for not fulfilling those expectations and ideals is exile into our own hell. It is a vicious circle that keeps us in a state of perpetual remorse about Should-haves, Could-haves, and Would-haves. It is not until we fully accept and honor that in every moment we did the best that we could—otherwise I do believe we would have indeed acted differently—and make peace with our actions and ourselves, that we can learn from our past and let it go.

I recommend to anyone interested in fully living in the present, that they explore any feeling of regret and remorse. The forgiveness we seek from the Divine is first and foremost for us to offer to ourselves and those we have judged. In so doing, we are generous with our hearts and closer to the fulfillment of our true nature.

Jesus Christ and the Virgin Mary have been my greatest teachers in the path of forgiveness. It is Jesus who has been quoted as saying "love thy enemy," a concept so foreign to the archaic tribal ways of his time that he was derided for it. And I will not hide how perplexed those words made me feel two thousand years later. Like most people I had lived a life of blaming, judging, and secretly relishing revenge. It wasn't until I moved to the United States that I heard the expression, "for every finger you point at someone, you are pointing three fingers at yourself," and from then on my judging of others became a powerful mirror of my own self-judgment. As I began to take responsibility for the experiences I was inviting into my life I started, little by little but increasingly so, to see that the people I had resented, resisted, and judged, were really my greatest teachers as they were helping me reconnect with wounds I would have rather kept denying and repressing.

Along the way my friend Inadevi taught me that *all* emotional reactions are okay and that to allow ourselves to experience them is indeed very healthy. So, after my initial reaction and resistance when something unpleasant or annoying happens to me, I ask myself what that experience is meant to teach me and eventually start seeing all other people involved as my teachers. Our best teachers *will* make us suffer, cry, and go through our personal hell, but while the lessons are being learned we can be grateful to them for offering us an opportunity for healing and growth.

I could begin to forgive and extend my love to those whom I had perceived as my worst enemies only when I let go of my limiting belief that who I was ended at my fingertips. When I saw myself no longer limited by my physical body, but that my consciousness extended as far as anything that I was willing to be aware of, experience, and take responsibility for, I then gradually started to expand until I reached a level of expansion where time and space became totally irrelevant, but in order to embrace that vastness I had to let go of discrimination and judgment so that I could see and embrace perfection in everything. That perfection and beauty cannot be seen with the eyes or with the mind but to quote Antoine de St. Exupéry in *The Little Prince*[27],"can only be perceived by the heart."

To forgive those who have hurt us is to take responsibility for our own experience, and to forgive others and ourselves for anything we had deemed in the past as unforgiveable is to embrace our own sainthood and holiness. In *ACIM* it is repeatedly written that all attacks are a call for love. Whenever someone calls for love it is because they live in fear, and the best way to support a scared child is to offer our love, kindness, patience, acceptance, and compassion. We all want these loving attitudes in our lives and the best way to receive that love, acceptance, and forgiveness is by offering them as often and generously as possible.

BELIEFS

When I attended my first Avatar© course I struggled on and off again with the most important premise of its teachings: beliefs create experience. Like most people I grew up assuming that experience was what had shaped my beliefs. It took me quite a while to readjust my viewpoint and see the full implications of that simple statement. Beliefs are basically anything that comes out of our minds: thoughts, judgments, and beliefs. These are the statements that create life and ourselves as we experience them. Because the mind always wants to be right, it distorts its perception

---

[27] de St. Exupéry, Antoine. *Le Petit Prince*. Paris, Gallimard, 1999.

of reality in order to validate its beliefs and assumptions, thus actually recreating reality accordingly. The same thing happens in the case of judgments: if, for instance, I put a fancy label on a bottle I may start wishing to drink from it, whereas my reaction would be rejection if instead the label showed a skull and bones.

At a deeper level, looking at what our lives look like gives us a perfect reflection of the beliefs we hold in our consciousness. Oftentimes people seem at a loss when confronted with a gap between the actual lives they live and the one they intended to live. They blame the difference on a million external factors when in reality there is simply a confusion and unawareness between what they *wish* they believed and the beliefs they actually hold in their consciousness, e.g., to wish for abundance and to actually and without doubt believe in the abundance of Life will necessarily yield different results. In our times of computer technology many people refer to the beliefs they hold but don't like as "programming." These beliefs are considered to be some sort of external brainwashing, particularly on the part of family members, teachers, and society at large. I personally don't share such a viewpoint, which I find disempowering, and prefer to view the beliefs held in the collective consciousness that have affected me as my own, i.e., the reflection of my own beliefs, or as the best possible scenario I could have chosen in order to deal with my own issues in this lifetime. A good example of this was choosing to be born gay in a Catholic environment: that social environment perfectly mirrored the shame I came into this world with. So, when it comes to beliefs I feel that the first step is to take full responsibility for them and see how they affect us in all aspects of our experience and lives.

The second step is to become aware of how conflicting beliefs prevent us from getting anywhere. Using again the analogy of computers, we cannot expect our laptops to function effectively if there are two conflicting programs running simultaneously. Rejection and condemnation of prevailing beliefs and dynamics in our society such as greed and power-over has so far done little to change our world and I doubt this will ever change. For me the path of change entails first and foremost the *integration* of such beliefs. Integration requires that we first of all take responsibility for our own beliefs rather than blaming others for them. We may not like them and we may not agree with them, but they are in our world and experience, and are therefore totally ours.

Lastly, in order to let go of such beliefs it is important to see and learn the important lessons such beliefs and the resulting experiences they created have afforded us. Let's take the example of wars: I firmly believe that we will keep on engaging in violent conflicts until we have learnt from them, perhaps the hard way but so it is, not only how destructive these conflicts are, but also the beautiful lesson about the unity of us all and of how we hurt ourselves every time we hurt others and the planet.

What we call "reality" is simply the expression of the beliefs we hold in our consciousness, and to change that reality the best way I found this far requires that we explore such beliefs so we can learn from them and integrate them.

MAGIC AND MAGICK

Since the dawn of time humans have engaged in magickal practices of all sorts. By "magick" I mean any attempt to *change* our experience, be it by trying to improve the weather according to our needs and wishes, or the way we feel about ourselves, and so on.

Magick, no matter how esoteric and complicated, is the reflection of a childish attitude that fails to simply accept things as they are. Spiritual and shamanic practices all over the world are full of such attempts to control and change our experience. To be more accurate I would have to say that we unconsciously imbue these practices with our secret need to change our experience thus turning them into magickal practices. The plant medicine path has not been immune to such distortion and unconscious manipulation: many people approach it with the obvious hope that by engaging in it everything will be magickally okay, meaning that nothing else is required of them other than show up, pay, puke a little and that's it. Such attitude is understandable but often results in the person being disillusioned because "nothing happened."

Spirituality as far as I am concerned is not magick and will never be, no matter how good our magick tricks are. True spirituality begins only when we have the courage to let go of such tricks and allow ourselves to be completely naked, vulnerable, and honest. Some years ago a young woman who had heard of me came to one of my ceremonies. She was a loving and lovely woman who had done it all before: yoga, Burning Man, meditation, and had even assisted in Ayahuasca ceremonies. In the middle of the afternoon I found her lying on the grass furiously working a large crystal on her abdomen. I asked her what she was doing and she replied that her belly was hurting and she, by using her crystal, hoped her pain would somehow go away. I told her to put her magick crystal away and simply welcome and *feel* that pain. Two weeks later she joined one of my retreats, which started with a San Pedro ceremony. The day before the ceremony I had warned her not to bring any of her magick tools and during the ceremony she confessed that being in ceremony without her tricks was the hardest thing she had ever done. And later in the same retreat I was the one to urge her to lie down instead of sitting up in perfect yet rigid lotus position so that she could surrender to the medicine in ways she hadn't thus far.

A subtler form of magickal practice is to smother with what people call love any aspects of themselves they don't feel comfortable with. That love may be genuine indeed but when it is extended out of fear or a desire to "get rid" of parts of ourselves because they do not resonate with our idealized selves, then it is no longer love. Call it what you want but for me it ain't the real thing: love that is manipulative just isn't love, no matter what we tell ourselves.

Now don't get me wrong: I have and continue to use magickal tools. Rituals, and by extension plant medicine ceremonies, and healings are full of magickal practices. Years ago during a channeling session I was told that I had been in the line of shamanic practices well before this lifetime and would, whenever my patients required because of their beliefs, play magick tricks in order to get the job done, but always with the awareness that I was using those tricks simply to satisfy my patients' need for showmanship (shamans and showmen have more than a few things and letters in common). For me ritual practices are a wonderful way to *focus* both our attention and will, and I use them in such a way and no other.

Real magic is the awareness that we *create* our lives from beginning to end. When we take full ownership of our essentially creative nature, then there is no need to change our reality in any way. To change our reality takes an enormous amount of energy and is often a fruitless pursuit, whereas we would do better using that energy to explore and let go of our victim little selves so that our true creative selves can shine fully.

Oftentimes we ask ourselves why we fail to change the way we feel and the circumstances of our lives. Instead of trying to change them I ask myself what the purpose of such experience may be, i.e., what is important for me to learn at this point in my life?

I am fond of saying to people that plant medicines are illusory medicines for illusory problems. Wanting to *change* ourselves is a symptom that we hold in our consciousness a belief or other that there is something wrong with who we are: plant medicine, like all meaningful spiritual paths helps us remember that beyond the beliefs and lies we tell ourselves about our inadequacy we are perfectly ok just as we are. And not only ok but actually divinely awesome. If we do fall back into old patterns or keep recreating scenarios we would rather not experience, and this is a major complaint from people who engage in plant medicine and other healing and spiritual modalities, is not because we are cursed or stupid, or because the practice is useless or we have not engaged in it in the right way, but simply because we have inadvertently tried to skip a few important steps and there are more important and valuable lessons to be learnt from our own patterns.

Another important reason for wishing to magickally change our lives is the fact that many of us pursue our lives from our egos, whereas in my opinion this life of ours is part of a much longer soul journey. The pursuit of happiness is for most simply the fulfillment of ego-driven desires and the avoidance of fear and pain. The soul journey is a journey of remembrance and embodiment of our true divinity. We may put all of our efforts and attention to the fulfillment of our egos, but whenever we fail to fulfill that agenda it is simply because our souls have a different plan and direction: a plan we chose very carefully well before entering these bodies. So when things don't go "our" way, the wisest thing is to stop (rather than keeping on pushing or knocking at a door that won't open) and ask ourselves what the situation *as is* may be trying to teach us.

SURRENDER

The biggest gift I have received from San Pedro over the years has been the gift of self-acceptance—acceptance of who I am or have been at any given time. Acceptance is one of the deepest expressions of surrender. It is not resignation nor defeat, but surrender. Rather than trying to change a past that cannot be changed or a present that asks only for honoring, accepting things and ourselves opens the space for learning, integration, and expansion.

The biggest challenge of plant medicine ceremonies is surrender. And one of the most important life lessons (as in, "in your own skin rather than on the page of a book") that plant medicine offers us in these days of compulsive control is surrender.

Many people on different spiritual paths tell themselves and whomever is willing to listen that plant medicine is a lower form of spiritual practice because it involves the ingestion of something, implying a reliance on something other than ourselves, as if meditation were not a tool, or breathing, or focusing one's attention through mantras or chanting. At the bottom of such judgment I have often found a deeply-seated fear of surrendering and of not being at all in control. I have found no more powerful way to learn and practice surrender than with plant medicines: to have no other option but follow the green rabbit wherever it may take us is an unrivalled experience of surrender among all spiritual practices and healing modalities.

The currently fashionable word for control is "choice." Some people on a spiritual/self-discovery journey that to me feels more like a business venture than anything else, keep telling themselves, often out of some insecurity and doubt, that they have a choice: the choice to feel this or that way about themselves and the world, and to live their lives accordingly. I agree that personal will, determination, and perseverance are most important qualities in order to manifest what we desire, and we do have a choice all the time. Every moment and experience is a choice, even when we decide to do nothing at all. But no matter how hard and intensely we try to tell ourselves that, for instance, we love ourselves, our deliberate programming will fall on deaf ears if that message collides with a belief that we just don't love or like ourselves. In such cases the sensible choice is to actually embrace and experience what we truly hold inside ourselves but have battled like heroes to deny, such as feelings and beliefs of unworthiness, inadequacy, and inferiority. And that choice is not really a choice at all, but a necessity that will have to be addressed sooner or later if real healing and growth are sought.

Under instructions from a healer I spent two months in 1996 on the beaches of Bali and Lombok walking every morning for at least an hour while repeating to myself, "I am totally loving and lovable just as I am." I am not kidding. I felt like Julianne Moore in the movie *Safe* by Todd Haynes: faking it 'til I would (hopefully) make it. It was a good beginning but it took me several more years to actually *be* and *feel* that loving and lovable. Much had to be looked at, embraced, cried, and purged out until I could heal and let go of the judgments I held against myself that prevented me from being and experiencing that love.

Surrender is as simple as giving ourselves the permission to embrace our true feelings and say, "I really hate myself no matter what I tell myself and others," or, "in all honesty I deeply resent my parents and siblings despite my efforts to avoid such feelings." Asserting our freedom of choice often belies a resistance to being simply who we are and embracing how we truly feel. As what we resist persists, what we think of as choice will sooner than later prove to be simple make-believe. I have experienced no greater relief and healing than under the influence of San Pedro whenever I would finally surrender and feel long-held repressed emotions.

Surrender is the stuff of true heroes, just like the forgiving of the unforgivable, which is why the lives of saints and enlightened beings are as fascinating and troubled as the lives of warriors. The mind will fight until the end for its supremacy and the closer we get to let go of our identification with our minds and egos, the stronger the resistance on their part becomes.

I am as guilty as anyone else of having entertained delusional fantasies about my spiritual life. Even when I started my shamanic apprenticeship in the jungle in 2005 I couldn't help but creating a Hollywood fantasy of what that process was going to be like, full of woo-woo and special effects. My first five months of apprenticeship, during which, as I had been told by my green teacher the Datura/Toé plant (*Brugmansia*), I was to receive everything I needed in order to start leading my own Ayahuasca ceremonies, turned out to be a long and tedious process of taming of my ego and little else. I write about all this because as powerful and healing plant medicines are, they will not shelter us from our spiritual egos and mind tricks. On the contrary, they will present us with the challenges and temptations of a hugely inflated ego that believes itself to be all-powerful and enlightened.

We can experience with San Pedro our true divinity and the divinity of all of Creation. This is always a welcome experience and initiation, but also one that can easily risk getting to our heads faster than a glass of champagne. The inebriation can lead even the best of us into self-importance, delusional messianic thoughts, and worst of all, a sense that we are above caring and that the rules no longer apply to us.

It is true that a solid and grounded expansion of consciousness brings about a new set of ethical standards that may seem beyond the established notions of good and bad, but these new standards are actually all about humility rather than attempts to self-aggrandize oneself. My own awakening has brought the awareness that no one is above anyone else and that no path is holier than any other. It has brought me to the end of the comparing and judging game that had served me to, as best as my ego could, overcome my own fears and insecurities. Surrendering to the fact that *ALL* Life is equally precious and treating all expressions of Life with that reverence and respect, not because we feel spiritually superior and therefore with an attitude of condescendence, but because we know that *everything* is part of the same luminous divine fabric: that's for me a sure sign of true spiritual elevation.

My favorite representation of true spiritual awakening is the scene in the first *Matrix*[28] movie by the Wachowski brothers where Neo takes the famous red pill and ends up waking up to a reality from which he had been until then completely unaware of. The awakening is not pretty at all: it is actually shocking and scary. Ignorance, denial, and amnesia are the sweetest of narcotics, and a drug I have sometimes wished I could resort to since my eyes and spirit have opened up to greater realities than the little construct of my busy mind. Of course awakening is all worth it and ultimately there is no other game truly worth playing, but it is not the pleasure cruise advertised in certain medicine and spiritual circles around the world. Surrender is a dying process: that dying can be ecstatic but also fraught with resistance and therefore full of suffering.

We all meet sooner or later in this process the door to a place within ourselves that because of pain, fear, or judgment we have vowed in the past never to open again. That same door that holds so much resistance is the door to our own awakening, but in the moment we

---

[28] Op. cit.

are not aware of any of it and all we can feel is dread. It is only with courage and faith that eventually we can go through that scary door and eventually enter our own Heaven. Those of us who have gone through that door can only testify for the rewards that await us on the other side, and encourage and support others in tangible and invisible ways to do the same, extending the same patience that is required along the journey, knowing perfectly well that there are no shortcuts.

There are levels upon levels of surrender, many of which we are often unaware of until we are face to face with the resistance to let go. For me the biggest, and therefore most challenging, leaps of surrender were around getting sick and physically die, and surrendering to anything I perceived as threatening to my own sense of individuality such as feminine energy as expressed by Mother Earth and Divine Love. Each one of us has their own story and path to walk and it is only by showing up that we can unearth our deeply concealed pains but also rediscover our most sublime light.

It was after a San Pedro ceremony years ago that a participant told me the following: "Javier, I think all this talk about the Universe being made of love is a bunch of bullshit. I believe the fabric of the Universe is irony." Well, I would say that in my experience that fabric, as loving in essence as it is, is not devoid of humor and irony. Actually, plenty of it.

It was one of such moments of deep irony that I experienced only in 2015. All of my life my main and highest priority had been personal freedom and from early on I rebelled against anything I would perceive as repressive and limiting of my freedom, often extending my solidarity to anyone and any people I perceived as similarly oppressed by society or religion. It wasn't until my late 20's that I realized that my deepest shackles were not out there but right between my ears, and that my beliefs and judgments were more effective than any army and police in keeping me small and scared. Only years later I found the following quote by C. G. Jung that blesses the home page of my website: "Your vision will become clear only when you look inside your heart; who looks outside dreams; who looks inside awakens."

The search for freedom turned into a longing for liberation and ended in a moment of true irony when I realized, after it was all done and dealt with, that there had never been a moment of true personal freedom along my spiritual journey and life. I realized I had set my journey long before my physical birth and that what I used to call "my personal will" was only the limited and desperate exercise to avoid the inevitability of my choices and express some kind of ego-centered independence and freedom. The ultimate surrender turned out to be the surrendering to my soul path and surrendering to my ultimate loving and divine essence.

SERIOUSNESS AND APPRECIATION

The spiritual path can often be overwhelmingly humbling: I have many times cringed with embarrassment at the arrogance and presumptuousness of my own mind and ego, which is why I have learnt not to take anything that comes out of my head too seriously for too long.

One of my most important teachers was fond of saying that seriousness is always a symptom that we are somehow missing the point of it all. Now, spirituality is a very serious business, right? Enlightenment and salvation are important matters that require all of our seriousness, right? Two years ago I went on a San Pedro walk with some friends up by the lagoons of Kinsa Cocha and at the end of the walk, rather than spend some time with the locals I decided it was better to watch the sun set on a nearby slope with two of my companions. At some point I shared with them the news that my career as a medicine person was in serious jeopardy. The reason was that I was on my way to the jungle to diet with my teacher and the diet was going to be with the plant Cielo Piri Piri, which, since my teacher had started adding to the Ayahuasca brew I was offering to people, had brought a welcome and refreshing energy of joy into my work and life. My intention for the diet was to embrace joy fully and let go of whatever stood in the way. I could tell right away that seriousness was one of the things I needed to let go of and that my work and life would be informed with a new lightness and humor that in many spiritual and medicine circles is easily frowned upon.

Once in the jungle I did take San Pedro by myself one day. I set out early in the morning and walked to the old Sachamama Center, which I hadn't visited in years and had been taken over by Don Francisco's assistant. As I quickly discovered the old Sachamama had also been taken over by the jungle, which will erase in no time any sign of previous human settlement unless assiduous work is done on a regular basis. I could hardly follow the path now overgrown and was reminded once again of the impermanence of life and of how quickly our footsteps on this Earth will be forgotten with the passing of time: here now, and gone and forgotten tomorrow. With that I could see how futile the seriousness that hangs over our lives is and how seriously I had had the tendency of taking not only myself but also all the thoughts that came out of my head. I could see how, out of my own beginner's insecurity and desire to do the best job I could do with plant medicines, I had in the past been excessively serious and how it was high time I let go of a good chunk of it.

Seriousness is often exercised out of fear of making mistakes, which is not that bad of a thing, but excessive seriousness really makes us miss point: the point being that life is continuous evolution and learning, and that what we call mistakes are part of that growth process. At some point later that day I even chuckled with God imagining Him/Her going, "Oops!" at some poor past choices. I told Him/Her I was sorry everybody had such a serious reverence, which is often just badly disguised fear and terror, for the Divine to the point of leaving the Divine without true friends and buddies with whom to joke about it all. It was an important ceremony for me, and one whose teachings I fondly remember.

Seriousness is an expression of the mind and its fears, and therefore has little to do with spirituality as I experience it. I was lucky to work over the years here in Peru with teachers who were only too eager to crack a joke, smile, and lighten up as often as possible. Their lightness of being, which does not mean in any way a lack of respect for their work, has been a very important medicine for me and one I am glad to share now with my own clients and friends. The rigidity of seriousness is easily felt in spiritual and shamanic circles where the emphasis is no longer on the celebration of our mix of humanity and divinity (a sure source of paradoxes and funny idiosyncrasies if there was ever one), but on doing things right and perfectly so. As the Sufis wisely point out, perfection is an idea of the mind and one that needs its opposite in order to assert itself[29]. Thus, the pursuit of perfection in life as in ritual by striving to adhere to complex ideas and actions, often results in a deepening of the mind's yoke rather than liberation from it. And this without even mentioning how the judgment and shaming for not doing things right is an even heavier weight on our spirits.

Spirit does have a big sense of humor. Life has a sense of humor beyond our imagination. Unfortunately, our fear of missing the train, of being stuck in some sort of hell, makes us miss the point altogether. And, yes, our lives can easily become serious business: our pains are way too "real" to laugh about, and our confusion is a constant source of worry, which we take very seriously indeed. But at some point along the journey all that seriousness begs to be let go of so that our spirits can rise freely and lightly. The smile and laughter on the faces of many spiritual teachers are witness to the accuracy of what I say: it is not a timid smile or a half-contrived chuckle, but a full-on laughter of lightness and joy.

When the mind is temporarily not as overactive under the effects of mind-altering substances such as San Pedro or Ayahuasca, many people who take themselves very seriously will shift from seriousness to a, "I don't give a damn about anything, everything is just a cosmic joke I am finally understanding the punch line thereof" kind of attitude. Well, even though a lesser

---

[29] I am grateful to Eli Jaxon-Bear for these insights from his book. Jaxon-Bear, Eli. *From Fixation to Freedom: The Enneagram of Liberation.* 3rd Printing, Ashland, Leela Foundation, 2006.

serious attitude is definitely welcome, I don't believe these people actually get the punch line at all. Not just yet at least, and not in its full splendor. To dismiss everything as an illusion or as a bad joke is just that: dismissive and belittling. To belittle illusion will not ever make it any less powerful over us. The heartfelt laughter of *appreciation* of illusion and of ourselves as the creators of such illusion is a different ballgame altogether. Deep appreciation for our creations and for Creation as a whole, no matter how transient and illusory these may be, brings a respect and love for Life that is anything but dismissive.

That same year in the jungle I was inspired to read the chapter of *Genesis* in the Bible. A copy in Spanish was around and I went for it, but not for long as I quickly found the language and its implications so demeaning to women that I didn't finish the chapter. But something stuck with me that day: as the biblical God starts creating this and that, after each creation He is quoted as "seeing that that (creation) was good." That got me into a lot of reflection as we are constantly in judgment and feeling remorseful and guilty about much of what we have created as humans in the last couple of thousand years, like polluting chemicals, famines, and such. It dawned on me that in the process of reclaiming our divinity, meaning the full awareness that we are part and extension of this amazing energy we call God, we are being called to express these divine qualities such as infinite love and patience, but also, as mentioned in the chapter of Genesis, to see that our creations, i.e., the manifestation of our creative energy, are good. And not just some of them, but *all* of them.

Jesus brought an important piece to this process by extending forgiveness to those who imprisoned and killed him. As I understand it, he did not do so out of some sense of moral superiority, but because he could see that no harm could be done to his spirit, which is eternal and beyond all harm. His crucifixion was not the too often lamented killing of his physical body, but symbolizes only the sacrificing of the mind that identifies with the physical so that the heart and the spirit can be free. His example is a teaching to us all as what was true for him is just as true and valid for us all as we are all Children of God. In the end we don't have to become or do anything, but simply let go of the serious agenda of our minds and welcome into our hearts and souls the truth of our divine essence.

So, the first step towards the opening of the heart is to let go of judgment and the extension of forgiveness wherever judgment had or has been held. As many people I have guided through San Pedro ceremonies have shared afterwards, oftentimes with heartfelt and ultimate forgiveness comes the realization that there was really nothing to judge and nothing to forgive, and that everything, all the hurts and atrocities, were simply part of a learning and healing experience. When we let go of judgment, then and only then we can finally appreciate our creations, dramas, and failures with the same enthusiasm we appreciate the most amazing sunset, friend, or work of art, and that appreciation brings us in alignment and resonance with the Divine.

The old paradigm has been about judgment and fear of judgment, but we are now more and more exposed to a new (and ancestral) awareness that says that Life is simply a way for the Divine to become aware of and experience Itself, and that this often-resented duality we live in is actually the means by which we are to become aware of our divinity. With greater awareness we can finally see that the apparently mysterious and scary master plan of Life is actually one of loving awareness and celebration, of play and laughter.

Some of you, as many of my clients have before whenever I have been singing this song, may say, "But what about the evils of this world? What about genocide and child sexual abuse etc. etc.?" "How can anyone possibly condone such atrocities? And isn't such condoning actually a way to support the perpetuation of such behaviors?" Yes, I hear you. And I am aware of the challenges of accepting, forgiving, and appreciating such occurrences. Somehow we fear that our forgiveness will only lead to more abuses and that to offer the other cheek is a terrible mistake rather than a plausible solution to the many ills in this world. It is not that easy to forgive and appreciate certain creations such as erotophobia, fascism of any persuasion, envy, or misogyny. But that is in my opinion the only way to the new world we all hope to create and experience.

It is easy to preach to the converted, to accept what we agree with, and to forgive the forgiving and forgivable. It is a whole other story to forgive the unforgiving and accept what we have deemed as unacceptable. I was sharing this with some newly converted Orthodox Jews in Tsfat during my first visit to Israel in 2013. They listened to my words in quiet disbelief but had to agree with me on some level when I told them that, as Albert Einstein once said, to expect different results by keeping on doing exactly the same thing is unrealistic.

We are being called to radically change not only the way we think but most importantly change the way we act in order to align ourselves with the changes we hope to see in our world. And here we are faced with one of the most recalcitrant aspects of the mind: its unwillingness to change, see things differently, and act accordingly. The mind just wants to be right all the time and create a future that is the carbon copy of the past. Imagination and surprise are not welcome in the world of mind.

I have mentioned earlier that when I attended my first Avatar© Course I struggled with the viewpoint that belief creates experience and not vice versa as I had always thought. I had held the popular assumption that the circumstances of my early life and family background had shaped who I was and how I experienced the world. To embrace the fact that it was the beliefs I held in my consciousness that were indeed shaping my experience was truly challenging. First of all, if I were to embrace that viewpoint I had to let go of all blaming and my previous cause and effect reasoning. And secondly, I had to let go of that part of me with which I had been intimately identifying all my life up to that moment and had acted out of the assumption that I was who I was because of external factors. Last but not least, there was the question of how far I was willing to own the consequences of this new viewpoint: my own life? The life of others? The planet? The whole Universe? It's been interesting to expand my awareness and consciousness little by little: occasionally there has been strong resistance but sooner or later always followed by surrender.

A corollary resistance voiced by many to extending acceptance, forgiveness, and appreciation is the urgency we often feel in regards to the damage we inflict on the environment. After all our own survival and that of our children is at stake, and that a very "serious" matter indeed. The spectrum of annihilation of not only the Earth as we know it but of our own species is cause of great alarm and fear. Something needs to be done and as quickly as possible if we wish to continue thriving as a species.

Once again our first approach has been judging and denouncing as loudly as possible whomever we feel is responsible for this damage, and that is ok but it's not taking us very far. All that denouncing and protesting is a way to drown out the deep guilt we hold in our hearts but rarely succeed in silencing altogether. Personally, I admit to myself that I am part of the damaging party, so rather than judge myself or governments and corporations, I offer myself some heartfelt forgiveness and do my best to minimize my ecological footprint. But also I do my best to help others become aware of how we all contribute to the situation and make them aware that solutions, however small, are available to us all the time. Often the helplessness that people experience in their inner lives is also transferred to a sense of helplessness in regards to their public and social life.

I am aware that one of the main things I teach my clients is self-empowerment: the awareness that we don't have to depend on anything or anybody in order to live our lives, and that we can become our best friends, lovers, doctors, and spiritual guides. Plant medicines do exactly that when engaged with under the guidance of people interested not in personal power or self-importance, but in the emancipation from our fears and limiting beliefs: they support us in letting go of our pains and fears, and help us reconnect with our strength, courage, and power so that we can take once again the reins of our lives trustfully.

BREATHING

When I was in massage school in New York in '91-'92 I heard a common and humorous saying in massage circles that people practicing massage therapy usually tend to move from massage to therapeutic breathwork and inevitably end up offering high colonics. Well, apart from the fact that I did end up leading Ayahuasca ceremonies, which are really high colonics for the soul, in the summer of '93 I went to Northern California for a Rebirthing training. The course was offered by the Body Electric School of Massage, which had been created by Joseph Kramer, the man who a year earlier had taught me the importance of breathing.

In my work with plant medicines the word I repeat most often is "breathe." Humans, just like all animals and plants, need first and foremost air in order to survive and thrive: we can be without food or water for days but not even a couple of minutes without breathing. Our first breath marks the beginning of our existence outside the maternal womb and that very existence comes to an end shortly after our last breath. Breathing is what we consciously and unconsciously do the most throughout our lives, and to me the way we breathe is a reflection of our attitude to Life. It is interesting that we all wish to live our lives more fully and healthily, and yet fail to nourish ourselves and

178

every cell of our bodies with the most important of nutrients: oxygen.

When we think, we have a tendency to breathe less than we ought to. Apart from the fact that when we are in our heads we are not really *experiencing* Life but just thinking about it, the lack of oxygen impairs our ability to think clearly. At the beginning of my San Pedro ceremonies I always remind people that nothing is expected of them except to breathe. Breathing is the easiest and quickest way to shift from thinking to feeling and experiencing, and the best way to help this medicine help us shift from our minds into our hearts: by breathing more deeply and fully we actually align our actions with the purpose of this medicine. The natural trepidation at the beginning of each ceremony is often mirrored by a shallowness of breath, so I often share that in ceremony I am always as generous with my breath as I hope the medicine to be generous with me.

Since this process is all about letting go, my recommended way of breathing is inhaling through the nose and exhaling through the mouth, and I encourage people to inhale as deeply as possible and to let out on the exhale whatever sound or moan that wants to come out. Each inhalation for me is a way of saying yes to Life, to our lives: the fuller the inhalation, the bigger the yes. And each exhale is a relaxing into our own deeper selves and a letting go into Life, trusting both to support us benevolently. A good way of experiencing such support is by feeling how the Earth supports us without fail as we sit, lie, and walk upon it. As we let go of our holding and control posture, and allow the Earth to support and hold us, we simultaneously relax into the medicine process with increased trust in both the Universe and San Pedro.

Awareness is often understood as a mental process whereby through our thinking we become rationally conscious and understand what is happening to and around us. For me awareness is a more expanded experience of simply experiencing, without any inner mental discourse *about* what I am experiencing, more akin the state that Zen Buddhists refer to as "no-mind," which is really, to keep things simple, just a feeling state. Alan Watts describes this awareness when speaking of Sam-yag-drishti or complete view, the first section of the *Eightfold Path* of the Buddha's *Dharma*, as a lively attention to one's direct experience, to the world as immediately sensed, rather than misled by names and labels.[30]

It is unavoidable for most of us these days to want to make sense of our experience even as we experience it. This presents unfortunately the challenge of trying to be in two different places at the same time, i.e., in our heads and in the flow of the experience. The therapeutic limitations of such predicament are clearly demonstrated in classic psychoanalysis with its focus on *understanding* why we function a certain way rather than *healing* and *integration*. There is always time to order experience and frame it in a way that helps us make sense of it, but in order to integrate past resisted experiences and aspects of ourselves I feel it is most important that we leave our thinking aside and simply allow ourselves to have a direct experience, particularly when emotional states are involved.

---

[30] Watts, Alan. *The Way of Zen*. New York, Vintage Books, 1989.

So many people will ask in disbelief, "What was that that I just went through?" right after a particularly strong cathartic experience with San Pedro. Let's just say that the experience would not have been nearly as profound and healing had there been a constant monitoring and commentating on the part of the mind.

Nothing can help us stay more in the present moment and experience what the medicine is inviting to experience than our own breath. I always recommend using the breath to *allow* rather than control our experience, to amplify feeling rather than constricting and managing it. The only exception to this rule is when we feel scared and our inhalation becomes rapid and shallow only to drive us deeper into a panicky state. In such cases I invite people to take long inhalations and exhalations until a certain trust in the process is restored.

In Praise of the Breath of Life

One of my favorite experiences in life is the sim-ple experience and contemplation, infused with gratitude and appreciation, of Life itself.

Either laying in my bed first thing in the morning, before going to sleep, or anytime during the day I simply breathe, taking the time to fully enjoy the experience of inhaling and exhaling, and allowing the breath to flow in and out until it is no longer me breathing but Life itself breathing through me.

I marvel at my lungs and how they are perfectly designed for humans to thrive on this planet. I see that this physical body of mine is in perfect harmony with and truly an offspring of this Earth.

I marvel at the perfect interconnectedness of all life forms and energies that with their dance create living beauty on a planetary scale.

I think of plants and how precious their gift of oxygen is, and then exhale to complete that circle by offering them my carbon dioxide, which will once again be transmuted into more plant life and more oxygen.

I marvel at the terrestrial atmosphere that not only reflects enough light to create blue skies in a million subtle shades of iridescence, but also holds the perfect combination of nitrogen and oxygen, which creates and maintains Life as we know it.

I am moved by the movements of rivers and oceans, the winds and the clouds, perpetually flowing into and out of each other, and I can feel their motions within my own self as we spiral across the Universe at hair-raising speed but in perfect calm, only aware of the planetary revolutions with the movements of the sun, the moon, and the stars in the sky. Night and day bringing new seasons, new ages, and new eons in pure play.

And as I inhale and exhale I am in awe of it all and feel truly privileged and blessed to be, to be here, right now.

I think of other planets in our solar system and then feel really fortunate and supremely lucky not to be at this moment anywhere else.

I feel into the mysterious interplay of stellar and galactic energies. So many suns out there in the sky!

I inhale all of this and with my breath I take in this miracle of which I am expression, embodiment, co-creator, and both spectator and participant all at once.

And finally I am flooded with gratitude and joyful bliss for having the open heart and mind to receive all these blessings and for the ability to consciously appreciate and enjoy this wondrous, beautiful, and dynamic Creation. With just one breath.

THE WORLD OF MIND

Rigidity

One of the most striking features of the mind is its rigidity. The mind, because of its awareness of death, holds fear around dying and seeks an unrealistic eternity in a world that is intrinsically impermanent. Its way of escaping from the flow of permanent change that *is* Life is by creating and retreating into a world of ideas and concepts separate from Life, which I call the golden tower of our heads. But even thoughts and beliefs are fleeting and subject to change, hence the increasing rigidity of the mind that tries to hold on to its own vision and ideas of ourselves, the people, and the world around us. Because of its dread of change, the mind seeks stability and always wants to be right, to the point of insisting on the validity of its assumptions by interpreting reality accordingly. Rigidity of belief and obsession with being right, even in the realms of religion and spirituality, is not a sign of wisdom but more accurately a symptom of an insecure and overreacting mind. Such rigidity is often camouflaged by the claim that, "things have always been this or that way" (an inaccurate statement if you ask me) and, "therefore need to continue being the same."

One of the many gifts of mind-altering substances is their ability to help us see our preconceived reality through a different viewpoint, and therefore see the relativity of our previously rigidly held assumptions and beliefs. These substances help us see that life as we experience it is not really rigid at all, but becomes solid through the workings and insistence of the mind. Anybody who engages long enough with mind-altering substances or meditation eventually comes to the realization that life as we perceive it is simply a creation of our minds and that the mind, just like everything else in this world and dimension, is not nearly as solid or permanent as it portrays itself. The mind is also a creation and therefore fleeting. It is only the deeper ground and source of Creation from which all creations arise that has in my opinion any permanence at all.

The need of the mind for stability and security finds an illusory solution in the creation of an illusory ego, which is just an *idea* of selfhood and not an ultimate reality at all. The frightened ego then expresses its attachment to stability by being rigid, an incredible stubbornness to its own viewpoint, and a need to be right.

The constant struggle against new ideas and the recurrent waves of condemnation of mind-altering substances and mystical experiences that are believed to threaten the social status quo, which is painstakingly created by the mind and expressed collectively as normality and sacred moral order, is luckily frustrated by the undisputed but never publicly acknowledged need of recurrent waves of inspiration and expansion of consciousness, without which any culture solely dependent on the intellect would eventually wither and die. This is what our present day return to plant medicines, mind-altering substances, and the search for unmediated spiritual and mystical experiences are all about: as threatening to the established order as these experiences may seem, they are also indispensable in infusing with new energy and viewpoints the sclerotic rigidity of the mind and the world and society it creates.

But as much as we profess our desire and need for change, our minds are proportionally scared of it, and that's something important to be aware of when engaging in any transformational process, including the work with San Pedro, as the rigidity of the mind may express itself through a multitude of resistances to any true transformational healing or spiritual process.

For me the only important requirement, apart from a minimum of physical fitness and psychological maturity, needed in order to engage with San Pedro and other plant medicines is simply a sincere willingness—not necessarily a readiness, but at least a willingness—to question the validity of any previously held assumption and belief. And by the way, I feel such an open attitude is one of the secrets to a healthy and fulfilling life.

Polarity

The dualism of the mind is the means by which we can perceive light from darkness, hot from cold, and so on. It is a most valuable survival and perceptual tool as it helps us see and feel through opposites. As helpful as this way of perceiving and experiencing may be, it is clear to me that there is a next step in our evolution: the ability to see through the heart and beyond all opposites. Transcending the polarities of the mind is to me a lot more grounded when we integrate our mind into the whole of who we are rather than with attempts to kill it or silence it forever. In this way the mind ceases to be an enemy but can be honored as the valuable tool and important stepping-stone in our evolution that it is.

Only a mind disguised as spiritual ego would want to kill itself with efficiency and as soon as possible—and only a mind would want and pursue what it cannot have, thus leaving the individual frustrated, impatient, and angry. It is ironic that in our quest for a quiet mind we often end up feeding that very mind in the process. Rather than resenting our minds and their endless chatter, I feel it's more beneficial to embrace and appreciate them for what they are.

The dualism of the mind extends to the polarity of our views: in order to feel good about ourselves we often resort to creating others as less than ourselves, and the *need to assert* ourselves as righteous often ends up in the creation of others as wrong and bad. A participant in a recent San Pedro ceremony had a long history of conflict and struggle, as well as a strong Warrior archetype. Because she was also an activist and sincerely dedicated to creating a better world, I shared with her my belief that that same warring stance that we believe will help make a difference is actually the *reason* why conflicts are part of our daily experience. If we are attached to our personality and identities, we will keep creating situations and attracting individuals with whom we can keep playing this or that game: instead of being part of the solution as we had wished, we end up feeding and recreating the problems.

Someone in a deeply polarized identity of, say, the victim, will keep creating oppressors as often as possible; and the same happens with any polarized stance. A larger-than-life example of this is the attachment of the American government to being a "herald of freedom and righteousness," which to me is simply a way to

186

gloss over and deal with the deep guilt over a still to this day continuing attempt at genocide against Native American people. In this need to assert themselves as "the good ones," American government agencies keep creating out of thin air an endless list of "bad guys" and "roguish nations": the conflicts which they claim to wish to solve are actually of their own fabrication[31].

Asserting such polarized identities is the best way to deny the fact that we have all at some point or another, in this or other lifetimes, been sitting on *both* sides of the fence. And it is the best way to relieve ourselves of the guilt associated with parts of ourselves and actions we have judged ourselves for and that we ended up unconsciously projecting onto the world. No matter what our minds say, such projections are quite okay but they do feed the problem rather than solving it, which is why the big problems in our societies grow bigger despite the huge efforts at *fighting* them. The best approach I have found this far is to explore and integrate the identities we have created and heal the wounds underlying those identities.

The holy trinity: Judgment, Shame, and Guilt

No greater rigidity of the mind is expressed than in the greatest duality of all: good and evil. Even though we, particularly in the Judeo-Christian tradition, claim the divine origin of our social, moral, and religious laws in order to ensure their legitimacy and justify their enforcement, the rigidity in the application and

---

[31] I mention this not as an easy rant against the American government but because observing dynamics on a collective scale is often very helpful in seeing how consciousness works on a personal level.

observance of such laws speaks more of a human mind than any divine agency. Our Western tendency to view everything in opposing dualities and judge everything as either good or bad, and right or wrong has colored with moral tones even our understanding of karma. The law of karma, which is actually devoid of any moral standing of good and evil, is neither human nor divine but a simple law of consciousness whereby "we reap what we sow" always and perfectly to the point that there is not even a need for humanly orchestrated justice.

From our infatuation with our own minds and its creation of opposing dualities—rather than the *complementary* dualities of Eastern and native Andean cultures—has arisen what I am fond of sympathetically calling "the holy trinity," which is composed of Judgment, Shame, and Guilt. They form a trinity because guilt and shame go inextricably hand in hand with judgment: whenever there is judgment, this gives rise to shame and guilt.

The idea of a judging divinity is in my opinion simply a creation of the human mind and unmistakably human in origin. Whenever I find someone in my San Pedro ceremonies in the grips of guilt I ask them if they really believe that God has nothing better to do for all of eternity than keep a watchful eye over us just to judge us, like S/He has nothing better to do. All I know is that if I were in such a position of omnipotence I would surely spend eternity otherwise, even though I do confess of having often judged myself and others in the past.

The bottom line is that all judgment is a creation of the mind and categories such as right and wrong, and good and evil are the creation of a mind that creates and believes itself to be godly and the righteous representative of divine wisdom here on Earth.[32] Whoever we believe and fear to be out there to judge and punish us is just a projection of our own judging selves, which is why only we can forgive ourselves. As Jesus Christ announced two thousand years ago, our sins have already been forgiven by God, meaning that in the eyes of the Divine our so-called sins are no sins at all and are therefore absolutely forgivable. If there is any lingering judgment, shame, or guilt, it is for us alone to forgive ourselves. As we loosen the grip of guilt through forgiveness we are also less likely to project our guilt and judgment onto others. Such projection, and we can see that more clearly on a collective scale in major war and religious conflicts, is for many the only relief from the sting of unbearable self-judgment and guilt. But there are options, and once we forgive ourselves from our hearts it is easy and natural to extend that forgiveness to others.

Scarcity

All dualities are tools of the mind, which uses them in order to discriminate. The statement, "it's cold today" has only meaning when contrasted and compared with the thought, "it was warm yesterday." The mind perceives reality through pairs of opposites in order to make sense of it. Without such discrimination everything simply *is*. It is only through the activity of the mind that we perceive Creation as ugly or beautiful, cold or hot, and so on. In this regard we can truly say that our minds

---

[32] We are not including here the universal laws expressed in the Golden and Silver Rules, which have been guiding most human tribes since time immemorial and by their universality speak of the wisdom inherent in human nature.

(re)create the world through categories, judgments, beliefs, and memories. Our view of the world is really a reflection of the beliefs and judgments we hold in our minds and more an accurate description of our inner landscape than anything else.

I grew up believing that the mind was a powerful tool for expansion and learning, and even though I don't dismiss and actually benefit from its analytical qualities, with the years I have increasingly become aware of how narrow and limiting its viewpoint can be. Even science has scientifically demonstrated how illusory the claim of objectivity is when applied to the rational mind: it turns out that the mind is more of a filter than a magnifying lens, and even as a magnifying lens it is far from being as polished and accurate as it would have us believe.

The mind, with which we normally identify, i.e., we believe that we are somehow the sum of our thoughts and the one who expresses them, is not really a "thing" at all but simply a conglomerate of discriminating and analytical patterns most often applied for survival. As a tool it is highly valuable, but its increasing predominance over other aspects of our being has come with a heavy price tag for us modern people: its repressive character over the physical, emotional, mental, and spiritual aspects of ourselves has resulted in an ever-increasing number and variety of human diseases and disorders in recent history.

Another consequence of its functioning is the constant comparing: it's the sign of a rampant mind when we can't help comparing ourselves to others. That comparison is always cause for negative self-judgment because even in the case of a positive outcome as in, "I have more than most," the mind can't help but also entertain the thought, "but someone else has more than I do." An overactive mind will always keep the golden carrot three feet ahead of us no matter what we do and how fast we run, and it will keep us in a state of permanent dissatisfaction, frustration, stress, and insecurity. The mind's false hope for a better and brighter future is a slim payoff for a present moment infused with fear and in a permanent state of scarcity. It is no surprise that in such a mind-oriented culture as ours the predominant belief we hold in our consciousness is, "I am not enough." This belief manifests in different variations such as, "I was/am not loved enough," "I am not good enough to be loved or to deserve to be loved," "I have not enough," and is projected whenever we believe that "others are not enough," "the medicine or the medicine person are not powerful enough," "my life as it is isn't fulfilling," "there is not enough time," and reaches its climax with our present day obsession and fear around dwindling natural resources.

We create our world from the beliefs we hold in our consciousness, and we manifest our fears as much as our desires, and the highly competitive world we live in is undoubtedly informed by a collectivity of minds that has forgotten that it is the source of it all, like a child having a nightmare but unaware that he is dreaming. I believe that if we decided to incarnate here at this time in terrestrial history it's because we felt the importance of exploring this important theme of mind-created scarcity, and as a part of the collective consciousness each one of us holds a unique piece of this belief.

The healing with San Pedro, or any other integrative process geared towards wholeness, does eventually restore the natural balance between the mind and the heart with the resulting awareness and experience of ourselves, others, and the world as being enough: an experience of actual plenitude and fulfillment which has little to do with contentment bordering on resignation, but of infinite possibilities and potentials, untainted by stress and fear, and joyfully welling up from within and without ourselves.

I always remind my clients to refrain as much as possible from comparing their experience to that of others during and outside ceremony: we are all unique individuals in a unique place along our journeys, therefore our experience with the medicine will be unlike anybody else's each and every time. To make such comparisons is ultimately a way of dishonoring of our own experience. When we gather the morning following a ceremony for a sharing and integration meeting I also make them aware that this is not a contest but simply an opportunity to share our individual experiences, see that we all have our own struggles, and see in the positive experiences of others the same potential within ourselves and be inspired by them.

Another insidious (I say insidious because often totally transparent and unconscious) aspect of the mind's workings is the creation of a spiritual ego: an ego that disguises itself as spirit in order to make up for its own smallness and insecurities. A spiritual ego is easily recognized by a need for self-importance and to aggrandize itself, an unquenchable thirst for knowledge, and an equally unquenchable hunger for "spiritual powers." In the realm of plant medicine it can take the form of always wanting to reach a higher spiritual high rather than sinking deeper within one's own being. This is the attitude of "plant medicine junkies" who go from ceremony to ceremony looking for "powerful" medicine people, "strong" medicine, and "special" power places to fill the inner void created by their own minds.

I cannot recommend strongly enough to explore the belief "not enough," and how this belief affects us individually, interpersonally, and collectively. Such exploration and the resulting integration is the surest and quickest way I know of to inner peace and true abundance.

Inadequacy

When we identify with and internalize the belief "not enough," this gives rise to feelings of inadequacy. Our modern society with its idols[33] of success, wealth, fitness, and eternal youth, is the best scenario to play such feelings of inadequacy as everywhere we turn to a huge billboard indicates that our lives are not all that they could be. The belief in our own inadequacy plays itself out in the wounds of rejection, abandonment, betrayal, humiliation, and injustice as at the core of all these wounds is a story of lack, of something missing. Our stories of woundedness are dramatic ways to play out our own sense of inadequacy; and when holding beliefs of inadequacy becomes intolerable we project them onto others, society, the world, even God, and by assuming the role of the victim as often as possible. But when we finally take full responsibility for our stories, we realize that these stories contain the seed of our healing and full awakening.

---

[33] I use the word "idols" as in "false gods" because these are not really ideals and therefore not sacred examples but ways for the mind to avoid the inevitable experience of the impermanence of our physical bodies.

It was surprisingly quite a few years after receiving what I consider the healing of all healings I described earlier[34] that Life gifted me with two instances where I was invited to explore whatever non-integrated aspects of inadequacy I was still carrying. In both cases it was a scenario of a client projecting their own inadequacy onto me, accompanied by resentment, judgments, and accusations.

The first time around I could see clearly that the accusations had been unfounded, but when I cleared the heavy energy that they had left behind it did reveal an *ancestral* fear of not having enough that was connected with ancient famines and the fear of not being able to provide for my kin. It was very deep, as if inscribed in my genetic code, and I was happy to release it. Two weeks later I realized that my recurrent feelings of inadequacy had first resurfaced in a big way when I discovered I was gay and bought into the belief that my sexual preference was an unforgivable sin surely to be punished with eternal hell. What I finally became aware of was that as a consequence of my guilt I had tried my best to be the best little boy in the world to make up for my "sin." Alas, since the sin was in my eyes unforgivable, then there was no way to atone for it no matter how hard I tried, hence the recurring instances of people expressing their dissatisfaction with me despite all my efforts. What I did finally see was how I had been projecting my own anger onto others for not being "perfect." Seeing that I had been holding on to an *idea* of perfection that was really intended to mask my own perceived flaws allowed me to let it go and be more genuinely accepting of myself.

---

[34] See *Healing by the Willkamayu River* in Part II.

Three months later someone else accused me of not being professional and not caring towards my clients. At first, even though it was true that the previous night I had been impatient and not as respectful as indeed I should have been towards someone during an Ayahuasca ceremony, I brushed off all accusations as an excuse for this other person to project his own inadequacy onto me. However, six weeks later the memory of this incident returned while I was in the jungle. At first I was once again dismissive of the whole story until I stopped my looping train of thought and asked myself why indeed had I lost my patience and handled my client in a less than lovingly manner. In that moment I realized that in my own frustrated need for perfection I had *also* projected that expectation onto others my entire life, often disguising it under rules of common sense or decency.

As a result of this whole healing process I could see perfection in everybody just as they are and see their perfection beyond any behavior, without trying to control them so that they would fit my idea of perfection or good behavior.[35]

Competitiveness

A competitive personality, particularly when expressed in a man rather than a woman, is usually praised as a good trait in our economically-driven/ survival-of-the-fittest world. A driving personality is undoubtedly useful in getting ahead in life, but when it is accompanied by feelings of self-judgment or fear

---

[35] This is not only an illustration of a healing process around inadequacy but also about the importance of integrating our projections as part of our healing process.

of not meeting one's own and projected expectations, this competitive personality often turns out to be a mask that hides deep insecurity and feelings of inadequacy. At the end of any race, activity, or achievement, after a brief moment of satisfaction the competitive individual will be assailed by doubt and starts looking for the next challenge in order to prove their adequacy and claim their right to belong and be loved. The need to prove to ourselves and to others our worth through deeds, to play to win each and every time, to monitor one's own performance, and make sure other people praise us for it are all indications of a need for validation that is meant to compensate for our own insecurities. Winning game after game is an endless pursuit when we are really unconsciously acting out the workings of a crazy mind, of which we have become the slave rather than the master. This is why spiritual disciplines devote much of their training and practice to the quieting of the mind and the taming of the ego.

In the end the only aspect of our selves that truly calls for healing is our mind and all dis-eases are just symptoms and expressions of negative judgments, limiting beliefs, and limited viewpoints. All of these mental constructs inform our being on all levels: physically, emotionally, energetically, and mentally. The healing we come to San Pedro seeking may express itself on any of these levels, but it is my opinion that the ultimate healing happens in consciousness on the level of the mind, without any particularly extraordinary kind of voodoo but with a disciplined and honest exploration of our own beliefs.

Taking Flight

The mind is a beautiful mirror of the soul: in the same way that the mind creates itself as separate, the soul is that part of ourselves that seems to be able to have an apparently linear succession of existences and incarnations until it reunites with the Divine. Just like the mind, the soul holds beliefs and thoughts of being separate from God, and its journey does not end until it regains full awareness of its own divinity, which results in the final letting go of all fears and desires. The liberation of the soul, "Jivanmukti" in Sanskrit, is the end of all purposes and dualities since duality's raison d'être has been fulfilled.

In the Hindu creation myth, the world of appearances and the mind that could perceive through dualities are said to have been created out of a totally undifferentiated state so that it could know itself, become aware of itself, and rejoice in its creative essence and the beauty of its own creations. Each soul is part of that primordial act of differentiation and separation, and each soul's only desire and purpose is to know itself as emanation and part of the Divine. Not until the moment of that total awareness is reached is there any freedom because the longing for our spiritual home will keep the soul journeying until it gets there. Of course our spiritual home is not a place in this or other galaxies, nor a place in this or other dimensions: our spiritual home is simply a state of awareness, a remembrance on all levels of our being of our essential unity and identity with the Divine.

Different spiritual traditions have called this experience with different names and nuances, and have developed different tools and disciplines to support individuals on such a journey. Strangely enough I believe it was my Zen master in a previous lifetime who invited me to explore once again the plant medicine path with the hope that I would be knocked off my comfortable meditation cushion and the formalism of religiousness, which I had fallen into once again. To extreme ills extreme remedies, and so I found myself purging and purifying myself with Ayahuasca and other plants in the jungle as well as continuing that process in the mountains of Peru with San Pedro. If it did seem like a good idea in another lifetime, I am sure glad I did not resist that invitation for too long and persevered long enough to reap its benefits and see the fulfillment of that ancient promise of awakening and of my soul's purpose. I believe that when Jesus said, "I and my Father are one" he wasn't expressing an exceptional exception but stating a universal truth and experience that is available to us all and is the inevitable destiny of all souls.

THEMES AND INTENTIONS RELATED TO THE ELEMENT OF AIR

Here is a list of important themes connected with the Air element that would be ideal to explore during a healing process with San Pedro:

- Judgments
- Shame
- Guilt
- Limiting beliefs
- Control and surrender
- Rigidity
- Scarcity
- Competitiveness

THE BRIGHT LIGHT OF THE STARS
– AUSANGATE, PERU – SEPTEMBER 2015

Over the years I had met many people who had visited Ausangate, the highest glacier (6,384 meters) in the Cusco region and therefore of great spiritual importance for the natives of this land, whose main way of spirituality, even when syncretized with Catholicism, is the relationship with mountains. Mountains, called "Apus," are perceived and related with as energies and spirits, just like plants are in the Amazon jungle. They are therefore believed to be alive. I believe that the main reason these mountains are so alive and powerful is because the people of this land have been actively and uninterruptedly interacting with them for thousands of years. With the arrival of the Spanish these sacred mountains have been converted into Catholic pilgrimage spots with new Christian figures presiding over them, but it's a just a thin new cover over an old book that won't go out of print in the collective and ancestral consciousness of Andean people.

An example of this is the festival and pilgrimage of Qoyllur Rit'I, which is the largest and most important spiritual and religious event in the region and takes place every year at Qullkipunku, a mountain 20 km north of Ausangate. The festival, which marks the disappearance and reappearance of the Pleiades in the sky and the birthing season of lamas, is now celebrated one week before the Christian holiday of Corpus Christi.

Day 1

Once again I am blessed to have Miguel as my guide along the journey. And with us is also José on cooking duties, and Abel and his wife with their three horses, who are my heroes as without them this journey would be simply impossible.

We begin our journey in the village of Tinqui. This is the first time I ever walk for as long (five days) and at such high altitude, but I feel confident and ready. Plus, I have an important mission as one of the main intentions of my pilgrimage is to make an offering to the Apus for the waters of the jungle. Since time immemorial people from the jungle used to make yearly pilgrimages to the glaciers of the Andes and make offerings to these mountains because they were aware that they were the source of their rivers down in the jungle. Such custom is unfortunately no longer in use, but as water, both in quality and quantity, has increasingly become an issue even in the Amazon region, where rivers are too low for navigation in the dry season and often flooding during the rainy season, I have decided to make that pilgrimage and offering myself.

An hour after we set off, Miguel opens his mesa[36] and brings out his bottle of San Pedro, of which we will drink for four consecutive days. Our first destination are the hot springs and camping grounds of Upis, right at the foot of Apu Ausangate. As we walk I can feel the strain of the high altitude combined with my daypack, which will have to be lighter from now onwards if I want this trek to be more pleasant. As

---

[36] The mesa is a medicine bundle containing a shaman's personal sacred objects, such as effigies, crystals, and feathers.

we walk I get a better picture of the mountain we are about to circle on foot and wonder how this will be possible in just five days as the mountain keeps looming larger and larger with each step.

Today is all about cleansing and purifying myself energetically and mentally in order to further my journey. Most important of all is the realization that my intended prayer for water in the jungle is a ludicrous one: instead I shift my prayer to one of learning how to manage our existing resources, and the courage and strength to apply our wisdom for such better management. It feels that asking for more and more resources is a way to stay in perpetual childishness whereas the prayer for wisdom and courage is a way to ask for support in the sometimes difficult process of growing up as responsible and aware human beings.

By late afternoon we arrive at our destination. I join Miguel into the hot springs of Upis, and we both take turns by the main spout to soothe our bodies and let go of any tension and heavy energy.

After dinner, we all retire to our tents and in the warmth of our beds as the temperature quickly dwindles after dark. In my tent I remain awake, still under the effects of San Pedro, thinking about the day's experience and all the insights and healing I have received in order to continue my journey.

Day 2

The following morning we are greeted by a magical mist on the ground, a clear sky above, and a rainbow circling our three horses. After breakfast Miguel and I start our walk as our helpers stay behind to dismount our camp.

We start climbing to the right of Apu Ausangate as our trek around the glacier will be in a counterclockwise motion. Halfway up the path that will take us to our highest pass for the day we stop to drink San Pedro by a small terrace with a view of Apu Qullkipunku in the distance. We keep climbing and every hour or so, and this will continue throughout our trek, the landscape changes dramatically with snow peaks, barren mountains, creeks and rivers, and an ever-changing sky of blue, against which flow clouds of all shapes and all shades of white and grey.

My focus is as always on my breath, each inhalation lifting me up the slopes and further opening my heart. I thought I might suffer from the lack of oxygen at such altitude but I realize that there is no such lack if I take the time to inhale deeply and fully, and make the occasional stop to catch my breath again. Miguel is keeping the beat as we have much distance to cover each day, but he's happy with my walking speed, which means he doesn't need to prod me along. The walk and the vistas roll by with unexpected ease: I take this to be a sign that we have done our homework and the Apus welcome us without excessive trials.

We spend the afternoon coasting the glacier on dry ground but with the snow and large lagoons of melted ice only a stone throw away from our path. Even though the glacier is receding due to global warming, it's nevertheless majestic in the sheer volume of ice and snow that still covers its slopes.

And then, all of a sudden, I seem to understand a deeper aspect of the fascination the natives hold about this and other nearby glaciers...The festival of Quyllur Rit'I is literally the celebration of the "star snows" as "Quyllur" means star and "Rit'I" means snow *in the Quechua language. I can feel the energy of our sun and that of infinite other stars impregnate the snow with their physical and spiritual vibrations. It is at this high altitude, with a less dense atmosphere and hardly any pollution, physical and otherwise, that the stars bless this planet and leave their blessings' imprint on the snow. As we now know, water holds vibrations of all kinds really well, so this ice and snow will eventually carry the blessings not only of water but also of the energies of the stars, carrying them all the way to the oceans and covering much of our planet.*

This morning Miguel opened the direction of the West and it seems most appropriate to make my offerings to Apu Ausangate today. Serendipitously our camp for the night is right by a large lagoon surrounded by snow on the mountainside away from us. As soon as we arrive at our camp I prepare my humble offerings and head to the lagoon's edge as the sun is setting. There I offer a cup of Ayahuasca, a couple of feathers of jungle birds, some tobacco, perfume, and drinking water. Together with my prayers of gratitude for the gift of water and asking for the courage to implement whatever wisdom in order to better manage such precious gift, I also offer a couple of songs; and at the end of it all a massive chunk of snow falls loudly into the lagoon, which I take to mean as a sign that my offering and prayers have been received.

Later that evening in my tent I see how instrumental both Ayahuasca and San Pedro are in this process of greater awareness and ecological harmony: these two medicines do in fact support us in letting go of our sense of separation and in helping us become aware that we are part of a greater whole, they open the ways for a different relationship with the Earth and all of its inhabitants.

Day 3

This morning we are to climb right away to the highest pass of our entire trek. A third of the way up, we drink San Pedro as our helpers and the horses pass by. The climb is made much easier by the sight of the top of the glacier and its giant snowy tips that look like crystals pointing towards the blue sky. Climbing entails breathing, which activates the medicine and opens the heart, so that by the time we reach the Apacheta Pass, so named because covered with mounds of rocks piled by travelers like ourselves, I feel expanded and happy.

Our lunch break is at the bottom of the valley ahead of us: a landscape of glaciers, purple mountains, streams, and lagoons. I have been camera-crazy since we first left Tinqui, and I can't stop taking pictures of this amazing land.

By the time we reach our midday destination for lunch I am simply ecstatic: on the way down I am once aware of my lack of either fear or desire. I feel elated and yet in calm plenitude. My soul is free from all attachments caused by fear and desire: there is no strain, no conflict, and nowhere else to go except within that awareness of freedom and its resulting joy. I take my lunch away from my companions to avoid all distractions and bask in this awareness until my entire being is filled with it.

We continue our walk that afternoon through a land interwoven by creeks and rivers that make their way down the slopes like whirling snakes, and more songs about water and plants connected with water come out of me spontaneously. When we reach our camp for the night I once again go the nearest river to sing to Oshún, Orisha of sweet waters, rivers, and lakes. I am full of gratitude for this unique experience, for its gifts, blessings, and teachings.

Day 4

Our last day on the medicine and the morning climb on the other side of Tres Picos, so called because it's a constellation of three contiguous peaks, turn out to be more challenging than I had thought. The climb seems endless as I don't know the terrain, and at the top some snow and rain make the already bare landscape even sterner. Today for me it's a day of looking at my life from such heights and to gain some clarity around some aspects of my work and my intention of taking a group once again to the jungle to work with my teacher. Clearer vision allows me to take stock of the situation, not to change it but to move in harmony with it. I realize that I am not willing and cannot compromise the vision of how I wish to conduct my work with plant medicines: it is too powerful and delicate to allow any kind of compromise. In the end for me this is a teaching about letting go of any path that no longer resonates with my truth and be at peace with it.

After reaching the highest and coldest spot along the day's walk, the landscape once again opens up to a valley filled with large lagoons of different colors, from emerald green to turquoise. We have plenty of time at our disposal before reaching the hot spring of

Pacchanta, so we take it easy. At some point we meet two women and their dogs, literally in the middle of nowhere, who have their crafts set up and awaiting us as if this were downtown Cusco.

I buy a beautiful weaving from each one of them and later on during a stop I offer one to Miguel as a gift. He has been not only an indispensable guide but he has been most attentive to my needs, to the point that I didn't even need to express them at all. I feel much gratitude for his generous heart and spirit, and very fortunate that he would share this experience and land with me.

Day 5

Our last day is just a half-day gentle walk back to Tinqui, where our taxi driver will pick us up to return to Pisac. Today we don't drink any medicine and, as we stroll through fields and small communities along the road, we share about our experience and possible new adventures and explorations of this land.

Last but not least, before we arrive at Tinqui we make our closing ceremony of giving thanks to the Apus and all the other energies that have supported us along this journey, and to release all of our prayers with tobacco. The journey is over and a new one begins.

VI

THE HEART

The Center, the Void, the Heart, the Circle

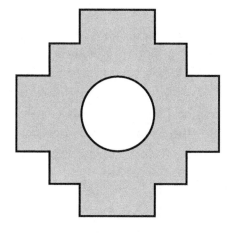

THE CENTER

The center of the Andean cross is an empty circle. The circle is a universal symbol of completeness and perfection. That this circle in the very center of the Chakana is empty indicates its immateriality: as the place of origin of Space (the four directions) and Matter (the four elements), it speaks of the spiritual origin of all physical manifestations, including mankind. The empty center is the place of the Great Mystery of Creation, a mystery that can only be known through direct experience rather than perceived and understood through the intellect, which is why the origins of this Universe can only be expressed through myth and not scientific explanations.

The first time I ingested Iboga, a powerful initiatory medicine from Gabon, Africa, now used therapeutically in the West to heal all sorts of addictions, I spent great lengths of time exploring over and over again the theme of the first creation, of creating (apparently) "something" out of (apparently) "nothing." At some point I even asked for help and guidance but received none, and only at the end of the night understood that my experience was to teach me the ludicrousness of my attempt to explain and understand that mystery with my mind in a cause-and-effect linear kind of way. I can try and describe it with abstract names and ideas that point at insubstantial principles, but no more than that. My error at the time came as a result of perceiving this world as a solid reality whereas many ancestral traditions assert that what we think is real is indeed just a dream. Any good movie will have us so identified with a story and so immersed in it that we forget we are watching a work of fiction; similarly, we are hardly ever aware that we are dreaming when we are asleep and having nightmares, and when we are awake we easily forget that our lives are more a dramatic and illusory experience than the solid reality we tell ourselves it is. In the end what we may perceive as "solid" reality, us included, is an expression of the creative intelligence of Creation, fleeting and yet amazing.

A couple of years after moving to Pisac I offered a prayer to the Universe wishing to fully engage in this world while retaining the awareness of not being of this world. Some four years later I realized my prayer had been fulfilled: I was more than ever in my body, enjoying and embracing the possibilities of this earthly experience, and yet consciously aware that none of it was "real." I wasn't detached, but grew increasingly amused and lighthearted about it. Of course there are occasionally dramatic situations even now that get me completely fooled and sucked in, but only for as long as I deny full responsibility for them. In this world of impermanence and illusions the only place that I return to over and over again and that feels real to me is my own heart, the heart of others, and the love that permeates every aspect of Creation.

THE HEART

In the Indian chakra system, the Heart Chakra (Ana-hata) is the central and midpoint of the physical human chakras and is represented by two intersecting triangles, one pointing upwards and the other downwards, merging together and surrounded by a circle. The image symbolizes the ascending energies of the physical, emotional, and ego-centered aspects of our being meeting and complementing the descending energies of our divine and expanded selves. It is a beautifully profound symbol of the integration of all of our perceived dualities, and the place of that integration is in the heart.

When before each San Pedro ceremony I tell people that in my opinion and experience this medicine is a heart opener, I also add that to me the heart is most importantly that part of our selves that welcomes and embraces everything, whereas it is the mind that discriminates and says yes to this and no to that. And it so happens that in the heart all judgments, dualities, and separation dissolve.

It is interesting that the image most used for Mother's Day is that of a heart as the Mother's archetype is one of unconditional love and acceptance. Hardly anyone has had the parents we wished we had had, but I truly believe it is everybody's journey to become the father and the mother we have always wanted. This process entails letting go of the blame and judgments we hold against our parents, and eventually cultivate within ourselves the positive archetypes of both Mother and Father.

The archetype of the Mother is indeed one of unconditional love, and is the expression of the Heart, of acceptance and nurturing, of generous giving and caring. When we open ourselves to both giving and receiving that motherly energy and love, all of our concerns dissolve as this energy is truly boundless.

The energy of the Mother is the quintessence of this planet Earth: its loving energy makes this planet the healing place that it is as love heals more than anything else. To open our hearts is to allow the energy of love to heal us through forgiveness, compassion, and acceptance. An open heart, just like the perfect circle in the center of the Chakana, is the expression of our full being, a being that is Love in its essence and expression.

Surrendering to our true essence is the only require-ment for self-realization. Letting go of our struggles and expectations, of our conflicts and idealizations, is the only way I know of to be able to rest within our hearts and finally be the loving beings that we are.

It was on the playa at Burning Man years ago that under the effects of MDMA[37] my heart opened up once again. This time I saw my heart as a lotus flower whose petals started opening up until they enveloped the whole planet with love. In that moment I realized that the heart is like a nuclear power plant: a source of infinite loving energy. In that moment I most importantly realized that love is not what I need but more accu-rately what I give and who I truly am. Until then I had loved only hoping to be loved back, and whenever I felt loved or loved someone, I would be holding an invisible checkbook inside my head. That afternoon I understood how much I had held my heart back with my limited beliefs about love. Generously giving of my heart was the only way to allow my own lovingness to flow and be, and the only way to receive that love generously from myself, others, and Creation. It was a radical shift in awareness for me, and one that has not left me since. The blessings of an open heart have kept increasing the more generous I have been with my love, my acceptance, and forgiveness.

Years later I was a participant in a native North American ceremony, during which I connected with my feminine energy like never before. I experienced that

---

[37] 3,4-Methylenedioxymethamphetamine, commonly known as Ecstasy.

energy as infinite and sweetly caring towards everything and everybody. I know today that energy to be the energy of the Heart in its motherly and nurturing expression, and to be limitless as long as I allow it to flow freely.

EMPTINESS

Just like the empty circle at the center of the Chakana, the space of the heart is hollow: an apparent void. I spent my adolescent years reading plenty of books on Buddhism and Taoism, and confess that for years the idea of Nirvana and the Buddhist Void as I understood them at the time terrified me: since I exclusively identified with my ego, the idea of letting go of it could only mean self-annihilation. What no text had explained to me—I guess because it was up to me to discover it firsthand, and that discovery was very much supported by San Pedro—was that the Void was not only a place of egolessness, but a place where the deeper essence of my being could shine again unobstructed by the noise of the ego. That much-dreaded Void turned out to be for me a place of Infinity, infinite possibilities, and infinite Love.

Like everybody before me, I have struggled and still struggle to put into words and coherent sentences my experiences of such egolessness, most importantly because in the Ocean of the Living Heart there is no-one really there: no mind to define and limit through categories, or make sense of it, and no sense of anyone in particular having that experience. The only "proof" is the experience itself unfolding within and without a self that has let go of all identifications and is therefore limitless as well as insignificant: truly everything and nothing.

In my younger years I was as deeply fascinated as I was scared of hallucinogens, so much so that it took me years before I would actually let go and have a classic psychedelic experience, and then some more before I would experience a total disintegration of my ego the first time I drank Ayahuasca. It is not the state of egolessness that is scary (because there is "no-one" left to feel scared anymore) but the journey *towards* that apparently empty space. During that journey the ego is still active and feels truly threatened as it undergoes disintegration, and often reacts with fear and all sorts of resistances.

That journey of letting go can be experienced to any degree under the effects of San Pedro and other mind-altering substances and entheogens. The power of that experience lies not in its otherworldliness, but in how it teaches and trains us in letting go in our daily lives: letting go of our identities, masks, and stories, letting go of our judgments and ideas, and letting go of our physical bodies upon the moment of death.

My dear friend Melody Fletcher[38]shared with me her belief that the increasing numbers of people who die after a long degenerative illness such as Alzheimer unconsciously choose to leave this world so slowly because of their fear of letting go, so that by the time their physical bodies cease to function and die, they are no longer consciously there to experience their own death. Having had my own fair share of fear of dying I can understand how some people may prefer to be totally unconscious instead of fully present at the moment of death. Letting go is challenging and often

---

[38] Melody Fletcher can be reached and her work explored at www.deliberatereceiving.com

met with dread and resistance. In the course of these years actively engaging with plant medicines I almost physically died once as part of my healing process and have experienced countless deaths on other levels. At times I have become indignant, upset, and totally discouraged as the Universe and my higher self were inviting me to let go of yet another part of me.

"Why? Even this? There will be nothing left!"

Precisely!

The disintegration and re-integration of the ego is for me the most delicate process in plant medicine as well as all other spiritual paths. It is particularly delicate with plant medicines because, once the process has started, it can either be resisted with resulting great suffering or it can be embraced, but it cannot be controlled. In my opinion this experience, because of its power and delicacy, is ideally experienced in as supportive an environment as possible and in the company of someone who has had that experience and can therefore offer the sometimes necessary and always welcome support, guidance, and reassurance.

IN SILENCE AND SINGING

The space of the heart is an empty space, meaning beyond all words and concepts, which is why even though this book is about the heart, the chapter about the heart is the shortest: as past mystics and sages have reminded us over and over again throughout time, we can only speak of the unspeakable by pointing at what it's not.

The heart is a quiet space because no longer drowned by the noise of the mind. What we may initially perceive as a silent place, if we are to dwell in it long enough, turns out to reverberate with a humming that turns into all of the songs of this Universe. When we no longer pay as much attention to the authoritarian voice of the mind, we can finally listen to the songs of our hearts.

Many people who come to my retreats have engaged in plant medicine in order to get a sense of purpose and some direction in their lives. I invariably suggest that they let go of that expectation and instead ask San Pedro to help them connect with whatever may make their hearts sing and let go of whatever may prevent them from singing that song freely and joyfully. The Sufi poet Rumi wrote that whenever we choose a path we needn't worry about whether the path is right or wrong (a symptom that we are in our heads), but ought to ask ourselves whether that path has a heart, i.e., whether it holds within itself the fulfillment of love and joy.

To let our hearts sing is our biggest priority. We may dismiss that priority with a million reasons and excuses and yet, whenever our hearts are not singing, when that loving energy is not fully flowing, our hearts grow sad and eventually we become sick. Many steps have been taken in modern societies to lessen the risks of physical heart failure, but cardiovascular diseases remain responsible for the most deaths worldwide for both men and women of all races. It seems to me that dietary and lifestyle changes, however important, are not enough to change the present predicament as they don't address the underlying and real causes of such diseases. These causes are not only a lack of education in regards to physical health and diet, but also the sad reality that many people simply don't live the life they know is good for them and, as a result, compensate for such unhappiness with behaviors that are unhealthy.

For me the most important requirement for a healthy life is to live a happy life: not a life necessarily devoid of challenges and pain, but a life that is rewarding and fulfilling. In order to gather the courage to finally embrace what makes our hearts sing, we often wait until we have literally nothing left to lose: when we are in the advanced stages of physical illness, or after yet another failure, financial or emotional. It would be great if we didn't need to go that far in order to reconnect with our heart's desire, but at least such drastic situations can help us reassess our priorities from our hearts and souls rather than our minds, and that is in and of itself source of great healing.

Non-Duality and Unity

It was with much surprise that engaging with A Course in Miracles turned out to be for me not only a powerful learning of forgiveness but also a radical course in non-duality. It was radical in that it didn't allow for compromises, and it had my head spinning for months around the unity of all aspects of Creation—not as an idea but as a reality. Its exercises and meditations drove day after day this unity awareness deep into my whole being until it informed my entire life. The process wasn't met without resistances, but I persisted until the world ceased to be just a reflection of me and began to be an integral part of me. The expansion of my consciousness went as far as anything I would experience or put my attention onto: I ceased to be my body, my thoughts, and emotions, and understood that I am my entire world and Universe, no longer separated, no longer apart from but one with everything and everybody.

It is ironic that when I decided to be of service to Ayahuasca and San Pedro I knew that decision to have been the first truly selfless decision of my life, and then some years later to discover that that selfless decision turned out to be a kind of selfish one because in my supporting other people in their healing and awakening I am really also supporting myself. I perceive myself to be like a cell of a large animal, i.e., the human species, and that animal to be part of the entire Universe. Just as any cell, whether healthy or diseased, affects the entire organism, I know that the healing of each single cell contributes to the wellbeing of the entire organism. As I am part of that organism I directly benefit from the recovered health of other cells, hence my indirect "selfishness." But truly I am not being selfish: I just rejoice the more people reconnect with their inner light and love because I know everybody else to be part of me and so their expanded awareness and the resulting joy add to mine.

Between saying, "we are one" and living by these words there is often a great divide that points to our actual sense and belief of separation. How often do we actually love our neighbors like ourselves? How often are we aware that their wellbeing is one and the same as our own? Certainly our lack of care towards others is often an indication of a similar lack of kindness towards ourselves, but it also shows how small we think we are, as if ending at our fingertips. The perception of ourselves as limited within the confines of our own flesh only adds to our feelings of inadequacy and anxieties. We *know* that unity brings strength and yet fail to cultivate that unity at all levels of our existence, within and without. The most we have been able to do so far is to identify with and feel part of a nation, a race, an ideology, or religion, but only to create an opposing and seemingly dangerous "other": our sense of unity is as limited as our perception of who we are. As we become increasingly aware of the limitations of such a predicament, I feel it is valuable for each one of us to explore such dynamics within our own selves as the separation we see in the world is an expression of the same separation within us.

Non-duality comes with the letting go of the supremacy of the mind and its constructs, through learning that ideas are useful ways to perceive reality but not the whole picture, and by being reminded that the map is not the road: the map of our realities may be made of light and darkness, but the universal landscape contains *all* light and darkness equally and without distinctions.

In the heart all separation ceases to be because in the motherly energy of the heart every part is honored and supported. Whenever we are in our hearts we experience wholeness and fulfillment, whereas when we feel separate all we do is care for ourselves as we fear that resources and love are limited, therefore doing our best to get our share of the pie before the plate is empty. Our self-centeredness quickly makes us forget that our thriving is directly dependent on the thriving of everyone and everything else, and even though our personal bellies are temporarily full, we end up diminished as a family, as a community, and as a planetary whole.

My relationship with San Pedro has taught me not only how to relate with myself in a more loving way but has also informed the way I relate to others and the Cosmos in general. Living in the Sacred Valley of the Incas has also taught me the importance of engaging in a loving and respectful way to the Earth and honor all aspects of Creation as living entities, including mountains, rivers, and winds, not as separate from me but as deeply interconnected aspects of the same Divine Intelligence as myself. This awareness has extended not only to ceremony time or this valley, but to all times and everywhere I go. Much of this Earth has suffered from increasing objectification and nothing has enriched my life more than this new loving relationship and attitude. Seeing all manifestations of Creation as alive, supportive, and benevolent rather than inert and threatening has made me so much more aware of the respect that they are due. In all human cultures there is a taboo about killing other human beings: seeing even rocks and mountains as alive and intelligent as my own self was the easiest way to learn to respect this planet and care for it ever more deeply and sincerely.

HUMILITY

One of the unexpected consequences of feeling at one with everything and everyone has been for me a deep sense of humility towards other people—towards all people. What a surprise it was for me to spontaneously drop all sense of superiority and inferiority, and finally experience true equality and identity with everyone! Along my spiritual journey I couldn't resist at times the temptation of feeling that because I had walked a longer distance along that journey I was a better person than others. When fraught with insecurities and self-judgment we always find ways to make ourselves feel better by putting others on a lower position, and I was no exception. But when those fears and judgments subsided I was also able to drop these secret hierarchies and be with others as equals. Not only as equals, but as brothers and sisters. Not only as brothers and sisters, but as fellow Children of the Divine.

In order to get there I had to accept that all my fellow human beings are my greatest teachers: I distinctly remember walking through the streets of Cusco for several months looking at people in the streets and seeing them as my teachers, at first dubiously, then tentatively, but eventually with certainty.

A teacher is anybody who can help us see our own divinity, and no teacher is more valuable in this process of reawakening than those people upon whom we project our shadow. In the end I realized that my greatest teachers were those who pushed my buttons most irritatingly, and that to them and to what they were reflecting back to me I needed to offer my greatest and loving attention. This is often not an easy route as those great but nevertheless annoying teachers can be easily dismissed with judgment, scorn, and rejection. But I persisted until I saw the truth and importance of the teachings I was engaging with, and in the end it was most rewarding to drop all judgment and hierarchies, sitting on the same level with everybody else, and seeing in everyone the glowing jewel in the lotus of their hearts.

The willingness to perceive everything and everybody as important as I am and as integral part of who I am has helped me expand my consciousness in the humblest and most profound of ways. As Gregory

Bateson put it after years of exploring earthly ecology, the smallest thriving unit is not the individual, nor the family or the community, but the entire Cosmos, which is why each part of the Cosmos deserves our loving respect and care. According to this awareness we can see that a brain cell is as holy and important as a skin cell around our sphincters, that a post office clerk is as important as the president of a nation, and that ants are as valuable as bees, flowers, giraffes, humans, and mountain ranges. Once again we are reminded by the story of the hummingbird about the importance of small things and the importance of even the smallest and apparently most insignificant of creatures, gestures, thoughts, and events.

THE POWER OF THE CIRCLE

In my longer retreats here in Pisac we have our first meeting in a circular sunken area in my garden and the first thing I do after we introduce ourselves is point out to everyone present how we are sitting in a circle with nobody above or below us. We have sat in circles since the beginning of time and the power of such circles has strengthened our tribes. In a circle we may have leaders, doers, people who voice dissent or agreement. What is important is not that different people hold different roles, or that some are esteemed to be of greater or lesser importance than others, but that the power of the circle is strengthened by honoring each point in that circle as any circle is made of the *entirety* of its points.

In our present modern societies we are organized in hierarchical pyramids. Such pyramidal configuration has benefitted our scientific progress and improved in some ways our material standing, but has often silenced and repressed anything and anybody that was not in alignment with the goals of such organizations. In a similar way, whenever we hold a hierarchical rather than holistic view of ourselves, we tend to repress or dismiss any internal voice of discontent or unease.

We are proud of our democratic ways but think and act in ways that are often tyrannical and oppressive, particularly with ourselves. It is by cultivating equality and democracy among all aspects of ourselves that we can grow strong again and create as a result a truer form of democratic societies in this world, and by honoring all of our inner voices equally we can engage in a real dialogue with ourselves. This dialogue needs not be a striving for a winning majority at the expense of other voices. We don't need to sacrifice our relationships or sublimate our erotic energies in order to pursue a career or other goals: in the new circles within and without ourselves we can strive to honor and fulfill *all* of our needs, physical, emotional, mental, and spiritual.

A mother instinctively supports all of her children whereas in our male-oriented groups we tend to support only the most seemingly effective viewpoints and members while dismissing everything else in the name of a goal or mission. The present planetary ecological challenges are a much-needed teaching to us all about the interconnectedness and unity of all Life: it is teaching us on a large scale that such hierarchical attitudes are not as beneficial as they claim to be because only when everything and everybody is honored as equally important is our thriving real and lasting. Our evolution is first and foremost an evolution in consciousness—political, social, and financial steps can and ought to be taken to support that shift in consciousness but will continue to be only empty gestures until we shift our own viewpoints and priorities from egoic self-centeredness to the highest good of the collective: this revolution will not be televised because it is unfolding inside our hearts.

THEMES AND INTENTIONS RELATED TO THE ELEMENT OF THE VOID

Here is a list of important themes connected with the element of the Void and Infinite Space that would be ideal to explore during a healing process with San Pedro:

- Fear of the Void as expressed in fear of surrender and dying
- Fear of the loss of individuality as we know it
- Fear of losing control and of embracing oceanic states of consciousness
- Fear of opening the heart to infinite Love and Joy
- Fear of living life fully and of taking the steps towards a fulfilling and joyful life

PILGRIMAGE TO CHAVIN – CORDILLERA BLANCA, PERU – OCTOBER 2015

Ever since I decided to lead San Pedro ceremonies I felt a strong call to visit Chavín de Huántar, a small town nested east of the Cordillera Blanca of Peru at the confluence of two rivers, the Mosna and the Huan-checsa. Chavín is considered by many the Rome or Je-rusalem of San Pedro: in this ancient site, which dates to at least as far back as 1200 BCE, archeologists have found the earliest unmistakable signs of the ceremoni-al use of San Pedro available to us today.

Chavín was an important religious and ceremonial center, whose symbology, cosmology, and spirituality deeply influenced all pre-Columbian cultures from southern Ecuador to northern Chile; and it operated as such uninterruptedly for two thousand years, just like and around the same time as the great Eleusinian Mysteries in Eleusis, Greece. Its location, halfway between the Pacific coastline and the Amazon jungle, made it an ideal meeting place for many different ethnic groups and a place of exchange of religious ideas, artifacts, and goods, including plants and Sacred Plants.

Exactly ten years after my first experience with San Pedro I fly to Lima and get on a series of bus and van rides that will take me to this sacred site for a long-awaited pilgrimage. Upon my arrival I realize that the timing is perfect and that I am ready in body and spirit to receive the teachings of this place.

Along the journey my first stop is at Harry Chavez place in Caraz, near Huaraz. Harry's art piece, "The Mandala of Joy," adorns the cover of this book, so it's a perfect way to start my visit to this part of the Andes. After a night with his family I continue on to Chavín. The final van ride from Huaraz to Chavín is full of quiet curiosity as I wonder what may happen once I get to my final destination.

The town of Chavín de Huántar is relatively small, which makes choosing lodging and restaurants easy; I check into a hotel by the main square and proceed to look for Sergio, the town's "official shaman", who officiates the spiritual part of the large celebrations that take place inside the archeological site a few times a year. Sergio is not at home that day but he unexpectedly shows up at my hotel the following morning while I am having breakfast. His visit is accompanied with the raised brows of the hotel owner, who I suspect from now on will perceive me as a Devil worshipper in this town that struggles to maintain its Catholic ways amid increasing interest for its glorious shamanic past.

Sergio invites me to his humble house nearby. He is a very gentle man, probably in his late 50s. As soon as we get there he makes a fire and we talk about my visit and his life. After a while he comes closer with a condor feather and proceeds to, I guess, cleanse me with it. My eyes are closed and as he swings his feather I am having visions of this ancient site as it used to be, with its high walls around the temple area decorated by giant stone carvings of feline heads. The modern understanding of these fierce feline heads is that they were meant to scare the visitors of this place so that the priesthood could manipulate them through fear, as well as the creation of a vengeful deity that demanded subservience and expected generous offerings. But my vision tells me that this interpretation is erroneous at best, and a projection of our current fear-based mentality at worst. What I do perceive is that this place was a place of the Heart and that these feline heads were an invitation to let go of fear: those who got scared and were unwilling to face their fears would have no place here.

Sergio confirms my intuition later on when he shares with me that the spot of the ceremonial site used to be a lagoon at the convergence of two rivers originating from two different nearby glaciers and that from the waters of this lagoon, just like the mythical origins of a Hindu god at the crossing of two rivers from the Himalayas, arose Wiracocha. Wiracocha is a central figure in many Peruvian pre-Columbian cultures: he is a superhuman being, often depicted as taller than the natives, and unlike the natives, with a beard, white hair, and blue eyes. In Inca mythology he is the Creator God, but he often appears here and there as a Teacher teaching the natives new technologies and ideas.

As Sergio shares this story, my understanding is that this is a creation myth about a new consciousness that arose from these waters and that this consciousness is a Heart consciousness. Chavín never had a power structure or fortifications of any kind: it didn't need them because at the level of the Heart no protection is needed as the fear that calls for such protection is long integrated and gone. I cannot help but associate such Heart consciousness with San Pedro, which grows plentifully all around this area and whose ritual ingestion was central to the ceremonies held here.

Not long after this experience Sergio surprises me once again by offering me a cup of San Pedro, which I drink despite having had a full breakfast and a cup of coffee. Soon thereafter we go on a walk that will take us to what used to be part of his family estate right above the archeological site and is now a beautiful healing center created by an American woman, Holly Laskey[39]. The healing center's construction is almost complete and they just had their inauguration

---

[39] Holly Laskey and her center can be contacted through: https://www.facebook.com/AncestralHighlands/

ceremony blessed with the ancestral music of Tito La Rosa, a most gifted Peruvian musician who specializes in pre-Columbian music and instruments. Holly welcomes us to her center, offers us some lunch, and then leaves Sergio and I by a circular man-made pond to continue our informal ceremony, which comes to a climax as thunder and lightning fill the sky on the other side of the valley.

The next day I visit the archeological site, which is beautiful and quite extensive. I am curious to see how this new consciousness manifested in the architecture of this place, but my deeper questions about the nature of this place have already been answered the day before, so there is no mystery to solve but just relax and soak in the energy and beauty of the place. Most moving of all is the sight of the Lanzón, the large statue that is believed to have been the most important effigy of this sacred site. Despite its big fangs the Lanzón is actually smiling: no fear-inducing deity here but the invitation to open our hearts and be joyful.

On Sunday I wake up early to drink San Pedro by myself and walk towards the community of Nunupata on what used to be the ancient path connecting Chavín to the Pacific coast of Peru and is also the way to Apu Huantzan, the second highest peak of the Cordillera Blanca and source of the Huanchecsa river.

I have no idea how far I will be walking today: the only thing I know is that at some point I will be sitting by this river, and that will mark my point of return. After a few hours I eventually find a path right after the village of Nunupata that seems to head towards the river below. It is there that I instinctively renew my marriage vows to myself made ten years earlier during my first San Pedro ceremony. To my surprise though, I end extending these vows of love and support to every-body and everything in my world as I am once again made aware that I am not my physical body and that my being extends as far as my awareness is willing to extend. It is a joyous moment and it's followed shortly by the spontaneous pronouncement of my vows of celibacy for all the Apus to witness. The work for the day is now complete and I start making my way back, this time pleasantly downhill, to Chavín.

I take the last day of my visit to relax and unwind at some hot springs near the town. On my way there I see on a large billboard the following message hand-written in Spanish: "Life is a journey to the center of your soul. It depends on you whether the path is prob-lematic or magical."

I am now ready to continue my life journey. "Chaupín," the original name of Chavín, means "center": the center of our being, which is symbolized by the heart. I feel very privileged to be finally sitting in the center of a new consciousness that has integrated fear, the need for seduction, and the seduction of power, and has opened the pathways of the Heart.

VII

BACK TO EARTH

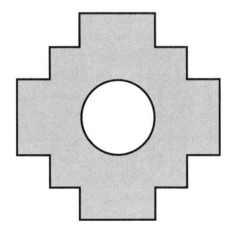

INTEGRATION

In his brilliant novel, *Fierce Invalids Home from Hot Climates*[40], Tom Robbins narrates the story of Switters, an interesting character who fortuitously spends a night in the Amazon jungle in the company of a shaman. The shaman has him drink a variety of native psychoactive medicines, and Switters has the time of his life exploring the secrets of the Universe, but also suffering the shaman's curse under which he won't ever be able to walk on the earth again.

This scenario is a familiar one for people who, either because of the ingestion of psychedelics or spiritual initiations, find themselves at odds with earthly reality afterwards, sometimes unable to integrate that experience, and sometimes ending their days as a recluse or in a psychiatric ward. Luckily for Switters, his experience leads him to a phantasmagorical and enlightening journey of emotional and spiritual growth that ends with his liberation from the shaman's curse.

One the main reasons for wanting to write this book on San Pedro was to write more extensively than I did in my book about Ayahuasca about integration, which for me is the most important and often most challenging aspect of the process with plant medicines. The Hero's journey does not end when s/he slays the dragon and gets the treasure, but when s/he returns home with the treasure and shares it generously. As epic as the journey until then may have been, nothing compares it to the challenges that may arise once back on familiar turf. And little prepares us for being transformed people when back in an all-too-familiar

---

[40] Robbins, Tom. *Fierce Invalids Home from Hot Climates*. New York, Bantam Books, 2000.

predicament that hasn't changed nearly as much as we may have during our absence.

A friend I had met in the jungle is fond of saying that, "the end of the ceremony is the beginning of the ceremony," meaning that a whole other process begins right after we have completed the direct process with plant medicines. This new process, which is really *integral* to the plant medicine process, is made all the more challenging because we no longer have access to these medicines and the support of the guide and companions with whom we had shared that experience. It is now up to us to figure it out, and often feel at a loss for lack of support and encouragement.

When I returned from India in 2002 after a most pleasant visit, nothing prepared me for the unexpected realization once I was back home that my life in Barcelona had come to an abrupt end. I became instantly aware that living there was no longer an option and yet had no idea of where to go next. It took me three years and a yearlong trip around the world before I would move to Peru. I wasn't desperate because at least I knew what no longer served me, but that awareness wasn't enough to clarify where I wanted to live next. It offered no answer—just questions, which were totally up to me to explore and find some answer to.

Such is the predicament some people find themselves in after engaging with plant medicines: one of confusion, disorientation, and most painfully, of further letting go on the everyday plane of existence. The dying and letting go of old resentments and identities we may experience under the effects of San Pedro are easy compared to the letting go of old friendships, relationships, etc.: this time around we are faced with practical decisions and actions, and that's where old fears and insecurities may resurface and sabotage a process of transformation already well on its way. That such obstacles may surface is an indication that there is more work ahead of us, and that is a good if disheartening thing. To dismiss or deny such obstacles only prolongs our suffering, whereas facing them with patience and humility can be source of important healing and great expansion.

Going home makes us aware in practical and unmistakable ways of what has been truly dealt with and what remains to explore. It is therefore not advisable to remain for too long in a "medicine bubble," but more important to get a serious reality check of our actual accomplishments while engaging with this or other medicines by returning to where we live and in the presence of those people with whom we had until then played out our wounds and neuroses.

In order to support this integration it is most important to adhere to whatever dietary and behavioral restrictions we have been required to observe in preparation for this process, and ideally *for as long as the process itself lasted*.

San Pedro often offers some deep physical cleansing that leaves our digestive system fairly raw. It is therefore important not to overwhelm and overwork our physical bodies with large amounts of processed and heavy foods. I tell my clients to keep feeding their body as if it was a baby: with gentle and easy to digest meals. Observing the abstinence from all drugs and alcohol is most important as well: the ingestion of such substances not only hinders the integration process by bringing it to a sudden halt, but can also seriously muddle our sense of self with unpredictable and often deleterious effects such as confusion and even depression. Sexual abstinence is also an important factor and a way to hold our energies and awareness inwards instead of dissipating them. Honoring these restrictions *without exception* is the best way to invite the energy of San Pedro to stay with us and support us in the integration process. And, trust me, we can use all the support we can get.

In our times of increased awareness towards what we eat, it seems important to remember that nowadays information is what we ingest the most, and that all the information we expose ourselves to needs to be processed as well. Information comes from all media, including the Internet, not only in writing but most importantly in images, which have a way of touching us in deeper and often unconscious ways. Some Silicon Valley executives now regularly go on "media diets", during which they limit and are consciously aware of the information they expose themselves to. One of the main reasons for my recovered health here in Peru is, I believe, due to the relative lack of advertising, my limited use of the Internet, and my discernment whenever I choose to watch a movie or read a book. Whenever I do expose myself to such sources of information I am just as aware of the possible effects of such exposure as I am aware of the effects upon my being of the foods and drinks I ingest. Being a little more conscious and discerning in regards to our media diets is a good way to prepare for a plant medicine process and an excellent way to create some space and silence in the weeks afterwards while the integration is still unfolding.

The return home is often thought of with mixed feelings of excitement and dread: the excitement of seeing again friends and family after feeling more than we had in a long time the bonds of love and affection that connect us, the excitement at the prospect of pursuing new ideas and projects, and the dread of falling back into patterns we now know more than ever no longer serve us. We are creatures of habit and old habits are notoriously difficult to let go of: breaking out of old habits and patterns is realistic only if we have valid reasons and exciting alternatives. Many spiritual paths focus on living in the present moment, and plant medicines ask of us that we honor who we know ourselves to be in that present moment and act accordingly, which often means being *creative* and daring to react differently to familiar situations. Falling back into old re-actions is normal and in such cases I advise people after their retreats with me not to beat themselves too hard or for too long should that happen. I encourage them to allow whatever reaction such recurrence may elicit, and then to take a fresh look at the situation and see what alternatives may be put in place instead. I have not been immune to such recurrences but eventually it became actually physically painful to act out of integrity: a sign that it was time to atone for acting out of alignment and to act differently.

Other people around us also become used over time to who we are and they may not welcome such changes either, particularly if we are no longer willing to dance an old co-dependent dance as we used to. Our new way of being may bring up for the people around us some insecurity and confusion, and in some cases even mistrust. It is therefore important to be gentle yet firm in our new ways so as not to cause unnecessary conflicts and backlashes. In extreme cases our change is met with such resistance that we may be forced to decide between an old and cherished relationship and the truth of who we are: it is a tough choice that no one would willingly invite, but sometimes there are no options but face that choice.

Over the years I have met clients who felt that their spouses and partners were no longer on the same spiritual journey as themselves, and who thought it highly possible that they would be breaking up with them as a result. It was surprising to me that partners would drift apart because of spirituality but understand that predicament better after experiencing it myself with friends who I feel no longer walk on a similar path as mine. It is not about the spiritual path itself, nor about feeling above anybody else, but at least in my case, it is about feeling that we no longer share similar attitudes towards Life, and it is up to me to make peace with the fact that our lives have literally drifted apart.

It is always sad to say goodbye to a loved one, particularly when they are still alive. Hope is the last thing to die and we do our best to save a precious relationship, often staying in it longer than any sensibility would allow. Sometimes we end up enduring repeated abuse only with the hope that, "things will get better with time." And when they don't and we have tried everything, the last thing that remains is the choice to finally give up and surrender to the fact that if we stay on things will continue as before, or decide to walk out towards new horizons. This same process may unfold in regards to any aspects of our lives: a job, the place where we live, or the way we live.

Should we know in our hearts that it is time to go but struggle to take that step, it is then important to explore the reasons why we are reluctant to take that step as well as our attachments to a past that no longer is. The letting go on the physical plane is often more challenging than the letting go we may experience under the influence of San Pedro, but it is part of the healing process and without it such process remains incomplete. As in all grieving process, this letting go is often first perceived as a loss, whereas with time we end up realizing that letting go is simply that process by which we create the space for new experiences and relationships to enter our lives.

Integration means the completion of something. Sometimes that completion is not about adding something that is missing and important, but about letting go of something that no longer serves us.

INTEGRITY

Integrity is the state of that which is "entire," of that which is complete. And by extension, its meaning entails also honesty.

When we are connected with all of ourselves and our thoughts and emotions, we may feel that we are juggling with too many knives and tennis balls. If we feel that our juggling act cannot be sustained for much longer, then it is time to deliberately let go of some of the knives before they fall on our heads or cut our hands. Life in developed countries easily gets very complicated as we pursue our careers, purposes, and our inner lives. We feel the conflict between our public and private needs, and often sacrifice one or the other. In my case I was fortunate enough to receive an important lesson during my first visit to the jungle in 2004: during an Ayahuasca ceremony the medicine clearly illustrated to me how important it is

236

to *align* every thought and action in order to achieve my goals as quickly as possible. Conflicting beliefs and an ambivalent attitude often slow down our progress to the point of being stuck. If that were the case, the quick way onwards is by exploring such beliefs and attitudes.

At the time of this experience in the jungle I was so bored with my own predicament that I was willing to do and let go of anything in order to move out of this stuck place of confusion. I had really nothing to lose and everything to gain by letting go of my old paradigm. I was fortunate to be engaging with Ayahuasca at a time when I had no obligations, no steady or fulfilling job, and no intimate romantic relationship. What I lacked then most importantly was an intimate relationship with myself, and that's what both Ayahuasca, and even more so San Pedro, helped me nurture and develop. When two weeks after leaving the jungle I drank San Pedro for the first time, I was ready and excited about furthering a loving and supportive relationship with myself to the point of getting married to myself.

I had to learn love all over again, and this time with me as my own primary partner. It has been a most interesting and rewarding process, and an ongoing exercise in letting go and deep honesty. At times the clarity and honesty have been outright brutal: I had to look at things I didn't want to look at and so that process required letting go of fears and resistances. But with time I have learnt to invite all of my inner selves to sit in the circle of my heart so that they all could be heard and honored equally.

Some choices I have made required of me the strength and courage to sacrifice certain things and let go of some relationships. In the West we still hold this idea of sacrifice as in, "Jesus dying for our sins": sacrifice is in our eyes a painful act. Suffering is in my opinion quite overrated and very old school, but with time sacrifice has taken on for me the original meaning of "making sacred," which needn't be a source of suffering at all once we let go of any resistance towards letting go.

San Pedro teaches us the challenging but amazing lesson of surrender, and the process with plant medicines is all about letting go of resistance so that our experience can keep flowing naturally and without obstacles. When we surrender to and honor our true feelings and what we hold as true in our hearts without resistance, then our path opens up again for us to walk on: this is living in integrity. To live in integrity, in love rather than fear of who we are, is pretty radical in our times of unconscious daily prostitution and betrayal of our truth. It takes courage to live according to our truth, and sometimes we may feel like we are alone along this journey. If it's true that no one can take those steps for us, it is just as true that the number of people who choose to live in integrity is constantly rising. Once again quoting from *The Message of the Hopi Elders*, "the time of the lone wolf is over." The open heart is about connecting with all of Creation and we are very fortunate to be alive at this time because once we let go of our fears and limiting beliefs, infinite possibilities are truly available to us.

One term for Teacher Plants such as San Pedro is "visionary plants": the visionary aspect of these plants is not in their ability to make us see otherworldly pictures, but in their supporting us to see deeper into our hearts and bring those visions into the world. When we see beneath the silver lining of consensus reality and free ourselves of the numerous no's and cannot's we hold in our minds and consciousness, we can not only see but more importantly experience and engage with a rich Universe that is pure potential.

We don't have to look for beautiful visions or an uplifting experience under the effects of San Pedro (I know I never do): our exploration and healing of old wounds and the release of old fears is all that is required to expand our consciousness and open our hearts with resulting feelings of elation and joy. Bypassing this stage of shadow exploration with plant medicines, or any other path or modality, will result in a possibly pleasant but momentary expansion that is bound to end sooner or later. When I started engaging with plant medicines it was very clear to me that I was not in it to have a good time but to make some important changes in my own life. I have nothing against having a good time under the influence of these medicines, but to me that's what they really are: medicines. And I never expect to enjoy my visit to a hospital, doctor, or dentist. What I do hope to experience whenever I drink medicine is to heal and let go of what no longer serves me so that a new awareness may arise to help make the rest of my journey not necessarily easier or pain free, but more meaningful and rich.

ATTACHMENT

The Buddhist teachings are based on a simple premise: attachment is the source of all suffering. I see attachment as the other side of resistance: attachment is fueled by desire and resistance is fueled by fear, with fear and desire being two sides of the same coin. I always explore, and invite others to do the same, both sides of this coin in regards to all aspects and manifestations of human consciousness.

The paradox of constantly seeking homeostasis in a constantly changing world is why attachment to anything, i.e., the hope that everything stays the same indefinitely, is the source of our suffering: we create our own suffering by wishing for something unattainable and wishing to hold on to something that is destined to pass as everything eventually does on this plane of reality. Suffering is the consequence of resisting that inevitable passing, and humans have throughout time developed and pursued various ways to deal with this impermanence: promises of eternal life and happiness are the surest way to sell any religion, ideology, or product.

Any chance for the ego to pursue and achieve immortality is really a tragic attempt to escape its own intrinsic mortality. Disguised as it may be, any attachment, including attachment to enlightenment, a peaceful world, or a happy life, will become sooner or later cause for stress and suffering. Behind those attachments, no matter how noble they may be, we will find a poorly disguised frightened ego full of expectations. Those expectations arise because of our attachment to the *fulfillment* of our intentions and hopes.[41]

Letting go of attachments that lock us in a past that no longer exists and have us worry about a future that we have no certainty about, is one of the most effective ways to embrace the present moment more fully. The impermanence of this life has with time taught me

---

[41] See Appendix I: *Intentions and Expectations*.

to let go of unrealistic wishes and to enjoy each and every moment as is and to the fullest.

People come to plant medicines with the hope of achieving something in the same way that we decide to act in this or that way with the hope that our actions will bear some desired result. And among people who join my retreats there are always individuals who well before the end of the retreat are already concerned and doubtful about their ability to sustain the level of clarity, courage, and determination achieved while under the effects of this or that medicine.

First of all, it is unrealistic to sustain to the same degree and indefinitely how we feel while under the effects of these medicines: these are peak experiences that most of us are not yet wired, physiologically as well as mentally, to experience 24/7. And it's not the goal of this process either, the goal being to return to our daily lives and implement the changes perceived as important and necessary while on the medicine. Secondly, it is just as unrealistic to sustain at home or in the workplace the same level of expansion experienced during a retreat and far away from our daily duties and environment. Eventually that elation will taper off in the same way that the effects of the medicine always taper off when we engage with it in respectful ways.

As I understand it, this process is not about attaining some eternal state of bliss but about coming out of it with more clarity and a more open heart so that we can engage with life with renewed enthusiasm and trust. The magic is not in the pill but in our rediscovered ability and capacity to live our lives as wholeheartedly as we can. Plant medicines, and San Pedro or any other medicine and substance are no exception, will not live our lives for us, but they can support us in reclaiming our lives in positive ways, e.g., they may help us heal the underlying causes of our dysfunctional diets but we may also still have to exercise and reduce our food intake in order to lose excess weight and keep our bodies limber and in shape.

The time after engaging in this process is most important as it is then that we are called to *act* according to the insights we have received under the influence of the medicine. It is also a time of possible "aftershocks": of instances where some old grief, anger, or fear may resurface. I encourage my clients after our retreats together to make the space and take the time to embrace and honor whatever may come up in the weeks following their visit here. It is easy to come up with excuses not to devote some downtime and contemplation in our lives, but our overall health depends on our generous care towards ourselves: taking some time whenever necessary to withdraw from all noise and distractions, and drop once again into our feelings and emotions is the easiest way to come out of our looping thoughts and confusion.

As the process begins long before the ingestion of any medicine, the process continues to unfold long after the effects of the medicine have subsided, which is why it is important to have some sort of support system in place for when we return home, that we continue to be gently connected to our needs, and open ourselves to receiving whatever care we may need. We may feel that it is time to start seeing a therapist of some sort, a counselor, or a massage therapist. Or we may open up to receiving the comforting care of friends and family. We may feel that it's time for a prolonged vacation, to reengage in our meditation or exercise practice, or a visit to an old friend or a familiar place dear to us. There are countless options but it all comes down to generous self-care, self-love, and staying present in the moment, i.e., what may have been a positive and nurturing activity in the past may not presently be our best option.

It takes some silence and a slower pace to connect with our feelings and emotions, so it is important to take the time to listen inwardly to them. Time is our most precious thing and to offer ourselves that time with generosity is an invaluable gift to ourselves as our overall health depends on such generosity.

COMMUNICATION

While engaging in this process I strongly recommend people not to fall in love, not to take any life-changing decisions, and not to make any important communication. This recommendation is also extended to a period of at least two weeks after their last ceremony. The reason is that we want to allow some time and integration before taking any action or making any statement that we may end up regretting or that may make people feel unnecessarily uncomfortable. Integration is about allowing the pieces of the puzzle to fall into their place in their own time. With time our perspective may become clearer and our ease may help others feel the same about us as well.

During the process with plant medicines we may become aware that it is important for us to have some honest communications with some people in our lives. It may be about expressing withheld discontentment, but also about sharing how much we love and care about them, or about the positive impact they have had in our lives. Expressions of gratitude are also very common: it is thanks to this and other medicines that I have learnt to cultivate the expression of gratitude, an expression that elevates both giver and recipient.

When it comes to sharing our feelings, I feel it is most important to be aware of the person we wish to speak to and put ourselves in their shoes for a moment to feel whether that person is actually ready to hear and honor what we wish to say, not necessarily to agree with us, but to hear us. If we feel that that person is not ready yet, that may call for some patience on our part. In regards to those people we feel may never be ready and open to hear us, I recommend creating a simple ritual during which we can invite in spirit that person and openly share what's in our hearts and minds.

Another piece of advice in the case of written communications is to save our letters as a draft, and reread and possibly edit them a few days after we first wrote them before actually sending them. What happened to me after my first time in the jungle may sound familiar to some of you: two weeks after I left the jungle I wrote what I thought was a loving and sensible email to my sister, only to receive a reply in which she shared her worry about me and warned me against the strange medicines I had been ingesting.

Our friends and families may get alarmed and worried by a sudden change in the way we express ourselves or by our actions following a healing process. They may react with support or they may react with suspicion and fear. Often timing makes all the difference.

Plant medicine experiences can make for very entertaining party talk and I am not shy about sharing the more ridiculous and funny aspects of this process, but I am a lot more discerning when it comes to sharing my more profound and personal inner experiences, and only share them when it is important to do so and with people I trust.

When we share our experiences it is important to do so without expecting any external validation: when we expect such validation, we are often met with skepticism and judgment. The bottom line is that no one but ourselves can validate our experience by honoring it as is, no matter how outlandish that experience may have been.

Last but not least, I encourage my clients to keep a journal during our retreats and recommend that they keep writing in the weeks after they leave. Writing is a wonderful way to integrate the process as it unfolds: it can be very helpful to put into words an experience that is often difficult to describe and make sense of. Rereading those journals after some time can also help us understand what was happening at the time and integrate the experience more fully.

ACTION

A journal is also a good record of the insights we may have received and of things we want to do after engaging with this medicine. It's important not to overwhelm ourselves with a long to-do list right after this process, but instead honor such insights and guidance even in the smallest of ways. For instance, we may realize that we wish to devote our efforts to global reforestation: such insight can be honored by simply being more aware of our toilet paper consumption. Once again, the story of the hummingbird bringing single drops of water to a wildfire and doing his best to help extinguish it can be an inspiration and reminder of the power of the smallest of gestures. In the same way, relationships can be easily rekindled with small acts of kindness and care.

Action is simply the result of allowing who we are to manifest in the world. What is important is not what we do, but the energy behind our acts and gestures. It is easy to fall back into a value system dictated by a perceived need to perform, and even easier to make ourselves feel inadequate by creating unmanageable goals for ourselves. My advice is always to take it easy, to show up whenever possible, do our best each and every time, and be at peace with the outcome. Our lives are stressful enough as they are and it's easy to feed that stressful attitude even with the noblest of pursuits. Stress is a debilitating factor and always a sign that the mind is once again running the show. Left and right, no matter what the situation, we are constantly told that there is no time and that things need to happen fast and right now. But hurried decisions rarely make for good ones and it is often better to wait some time for things to be processed also on a sub- and unconscious level before taking any step further.

In my own daily life what has made the biggest difference has been being more closely connected with my emotions and feelings (and as a result my intuition, too), not to mention a greater ability and willingness to receive. As a result of these shifts, it has been much easier to make life choices that were nurturing and in alignment with my needs and desires.

Reconnecting with my heart and deeper self has also brought me to question and shift my priorities in ways that are supportive of my health, physical, emotional, mental, and spiritual. I find myself living in an environment that would have been unthinkable in the past, and yet, I am healthier and more vibrant than I have ever been.

The awareness that I can support others only when I am myself well[42] has made self-care the highest of priorities. It may feel tantalizing to go back into the world with the awareness that much needs to be let go and changed, but we can reframe such challenge as a wonderful opportunity to be caring and loving towards ourselves.

PLAY

As I was reading *Surfing Aquarius*[43] by my friend, astrologer Dan Furst, which is about the Age of Aquarius we have just entered, I was amused by how the many themes I have emphasized in this book resonate with the themes of this new astrological age, the theme of personal responsibility highest among them. Aquarius is an Air sign, meaning also that it has a great ability to dream and envision. The challenge is to keep the feet on the ground and take the necessary steps to manifest those visions: to align our thoughts and actions in order to bring Heaven down here on Earth. Such challenge will be much easier to engage in if we

---

[42] Think about those airplane safety instructions where the adult is asked to put on the oxygen mask before they take care of a child sitting next to them.

[43] Furst, Dan. *Aquarius Surfing*. San Francisco, Weiser Books, 2011.

remind ourselves not to take it all too seriously, seriousness being a sure indication that the mind and not our
heart is on the driver seat.

Believe it or not, in most cases when someone asks
me what they can do after a retreat to further their spiritual journey, my answer is: relax and play! My advice
is to engage as often as possible in non-competitive
activities, physical exercise and sports that require as
little thinking as possible, and most importantly that
are fun and enjoyable. Anything enjoyable and that
stimulates breathing and our physical hearts, such as
running, swimming, dancing, and good sex, is helpful
in keeping our spiritual heart open and thriving.

Meditation for people who are very much in their
heads is like wanting to climb the Himalayas without first
adapting to the high altitude: better to go on actual
treks and nature walks to soothe the mind and keep our
feet and awareness on the Earth. Actually, spending
as much time as possible in Nature is the easiest way to
relax our minds, Nature being the greatest healer and
a most profound teacher.

For people with a competitive personality, my
recommendation is to focus on the experience itself
rather than on the goal—e.g., in the case of a yoga
practice, the focus is shifted from achieving a posture
to gentle awareness and breathing. Kripalu Yoga is a
wonderful example of this attitude. And of course, any
Five Rhythms and the many kinds of ecstatic dancing
events offered worldwide are always my favorite:
nothing beats the opportunity to dance with other
people without any expectation whatsoever about
what that dancing ought to look like and in a friendly
environment of acceptance and playfulness.

The expression of gratitude, from giving thanks before a meal to donating to causes and projects close to our hearts, and volunteering, are all an easy and practical way to let go of our ego-centeredness and live in the beautiful awareness that we are not alone and that the thriving of others contributes to our own.

Not to crowd our days with too many duties and goals is the first step towards creating time for play. Know that play is an essential element of health, including spiritual health, and as Jesus reminded us, it is only when we become like children that we will be able to enter the Kingdom of Heaven.

One of the Andean teachings I received soon after moving to Peru is about the integration of all levels of reality: it says that wisdom isn't worth much at all unless it is expressed and manifested on the everyday level of reality. It also says that if power and courage aren't illumined with Divine Light and Love, it can easily become dangerous. The goal of human endeavors is then a courageous and powerful course of action informed with wisdom and blessed with Divine energy. It may seem like a difficult equation to solve, but it's doable because true wisdom makes apparently complicated situations and predicaments really simple, and honoring such wisdom is therefore easier than we think. We don't need oracles and mediums to tell us what to do: more often than not all we have to do is connect with the wisdom of our feelings and emotions, honor our truth, and act accordingly.

Most important of all is to remind ourselves that we are *always* on the right path, even when we feel most confused and lost. Along that path I am fond of reminding myself of the sweet words of R.L. Stevenson, and that "to travel hopefully is a better thing than to arrive." May the wisdom of your heart and of San Pedro bless your path now and always.

THEMES WORTH CONTEMPLATING SIX MONTHS AFTER ENGAGING WITH SAN PEDRO

Here is a list of themes worth contemplating about six months after engaging with San Pedro:

- How does my life differ now from the life I had envisioned six months ago?
- What may be the limiting beliefs that prevent that vision from manifesting?
- Have I been asking for and receiving the support I need?
- What are my needs at this point of my life? And how can I go about meeting these needs?
- Who and what are my support system? Am I allowing myself to receive the support I need?
- How much time do I dedicate to playful and enjoyable activities, and expressions of gratitude?

THE VISION OF THE HEART
– IQUITOS, PERU – JUNE 2015

It was kind of funny that I should begin the writing of this book about a medicine from the mountains in the heat of the jungle, but that's exactly what happened. In June of 2015 I returned to Sachamama, my teacher's healing center outside Iquitos, for yet anoth-

er shamanic diet and with the intention of beginning in earnest the writing of this book. That year I was going to diet the Chakruna plant (Dyploteris Cabrerana), the only plant in my teacher's brew of Ayahuasca I hadn't dieted yet. The Chakruna plant is the one in the Ayahuasca brew that contains DMT (N,N-Dimethyl-tryptamine), a powerful psychedelic compound of the tryptamine family which is largely responsible for the visions under the effects of this medicine.

Even though I have had my fair share of visions over the years, I don't see them as the most important aspect of this process to the point that for me sometimes they can be more of a distraction than anything else, so the same night of my arrival at Sachamama I speak to the Chakruna spirit during an Ayahuasca ceremony and tell her that I am not here for fancy visuals but for deeper vision. Vision of what exactly I have no idea: only time would tell.

As I begin my diet I also begin writing. My diet process takes me to places inside and outside myself I had been reluctant to see, in particular some judgments of others and of some aspects of my feminine side. This exploration leads to amazing healing and a deeper integration of my masculine and feminine energies. What soon into the process begins to transpire is how this diet is not only a Chakruna diet but a combination of both Chakruna and San Pedro, simply because I am writing and thinking about this other plant for several hours each day. The two plants and their energies are dancing together in surprising ways, informing and complementing each other. I am not fond of mixing medicines for the sake of novelty and it was definitely not my intention to do so, but there I am and it's a beautiful dance.

Two weeks into the diet I drink San Pedro in the daytime. Over the years I have enjoyed drinking this medicine as part of my diet process in the jungle. It is not something my teacher is used to, but he has always trusted my choices. It is interesting that what began as my singing and taking the energies of plants and trees native to the Amazon all the way to the high mountains of the Andes has also turned into my bringing San Pedro to the jungle.

San Pedro always adds something unique to my diet and this time was no exception. What happened was that at some point my old story of abuse of spiritual power returned in the form of some unintegrated fear connected with it: I became aware that as a result of old guilt and shame from abusing my power and position in previous lifetimes, I had been reluctant to shine fully for fear of making the same mistake again, and in so doing I had been hiding my light and beauty as much as my shadow. It was ironic to experience in my own skin the truth of Marianne Williamson's words, "Our deepest fear is not that we are inadequate. Our deepest fear is that we are powerful beyond measure. It is our light, not our darkness, that most frightens us."[44]

Becoming aware of this shame and fear allowed me to let them go. In the hour that followed that letting go I experienced infinity within and without, and the deepest of connections with everything across time and space. Not long after that I realized that I also needed to let go of the part of me that had created itself as limited and inadequate, and of not knowing and not being able to see. I stood by the railings of my hut and cried as I was offering my farewells to this old

---

[44] Williamson, Marianne. A Return to Love. New York, HarperOne, 1992.

part of myself that had fulfilled its purpose and taught me to embrace my brilliance and gifts.

By the end of my diet I felt quite complete and so I went to my last Ayahuasca ceremony with the simple intention of giving thanks to the medicines, the plants, and the energies of this healing place. Later in the ceremony I left the Ayahuasca temple to go visit and pay my respect to the Chakruna bushes nearby, which I had visited and sung to many times during the diet. As I stood there expressing my gratitude I unexpectedly felt a strong ray of energy coming from the bush in front of me penetrate my head. For a few seconds I could perceive with my inner eye my whole brain radiating with an intense blue light, and soon after that I received a vision: the vision of the Heart, a gift for me from both the Chakruna and San Pedro. In this vision, which involved no visuals at all, I could see the unmistakable perfection of everybody's path and journey, including my own.

We often experience such deep insights, and with time their relevance seems to dissipate until forgotten, but not this time. In the days, weeks, and months following this revelation I kept seeing that perfection. The awareness of the perfection of everybody's journey has since informed my work with plant medicines as well as my own life: all regrets and remorse are easily let go of with the awareness that every decision, action, and circumstance was always the perfect one, and that there is nothing to be fixed or changed about our past and present predicaments except our own attitude towards them.

APPENDIX I

A SAN PEDRO PRIMER

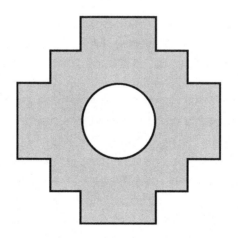

PREPARATION

The preparations before drinking San Pedro entail first and foremost information: reading this book is a good way to start gathering information about this process, as well as any information about where and with whom to engage in this experience. Personal referrals are always the best source of information, even though what worked for someone may or may not work for us.

I do not recommend that you drink this medicine by yourself the first time, actually not until you are thoroughly familiar with this medicine: as innocuous as this medicine may seem to us, it is a very powerful medicine and engaging with it carelessly can have long lasting negative effects.

You may die because of an accident while alone in Nature or even in the comfort of your own house. You may become paranoid and take hasty and bad decisions as a result. You may experience an ego death or uncover deep trauma for which you may be totally unprepared: these experiences can be very healing but without proper care and support they may instead turn into traumatic ones.

You may lose complete touch with reality and grow increasingly delusional to the point of not caring anymore about simple things such as your family and children, or your job, as has happened to the husband of a woman who contacted me years ago. Her husband had bought some San Pedro powder in Peru after drinking Ayahuasca in the jungle and had started drinking it by himself without any supervision. I don't know how the story ended but when she contacted me her husband had become so detached and delusional that he was unwilling to engage in regular 3-D reality at all. As enticing as this scenario may be to you, it isn't: this is the kind of experience that in the long run may have you spend the rest of your life in a psychiatric ward. If you insist on drinking this medicine unsupervised by someone who knows the territory well, at least have a trusted friend sit with you but without drinking so that they can help you should you need them.

I firmly believe that if we engage with San Pedro wholeheartedly there is no need to add any other medicine to it, but if you wish to mix medicines, I would recommend you do so ONLY when you are very experientially familiar with all of them. Through research make sure that all these medicines are compatible with each other and their conjunct use does not result in an overload of chemicals that may result in a heart attack or respiratory failure.

A regular dose of San Pedro has the stimulatory effect equivalent to two cups of strong coffee. For people with heart, circulation, or respiratory problems, it is imperative that you do not stress your body to the point of endangering your health and life. People with high blood pressure, with a weak heart. and are overweight are particularly at risk, even more so when they drink this medicine at high altitude.

Mescaline, the main psychotropic alkaloid in San Pedro, is notoriously difficult for the human body to metabolize, so people with seriously weakened liver functions are discouraged from drinking this medicine so as not to overload an already impaired organ.

If you take any medications, please check that the drinking of this medicine is compatible with all of them. The use of antidepressants and other substances that affect the chemistry of our nervous system in any way, as well as any medication containing stimulants (including over the counter decongestants), is to be discontinued well before engaging with this medicine. The weaning off from prescription drugs ought to be ALWAYS supervised by the same doctor who prescribed them.

It cannot be stressed enough how important it is to adhere to these recommendations, even when someone who claims to know what they are doing, even an experienced medicine person, or through peer pressure, tells you otherwise. It is always a sad thing when people seriously endanger themselves, sometimes to the point of dying, when these occurrences can be easily avoided through the exercise of discipline.

Dietary preparations include refraining from pre-packaged foods, chilly and spicy/hot foods, deep-fried foods, alcohol, and all recreational drugs. These restrictions should be implemented starting at least one week prior to drinking this medicine. For those used to daily caffeine use, including chocolate, which is both a stimulant and difficult to metabolize, please start lessening your daily intake as it is highly recommended that on the day you ingest San Pedro no caffeine, including chocolate, be consumed. Some people combine San Pedro with chocolate or cacao: if your liver is weak you may want to limit your chocolate and cacao consumption to a minimum. You should also refrain from all sorts of sexual activities starting at least three days before drinking San Pedro.

In our times we ingest more media and information than we breathe, drink, or eat. It is therefore important to be aware of this source of "food" and remain aware of how it affects us. Reducing our information intake is a way to make the space within ourselves in preparation for drinking San Pedro, as well as during and after the medicine process.

All of these recommendations are of course arbitrary but their validity and importance are proven through centuries of experience and experimentation as an effective way to prepare one's body and mind to the experience ahead. In the case of a prolonged process with this medicine I always recommend observing these dietary and behavioral guidelines without exception for as long as the process is going to be, before AND after the process.

Our willingness and commitment to follow these or the recommendations of the people who will lead you in ceremonies with San Pedro is of paramount importance. Should you not be inclined for whatever reason to follow them thoroughly, it is imperative that you let your guide know and let them decide whether they are comfortable with your decision. Failure to comply with the required and agreed upon preparations may endanger not only your life and the positive unfolding of your experience, but may also endanger the experience of whoever may be sharing it with you.

(Mind)Set

The modern Western psychedelic tradition has taught us the importance of set and setting in all experiences with mind-altering substances. It has taught us how a mindful choice of set and setting can make all the difference between a positive and a traumatic experience. By "set" our psychedelic grandfathers really meant "mindset," i.e., the mental and emotional state one experiences coming into the experience itself, which includes also our intentions and possible expectations.

We do manifest whatever our attention focuses on and this medicine often magnifies whatever we may hold in our thoughts and consciousness: if we engage in this process with fear or suspicion, then the medicine will probably enhance those feelings. Signing up for this process already sets the process in powerful motion: just the prospect of ingesting this medicine starts bringing up all sorts of thoughts and emotions and it is valuable to take those leads seriously as an important part of the process.

When I decided to drink Ayahuasca for the first time I was immediately aware of my own fear: not fear of the medicine but of whatever I might have hidden in the past from my conscious awareness that this experience may reveal. In the three weeks preceding that ceremony I explored those fears with diligence, to the point of arriving at the ceremony completely ready and open to receive what the medicine had to offer me.

So it's important to start paying attention to our inner landscape as soon as we sign up for this experience and bring whatever themes may come up as *part* of our intentions rather than dismissing them.

When engaging with this or other medicines for the first time there is often some trepidation caused by the novelty of the experience and its unforeseeable unknowns. I find it always rewarding to offer my trust to the medicine before and during the experience, no matter what the experience turns out to be. And I remind myself that the medicine is working *for* me and not against me, even when the experience is really difficult, challenging, and unpleasant. I highly recommend to first-timers that they choose as safe and supportive an environment for their first ceremonies: knowing that we are relatively safe and supported greatly helps lessen our trepidation and facilitates our surrendering to the medicine. For people who have engaged with this medicine before, the biggest trap is to believe that they *know* what is in store for them, how the experience will unfold, and most insidiously, what to expect. The wisest attitude is to dismiss such thoughts and expectations as illusory because the truth is that we don't really know what the future holds for us. This is supposedly a transformational process and as a result it's important to be aware that we are no longer the same person who drank this medicine in the past and therefore our experience will most likely be different. The best that we can do is to keep approaching this medicine with an open mind and heart, and always with the same respect and humility as the first time. Relaxing our discipline and not following the important preparatory guidelines will eventually result in a lessening of the power of this medicine, and sooner or later such attitude may entail less than optimal or even negative repercussions.

Personally, the more I engage with this medicine the more attentive I am in following the rules of the game. I have witnessed enough instances of lassitude and disrespect, and the dire consequences thereof, on the part of other plant medicine people and clients, to wish to end up in the same situation. We can use the wealth of wisdom gathered by people before us through trial and error so that we don't have to learn the hard way and can continue to benefit from this medicine each and every time. I have also seen enough unconscious and undisciplined self-appointed sorcerer apprentices to know the difference between sensible and respectful exploration of our inner world and dangerous foolishness. It is important to be aware that our physical, emotional, mental, and spiritual health are at stake, and that this is a powerful medicine that can easily turn into a poison if approached carelessly and disrespectfully[45].

Dosage

There is hardly ever anything enlightening about overloading our nervous system to the point of overdosing, either to the point of dying or of being totally overwhelmed by the experience and experiencing prolonged bouts of paranoia. As harmless as San Pedro is when approached respectfully, very few experiences can be as painful and harrowing as ingesting more of this medicine than we can handle. I am always on the cautious side when giving this medicine to someone for the first time and ALWAYS wait a full ninety minutes before possibly offering more[46]. I am even more careful with people who wish to keep drinking more medicine after a second dose: oftentimes I can see and sense that they have already had plenty of medicine even though they say they don't feel much. San Pedro does NOT produce a transcendent experience: it merely acts as a key to open doors to our inner and outer landscapes, and then it is up to us to engage in that

---

[45] The Greek term for medicine is "pharmakon", which means both medicine AND poison.

[46] And I ALWAYS go cautiously whenever using a new batch of medicine.

experience. Drinking more medicine with the expectation that the medicine does all the work is in my opinion an erroneous approach.

Breaking the Fast

Whenever I lead daytime San Pedro ceremonies I expect my clients to avoid all foods in the morning and restrict their breakfast to non-caffeinated teas, honey, sugar, and water. In the case the ceremony starts in the evening I prefer to eat lightly during the day and fast for at least six hours before ingesting the medicine.

I allow no drinking and no eating in my ceremonies until I feel that the person is ready to break their fast. Usually about four hours after their last cup of medicine a person is ready to start drinking and eating again, but sometimes the cleansing process is longer and breaking our fast can bring that cleansing to an abrupt stop or complicate it unnecessarily. The main guideline is: if the stomach feels upset and unsettled, exercise patience until it feels ready to receive food and drink. Breaking our fast when the stomach feels settled will not hinder our experience, if anything it will give us the energy to continue engaging in the process.

Because the alkaloids in San Pedro take long to metabolize, I recommend bringing to the ceremony only light foods such as fruit (but no avocadoes and no citrus), breads, light pastries (without chocolate), cookies, and crackers. Fried chips of any kind as well as snacks containing nuts are not recommended because of their heaviness. What IS important is to keep hydrated once we are ready to break our fast. Sometimes people feel that not breaking fast is conducive to a better or deeper experience when in reality it leads only to dehydration and confusion. Breaking fast is a good way to reconnect with our bodies and ground ourselves. I am aware that oftentimes one doesn't have much of an appetite, but making a little effort usually makes for a more grounded experience. The recommendation to eat lightly on ceremony day extends until the end of the day, including dinner. Dinner can be filling and tasty, but not heavy.

INTENTIONS AND EXPECTATIONS

Throughout this book I have spoken about and suggested various themes for intentions as well as spoken about the pernicious holding on to expectations. A frequently overlooked aspect of this work is the subtle yet radical difference between intention and expectation. Intention is, as far as I am concerned, a very important part of this healing modality. Taking the time to become aware of the reasons we go to San Pedro helps us focus on ourselves and the process ahead.

As we receive only as much from this medicine as we are willing to put into the experience, focusing on our intentions before each ceremony is a way of devoting some time and attention to the experience ahead. Preparing our intentions for a ceremony helps us understand the real reasons for approaching this medicine and opens the way to receive the healing we are longing for.

I used to be fond of telling people that plant medicines don't necessarily give us what we want but most importantly what we need. This statement no longer seems to me totally accurate: I now feel that if we approach plant medicines with a pure intention we can trust that whatever happens during any ceremony is somehow in alignment with our intentions. It's just that oftentimes before we can work on the specific themes that are part of our intentions the medicine may invite us to first face and explore all the obstacles that prevent us from being truly ready to address the themes of our intentions. This is often a source of frustration for the ego, which has somehow hoped for and is attached to certain results in unconscious ways. Sometimes we go to San Pedro with a desire for certain visions and experiences but the medicine may point us in a totally different direction and without much space for bargaining. Such events ought to be dealt with surrender rather than stubbornness because what we are dealing with is not intention but expectation. All expectations are a product and an aspect of the ego-mind and when we let go of our expectations we can finally open ourselves to a greater universal intelligence rarely provided by the limitations of the mind. The plant has an uncanny ability to know exactly what we need and we should let it do what it knows best with as little resistance as possible.

At the beginning of a ceremony I ask all participants to offer their intentions to the medicine and the Universe, and then let them go. The medicine may take us right where we wish to go and our intentions may be fulfilled; other times the medicine may see the importance of our intentions but also the need to explore and heal other aspects of our lives before addressing the themes of our intentions. This may happen during one single ceremony or over the course of several.

A woman told me of how towards the end of an Ayahuasca ceremony she expressed the wish to explore a certain issue that had been part of her reason for drinking the medicine that night. The answer she got from the medicine was a simple but irrevocable, "Not tonight, dear." Surrendering to the wisdom and healing power of San Pedro can be challenging but not impossible: one has simply to acknowledge and remember that the choice one has taken is the right one, that both set and setting are ideal and conducive to allowing oneself a certain degree of vulnerability, and that ultimately one is in safe hands, both those of the medicine and of the people leading the experience.

INTENTIONS AND EXPECTATIONS: THE DANCE BETWEEN SURRENDER AND ACTIVE PARTICIPATION IN THE PROCESS OF DRINKING SAN PEDRO

In my work with people drinking San Pedro I always recommend taking some time before each ceremony to feel what one wishes to receive from this medicine. This is a way to initiate the process and to focus on what themes one wishes to address or be addressed during the ceremony, and it helps figure out what are the reasons for engaging with this medicine and how to best go about it.

As I said earlier, before one drinks I ask everybody to offer those intentions to the medicine and the Universe, and then let them go and see what happens. My recommendation is to bring up those intentions again during the ceremony and to start exploring them with the help of the medicine only in

266

the case they haven't yet been addressed and when the effects are no longer as strong and there is nothing else going on in one's experience, but always without any expectation that our intentions may be fulfilled. Drinking San Pedro is first and foremost an exercise in surrender and acceptance of what the medicine has to offer, but at times it also asks for our active partic-ipation in the process. The dance between surrender and active engagement is often an intricate but not impossible one.

Sometimes people get upset and frustrated because in their eyes "nothing happened" or their intentions weren't addressed. Attachment to the fulfillment of our intentions and the resulting anger or disappointment, are signs that the mind is subtly at work and that an element of unconscious expectation has crept into the experience. When addressed with calm and awareness, one can often identify in such occurrences very familiar patterns such as self-sabo-tage, the tendency to set for oneself unrealistic goals, or the wish to overlook some basic psychological issues that nevertheless end up showing up in our experience whether we like it or not. Among these psychological issues there are often childhood issues of projected expectations and the anger and disappointment for failing to meet them, which in most cases result in deep anxiety and feelings of unworthiness. As we can see, the results of ingesting this medicine, whether we like them or not, always point to unresolved issues that can probably benefit from being addressed and let go of as part of the healing and transformation process.

With San Pedro I feel that a more active engage-ment in the process than for instance with Ayahuasca is often beneficial. I personally start exploring the themes of my intentions right after drinking the medicine instead of waiting until it takes full effect. I bring my conscious breath a few notches above usual and prefer to keep my eyes closed as much as possible in order to better focus on my inner experience and feelings.

SETTING

" Setting" refers to the physical and social environment of the ceremony or retreat, and it speaks of the importance of a safe environment, created and sustained in order to support the most beneficial experience.

I prefer to be outdoors when drinking San Pedro and a few years ago I received a strong message that it was time to limit my ceremonies to my own healing center. Up until then I had enjoyed taking my groups to the nearby river and occasionally to some pre-Columbian ruins and sacred sites, but that was no longer an option as I realized that engaging in this process with groups of people on public land, and with people often crying, screaming, and purging, was not ideal nor respectful of the local people. Once I connected with the power of sacred sites I also realized that it was better not to hold ceremonies there anymore as these places often require a much greater degree of preparation and purification in order to hold plant ceremonies with their blessings.

When outdoors and away from immediate help, safety is most important and I recommend NEVER drinking San Pedro in a place we don't know intimately. Being aware of the history and nature of a place, whether untouched or used in the past as a burial site or sacred space, informs us about the necessary etiquette when visiting it and whether it is appropriate that we visit it in the first place. An example of this are the mountains of Peru, which are not just mounds of rocks but are experienced as grandfather and grandmother Spirits, and are revered, connected with, and walked upon with a specific code of behavior. Failure to comply with this etiquette often results in bad "accidents" and sometimes tragedies.

San Pedro teaches us about the interconnectedness of everything and the importance of being in harmonious relation with our environment. Learning about and respecting the ancestral laws of the land wherever we are is the best way to ensure that the land and all visible and invisible energies that dwell in that land are benevolently supporting and guiding us. A simple but heartfelt prayer and offering is often all that is required of us: such simple gestures help us be mindful of the reality that we are not alone and that our wellbeing and safety depends also on our attitude and behavior towards what surrounds us.

Lastly, the more remote the area, the more aware we need to be about getting home safely and in time—this may sound obvious but our perception of the passing of time can easily become impaired under the influence of this medicine.

We may create a beautiful room with incense and a comfortable pillow to meditate, but the room cannot and will not do the meditating for us. In the same way, the setting we choose can be conducive to a positive experience but will not guarantee it in any way. Blaming the surroundings or the people we chose to share this experience with will do nothing to improve the quality of our experience as in the end the way we perceive and experience the world is only a reflection of ourselves. Expecting a perfect setting and ceremony, and then feeling disappointed and judgmental if our expectations are not met, is only a projection of our own feelings of inadequacy and self-criticism. Sometimes people bring up assumed "standards" as to how a "sacred" ceremony ought to be conducted and express high and mighty judgments if those standards are not met. I agree that the quality of each ceremony ought to be as high as possible in order to ensure its positive unfolding, but judgment is judgment and three fingers are always pointing towards the person who expresses such judgment. The quality of the social environment in which this process takes place is of equal importance as any ceremony and retreat is really the co-creation of everybody present no matter what his or her role may be.

Under the influence of San Pedro one is not immune from projecting undesired aspects of oneself onto others or the environment—actually, those projections are often larger than life and people do occasionally get upset and very judgmental of others. This is a classic blessing in disguise as others are so generously willing to host our projections so that we can see through them, gain deeper awareness of our patterns, and eventually release them. A San Pedro ceremony is like an enhanced version of daily life and in it some familiar and some secret aspects of ourselves make their appearance. It is a good thing to remind oneself of certain pitfalls one may have a tendency to create over and over again, such as giving one's power away to some authority figure, e.g., the medicine person leading the ceremony, or certain negative judgments about people or situations. As with all other emotions coming up during a ceremony, simply sit back and lovingly watch yourself and your ways of being: are these recurrent themes in your life? Are you happy simply reacting to them in your usual way or would you rather take advantage of the situation and look at them more closely, and perhaps find and heal the reasons for such behaviors?

There are no coincidences and often we find ourselves sitting in ceremony with exactly the kind of people needed to heal certain aspects of ourselves, no matter how annoying their presence may seem at first. This reminds me of a story a friend related to me about an Ayahuasca ceremony where someone had been screaming for a very long time. After a while someone angrily reacted by saying out loud, "Shut up! You are ruining my experience!" to which my friend wisely responded, "He IS your experience!" Assuming total responsibility for ourselves, our choices, and experiences is the sign of true maturity, whereas blaming everything and everybody else only keeps us in a place of powerlessness and unconsciousness. So, if you start getting all upset at somebody, be grateful and remember that a new powerful lesson and chance for healing has just begun!

Of course, we hardly ever react with enthusiasm in such cases. On the contrary, we start resenting people for mirroring back to us aspects of ourselves that we don't like and have invested much energy in avoiding. As we are with ourselves, so are we with others: we judge, chastise, ridicule, reprimand, and generally reject others because their behavior reminds us of parts of ourselves we'd rather not look at. It happens all the time, including among people who have gathered to drink San Pedro: insecurities, fears, judgments, envies, jealousies, group dynamics, power plays—all the dramas of our personal lives can be acted out with any group of people. Because of the temporary altered state of consciousness induced by this medicine, people often say after a ceremony that, "they're going back to their lives," when actually there is never such a separation, and indeed the picture we gather of all the thoughts and emotions we experience during a ceremony is far more complete and accurate than the edited version of ourselves we are constantly trying to sell to others or ourselves.

Eventually the ceremonial space turns into a hall of mirrors where both cherished and resisted parts of ourselves make their appearance. Once in the jungle I left soon after the closing of a ceremony with a friend who seemed rather annoyed with the prolonged humming of another participant. It was clear to me that leaving the space was the easiest solution available and we gently made our way back to our huts while of course discussing proper and improper ceremonial etiquette. My friend pointed out the need in his opinion for a common set of rules that, when observed by all and at all times, would not only benefit each participant but the flow of the ceremony as well. Misbehavior then, I gathered from his words, would not only be offending to others but also to the ceremony itself. I pointed out to my friend that seemingly he had been the only one bothered by this other person's humming and that therefore it wasn't exactly a public case but a very personal one. I also reminded my friend that one of his main intentions for being in the jungle was to let go of self-judgment and the insecurity that results from lack of self-acceptance. We talked about the ways we project onto others our own self-criticism and in the end what could have been another pointless rant about the lack of respect and education of others became a precious opportunity to explore the theme of inadequacy.

San Pedro ceremonies are fairly simple rituals. My friend and teacher Joseph Kramer explained to me years ago that a ritual is basically something "with a beginning, an end, and something in the middle." For me that "something in the middle" ought to be as empty and uncluttered as possible in order to give a blank slate upon which each participant can project their own personal stuff, *and* supportive of one's becoming aware of one's own projections. San Pedro ceremonies are not performances but occasions where our hurt selves can come out without fear of judgment or rejection. In my work I ask each participant to hold their space, i.e., not worry about what goes on around them during the ceremony, but also remind them that we are among sisters and brothers, and they should not feel self-conscious but just let themselves be exactly as they need to be.

Rather than being performances, healing ceremonies are an opportunity to let go of our perceived need to perform. If we stay in "performance mode" we are really in an identity, which often prevents the medicine from touching us where we need it most.

It is very easy to get distracted from the gentle voice of our hearts and therefore I invite people to do as little *as possible* during a ceremony: playing music, singing songs, and engaging with our favorite sacred objects may be just the right thing, but oftentimes it is a way to distract ourselves rather than just *feel*. My general advice is to simply be aware of whether whatever it is that we are doing is *conducive* to our healing experience. If it isn't, then it's best to let it go.

I took the time to write this book to support others in making the most of this medicine, and the foul taste of San Pedro is an invitation to make the most of each and every ceremony as plants are giving of themselves for this purpose and no other. Maintaining an attitude of respect and gratitude can only help us not take anything for granted and let go of our consumerist ways, which not only unnecessarily deplete the environment of important natural resources but also further poison our spirit. Maintaining an attitude of respect and gratitude will also contribute to the power of this medicine so that it can keep blessing our lives with its teachings and blessings.

APPENDIX II

EMBRACE OF THE SERPENT

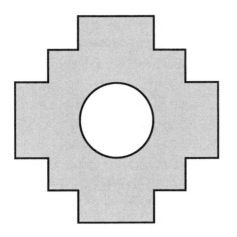

As we come more and more in contact with native people and cultures, we can't escape the fact that the consequences of such meetings go both ways. It is often enough a positive exchange but, if I may say so, we Westerners can seldom resist the temptation of wanting to "improve upon the lives of the natives" in always well-intentioned and usually damaging ways.

Unfortunately one such area is the Western intervention into traditional plant medicine shamanism: we come to San Pedro or Ayahuasca with our arrogance, impatience, and westerly ways, imposing our belief that more and faster is always better. We go to these medicines thinking that what we are ingesting is a compound of miracle molecules when in actuality what we are drinking is neither just mescaline (the psychoactive ingredient of San Pedro) nor DMT (the visionary molecule of Ayahuasca), but a whole plant with a much more complex vibration than the sum of a few molecular compounds, the wisdom of the psychic space of the place where they are from, *and* the wisdom gathered through time by all the people who have engaged with such vibrations.

To think of these medicines as inert psychoactive substances is wildly reductive. I think this is what Maria Sabina, the Mexican curandera who worked with Psilocybin mushrooms, referred to when she said that her medicine had lost its power after Westerners started ingesting it: by seeing these plants as simple chemicals we reduce them to something much smaller, and therefore less powerful, than they really are. Luckily the foreigners who approach these ancestral medicines with such small-mindedness seem to be able to expand their appreciation after ingesting them.

Personally, the bigger cause for concern lies in changes traditional plant medicine keeps incurring in order to satisfy the appetite of money-bearing foreigners. Nowadays programs are offered that are so intense and excessive by any traditional standards and common sense that I doubt the native people offering them would ever encourage any of their family members to follow them.

In order to make money, natives and foreigners alike are willing to speed up a process that has time and patience as its most important requirement in order to unfold positively. Nature has a slow rhythm and, no matter how quick the transformation plant medicine is able to offer, we still need to offer this process the necessary time for it to unfold beneficially.

In the case of San Pedro, which takes longer than most plant medicines to be metabolized in the body and therefore has long-lasting effects[47], I don't recommend more than five ceremonies over a period of two weeks, followed by at least another two weeks of integration afterwards, and this with as little activity between ceremonies as possible, adequate nourishment, and plenty of rest.

Plant medicine as I understand it is as much about the expansion of consciousness as it is about being able to ground that expansion and wisdom into the body and our everyday life. As I've witnessed in individuals who have abused this medicine with excessive frequency and lack of proper integration, the result is not clarity but confusion, often leading to paranoia or a dangerously delusional state.

---

[47] An average experience with San Pedro lasts between 8 and 15 hours.

277

To underestimate the power of San Pedro and engage with it indiscriminately does bear consequences. To approach it with caution and respect each and every time, and under the proper guidance if someone is not experienced or not mature enough (psychologically and mentally) to do it by oneself, cannot be recommended highly enough. In the end it is always better and easier to prevent the damages of possible abuse than mend them afterwards.

In 2016 what I consider to be a most important Columbian movie, *Embrace Of The Serpent*[48], was released on DVD. I quickly ordered a copy and was impressed not only by the story and the cinematography, but also by the poignancy and relevance of the themes explored in it.

The movie is about two historical yet fictionalized Westerners, Theodor Martius, a German ethnographer from the 1800's, and Richard Evans Schultes, who is considered by many the father of modern ethnobotany. Both characters explore the Amazon forest for their academic studies but they are both also looking for something they need: the former is dying and is looking for a cure, the latter has been engaged by the U.S. government to find ways to grow rubber trees during WWII after Malaysia and its rubber plantations were taken over by the Japanese. These two characters exemplify what motivates to this day most foreigners when they go to the Amazon: the search for healing and natural resources. In both cases their (and our) needs are pursued with a classic Western attitude imbued with disrespect, greed, impatience, and ignorance.

---

[48] Guerra, Ciro. *Embrace Of The Serpent*, DVD, 2016, Brooklyn, Oscilloscope Pictures.

The jungle is a very powerful yet delicate environment and ecosystem where all beings, plant, human, and animal alike, thrive thanks to their harmonious symbiosis. The movie depicts the many mistakes these two Westerners make as they enter this unknown environment because of their lack of respect, humility, and wisdom.

The first lesson these two men need to learn in order to continue their journeys is that they are travelling in the jungle with too much baggage, too much stuff. That baggage is an example of our Western attachment to things and objects, and is a good metaphor of our attachment to the physical and the material, which often ends up slowing down our spiritual journey. The other aspect of such baggage is the mental and cultural baggage we bring with ourselves wherever we go, among which is our belief that we know better than and are intellectually superior to others. Both men are repeatedly invited to let go of such baggage, their technologies, and their mindset, so that they can connect and learn from the jungle directly and without mental constructs that, as valid as they may be back at home, are now rather useless. In order to learn any student is required to be humble and have an open mind, but this movie shows us that even these two men of science are not in the Amazon to learn but to *get something* out of it, and how the pursuit of our appetites and needs make us blind and disrespectful of everything else, even to the point of endangering our own lives.

People of European descent have held this dangerous and aggressive attitude towards foreign lands and people since modern Western colonialism began in the 16th century. Even though colonialism as such is a thing of the past, it has been replaced by so-called free trade agreements where Western countries still have the upper hand. The most insidious aspect of colonialism, which is about objectifying and exploiting people and natural resources, is unfortunately still quite alive today. It is so pervasive that it even colors our attitude towards native cultures, religions, and spirituality.

In *Embrace Of The Serpent* neither of our two white characters can dream: they are so in their minds that the vast realms of the unconscious, of archetypes, and myth are totally unavailable to them: despite their technological superiority and money they are perceived as hungry ghosts, barely alive, and asleep. They roam the jungle like hungry ghosts looking for something to assuage their hunger, spiritual and physical, but they do so without respecting the ancestral laws of the jungle over and over again, stubbornly holding on to the very cultural and psychological predicament that is the cause of their hunger. And in their stubbornness they bring death and devastation wherever they go, spreading their spiritual disease instead of healing it. In the end Theodor Martius dies in the jungle and Richard Evans Schultes is forced to let go of his agenda and expectations altogether in order to receive the real gift that the jungle has to offer him and his people.

In the movie it is said that sacred plants (and all plants are sacred in the jungle) are in the Amazonian tradition not to be cultivated, meaning that they are not to be exploited and traded in the way we Westerners think; and that the way to connect with them and receive from them is a matter not of money or convenience, but of being spiritually and psychologically ready. That spiritual and psychological maturity will ensure that those gifts end up not being traded and benefitted from for selfish empowerment, but shared for the benefit of all.

So what are the important lessons for us all that history and this movie offer to us? The most important lesson for me is about letting go, whenever we engage with another culture and are visiting another place, of our Western materialism and utilitarianism, which make us perceive everything as a commodity to own rather than honor.

In regards to ancestral plant medicines such as San Pedro and Ayahuasca what I have seen happening is an increasing attitude of manipulation and distortion of the use and purpose of these medicines by foreigners both here in South America and elsewhere. A symptom of such manipulation and distortion is clear in the lassitude towards dietary and behavioral restrictions, and in the mixing and matching of medicines and processes in order to speed up the process or avoid certain aspects thereof. An example of this is the increased popularity among foreigners of Rapé, an Amazonian sacred snuff used as a ceremonial cleanser and medicine: foreigners all over the world can be seen nowadays using this medicine outside of ceremony and administering it to themselves and others without the guidance of someone truly knowledgeable, and they often use it in plant medicine ceremonies in order to speed up the purging process so as to avoid the unpleasantness of nausea. The first case speaks of our arrogance in insisting upon using medicines and spiritual tools without the proper training and often distorting their use; the second scenario speaks of our unwillingness to honor ancestral ways that have been developed over millennia and of our determination to use these medicines in any way we wish in order to avoid whatever aspect of the healing process we deem unpleasant or time-consuming. Once again we exercise a kind of cultural colonialism that is not only disrespectful but also potentially very dangerous, and in so doing we often fail to receive the very healing we say we seek.

I believe in constant evolution and I am not against change and progress, but I honestly don't see how people without extensive knowledge and experience with these medicines can beneficially change ancestral methodologies from one day to the next. This is not in my opinion evolution but manipulation, and a manipulation that distorts something very precious and valuable as it is. If we don't refrain from our colonialist and consumerist attitude, we risk destroying yet another important part of our human cultural heritage, not to mention the diluting and lessening of power of ancestral medicines. The best way to avoid such negative repercussions is to resist the urge to improve upon what other cultures and people have been doing for so long in the name of effectiveness and progress, and as if we really knew any better, and approach them instead with respect, humility, and patience. Plant medicine is not for everybody, meaning also that if we are not willing to honor this process and its ways, then it would be better for our own sake and health not to engage in it at all.

Moving through and beyond our Western paradigm of ego-centered consumerism and appropriation is in itself part of the healing that we seek as individuals and as a collective, and in my opinion the only way to receive the real gifts that these ancestral medicines and cultures have to offer us as modern people, just like it happened to our fictionalized Richard Evans Schultes at the end of *Embrace Of The Serpent*.

APPENDIX III

SUSTAINING A CULTURE OF SAFETY AND AWARENESS IN PLANT MEDICINE

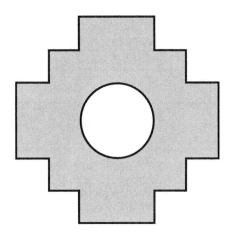

The increased popularity and use of San Pedro and other plant medicines worldwide, despite their illegal status in many countries, entails a necessary raise of awareness towards safety. I say "necessary" because the rising numbers of people engaging in this process makes what used to be an under-the-radar phenomenon a matter of public health and safety. In some countries plant medicines are tolerated despite their illegal status, but that tolerance may quickly disappear and be replaced with repression should people die or end up in psychiatric wards in significant numbers.

The illegality of these medicines makes them also unregulated and not subject to any quality control whatsoever, which in my opinion means that it is up to all of us to exercise discernment whenever we engage with them, at home and abroad, if we wish to avoid any future repressive governmental reaction. I feel this is a wonderful opportunity for us all to take responsibility for our own lives and health, and I believe it is possible to sustain a culture of safety in regards to plant medicines.

Taking personal responsibility each and every time we engage in this process will have the immediate and welcome result of lessening the amount of useless gossip and judging in medicine circles: whenever we take responsibility for our choice of ceremonies and plant medicine people, then any complaint and judgment appear in all their ludicrousness. The awareness that we get exactly what we sign up for and that what we sign up for is not necessarily what we want but what we need, opens the space for a true ownership of our judgments and projections, thus furthering the healing process.

I have seen and heard over the years how the deflecting of responsibility, by expecting some sorts of unspoken and unwritten quality standard to be present whenever and wherever we choose to engage in this process, or through some naïve assumption that plant medicine circles and their members are somehow exempt from human imperfections and flaws, has not really helped improve the quality of the plant medicine world in any way. Perhaps then it is time to let go of such expectations and assumptions of others, and take greater care whenever we choose a ceremony or retreat.

For this purpose I offer here a series of questions, one for yourself and the other for the prospective ceremony leader or host, that may help you better assess whether this or that experience meets your needs for safety and support. The biggest challenge around making the right choice for ourselves is that too often we are quick to dismiss our gut feelings and just go ahead and pursue what we want despite some clear signs that point in the opposite direction. Over the years I have become increasingly discerning about where, when, and with whom I engage in this process: as limiting of choices as my discernment may be, I am very happy to exercise such discernment each and every time, even at the cost of foregoing some very interesting and alluring experiences. I exercise the same care that I would in the case of choosing a dentist or surgeon, and why wouldn't I since this is about my physical, emotional, mental, and spiritual health? And whenever I am in doubt I simply say no and stay home. Getting out of our comfort zone is one thing, and foolish risk-taking is another thing altogether.

These questionnaires are based on a list of questions created by Michael Costuros of Entrepreneurs Awakening[49] when he started bringing groups of entrepreneurs to work with me and plant medicines

---

[49] http://www.EntrepreneursAwakening.com/

here in Peru. Michael's focus on quality and safety for the people who join his retreats is exemplary but not the norm in the world of plant medicine. The creation of such questionnaires has been his way to make prospective participants more aware and more actively engaged in making sure that they make the best choice for themselves. If we approach this process with greater responsibility, discernment, clarity, and honesty, we can continue to sustain a level of health and safety in our medicine circles that will benefit not only ourselves and our communities, but the collective consciousness as well.

Questions for Oneself Before Signing Up for a Ceremony or Retreat

- What is my general state of health? Do I feel physically fit enough to experience a possibly challenging healing experience?

- What are the medications and supplements, prescription and non-prescription alike, that I have been taking recently? Are any of them contraindicated in the case of ingesting San Pedro?

- Have I had any surgeries in the previous six months that may require some more healing before I engage with plant medicines again?

- What has been my consumption of recreational drugs, alcohol, and caffeine (including chocolate) recently? Am I willing to abstain from all of them before, during and after the medicine process as required by my host?

- Do I have a history of depression, bouts of paranoia, or mental breakdowns that indicate that I am not psychologically ready to engage in this process? Am I open to discuss any such trouble with the host before they agree to allow my participation?

- In the case of a single ceremony, am I willing and can I set aside a minimum of 12 hours before AND after the ceremony without social, personal, and professional commitments of any kind so that I can mentally and emotionally prepare for the ceremony and have a minimum of time afterwards to begin integrating it with ease?

- Am I willing to be off-line and off the phone for the entire duration of the ceremony and possibly a few hours before and after?

- What are the reasons for my wish to join this ceremony or retreat? (You may want to take some time and even pen and paper to list all the reasons and then see whether these are good enough to sign up or not. For instance you may find that one important reason for joining a ceremony is that you are a little bored or lonely. If that were the case you may want to invite your friends over for dinner instead.)

- What do I hope to receive from this experience? (If you realize that what you are seeking can be easily found in other ways, then I would forego the medicine approach.)

- What is my support network for after the ceremony/retreat?

- In the case of joining a group I have joined in the past, is there any ongoing dissatisfaction about such group? Are there any unmet needs that are important for me to talk about with the group, host, or ceremony leader before I join them again? Are there any projections that would benefit from some exploration before signing up?

- Do I feel that such community is still the best place for me to engage in this process, or is it time for me to find another?

QUESTIONS FOR THE HOST AND/OR THE CEREMONY LEADER BEFORE SIGNING UP FOR A CEREMONY OR RETREAT

- What is the size of the ceremony or retreat group? (I believe that if someone is looking for healing and is in need of support, no ceremony or retreat with more than 20 participants can realistically provide such level of support, and would therefore refrain from joining them.)

- What are the facilities and services offered? (These include overnight lodging, bathrooms, and transportation)

- What is the monetary or energetic exchange required?

- Who are the people leading and assisting the ceremonies? How long have they been offering ceremonies? What has been their training? What tradition did they apprentice in and for how long, and what tradition are they following now? Do they have a teacher they have learnt from and who has given them the permission to lead public ceremonies with this medicine?

- Where does the medicine offered come from? Has the medicine been harvested in sustainable ways? How does the community where the medicine comes from actually benefit from this exchange?

- In the case of people leading the ceremonies who speak a different language than ours, will there be a sober interpreter at all times during the facilitators' visit?

- When is the medicine person arriving at the site of the ceremony? And how long are they staying after the closing of the ceremony? (I feel it is most important to be able to talk to the medicine person before and after the ceremony if one feels the need. Ideally the medicine person would be available until noon the day after the ceremony in order to address whatever question or need.)

- What kind of preparatory information and guidance is provided before the ceremonies?

- What kind of support in regards to integration after the ceremonies is offered?

- What is the screening process on the part of the host like? Does the host meet personally with each participant?

- What kinds of songs are sung during ceremony?

- What kind of support and healing is provided to every participant during the ceremony or retreat?

ENDINGS

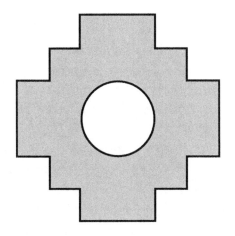

EPILOGUE

A ldous Huxley was fond of quoting William Blake's words, "Gratitude is Heaven itself"[50], and I think of no better way to end this book than by thanking everybody who has supported me in writing it.

First of all I want to thank the Spirit of San Pedro for guiding and giving me the strength to write this book— my only hope is to have listened and followed his advice well. And I want to thank you, reader of this book, for giving me the opportunity to write this book and thus deepen my connection with this important medicine.

My deepest thanks to Don Francisco Montes Shuña of Sachamama Ethnobotanical Garden in Iquitos for being such a gifted, generous, and wise teacher in the realm of Amazonian plant medicine and spirituality, and all the spiritual Teachers who keep guiding me on my path.

Thank you to all the plant medicine people I have had the honor to work with and learn from here in Peru: Jose' and Rony in Pucallpa, Leoncio Garcia, Kevin Furnas, Fredy "Puma" Quispe Singona, Lesley Myburgh, Miguel Mendiburu, and Luz Maria Ampuero, who has beautifully assisted me in all my San Pedro retreats this far[51].

Thank you to Harry Chavez in Caraz for his beautiful and inspiring art; to David Sylvian, whose music has accompanied my life journey for years and whose lyrics inspired the title of this book; and to everybody in my life for their precious help in bringing this book to completion, in particular Jesse Krieger and everybody at Lifestyle Entrepreneurs Press.

---

[50] Huxley, Aldous. *Moksha*. Rochester, Park Street Press, 1977.
[51] Luz Maria Ampuero can be contacted through www.nunaayni.org

Thank you to Diane Dunn and everybody at Paz Y Luz Healing Center in Pisac for their support of my work over the years.

Thank you to my parents, Luisa and Ignacio, to Jeff Rose and his deceased parents, Connie and Perry, without whose generosity the Ayaruna Center and this book might never have seen the light of day, and to my extended family of friends for their love, generosity of heart, and unconditional support.

Thank you to all the people who have supported my work all these years, and to all the people who have sat in ceremony and shared their beautiful energies with me: you have been the sweetest of medicines and best of teachers!

And finally, thanks once again to you, dear reader, for reading this book—may this be the beginning of wonderful new adventures in the sweetness of your hearts.

Pisac, Peru. February 24, 2017

BIBLIOGRAPHY (WORKS CITED)

A Course in Miracles. Wisconsin Dells, A Course in Miracles International, 2007. **Print.**

Bourbeau, Lise. *Heal Your Wounds and Find Your True Self*. Saint-Jerome, Editions E.T.C., 2001. **Print.**

Box, Ben and Steve Frankham. *Cusco & the Inca Heartland*. 4th edition. Bath, FootPrint, 2008. **Print.**

Cronenberg, David. *A Dangerous Method*. Culver City, Sony Pictures Classics, 2011. **Film.**

de St. Exupéry, Antoine. *Le Petit Prince*. Paris, Gallimard, 1999. **Print.**

Fromm, Erich. *The Art of Loving*. New York, HarperCollins Publishers, 2000. **Print.**

Furst, Dan. *Aquarius Surfing*. San Francisco, Weiser Books, 2011. **Print.**

Huxley, Aldous. *Moksha*. Rochester, Park Street Press, 1977. **Print.**

Jaxon-Bear, Eli. *From Fixation to Freedom: The Enneagram of Liberation*. 3rd Printing. Ashland, Leela Foundation, 2006. **Print.**

Kalschein, Donald. *The Inner World of Trauma*. London, Routledge, 1998. **Print.**

Kerr, John. *A Most Dangerous Method*. New York, Vintage Books, 1997. **Print.**

Ladinsky, Daniel, trans. *Love Poems from God*. New York, Penguin Compass, 2002. **Print.**

Naranjo, Claudio. *Character and Neurosis*. Nevada City, Gateways Inc., 1994. **Print.**

Regueiro, Javier. *Ayahuasca, Soul Medicine of the Amazon Jungle*. Las Vegas, Lifestyle Entrepreneurs Press, 2017. **Print.**

Robbins, Tom. *Fierce Invalids Home from Hot Climates*. New York, Bantam Books, 2000. **Print.**

Rosenberg, Michael B. *Nonviolent Communication*. Encinitas, PuddleDancer Press, 2015. **Print.**

Wachowski Brothers. *The Matrix*. Burbank, Warner Home Video, 1999. **Film.**

Watts, Alan. *The Way of Zen*. New York, Vintage Books, 1989. **Print.**

Williamson, Marianne. *A Return to Love*. New York, HarperOne, 1992. **Print.**

URL INDEX

Ampuero, Luz Maria: www.nunaayni.org

Chavez, Harry: https://www.facebook.com/harry.chavez

Costuros, Michael: www.entrepreneursawakening.com

Dunn, Diane: www.dianedunn.net

Fletcher, Melody: www.deliberatereceiving.com

Kramer, Joseph. *Heartful Erotic Touch*: www.eroticmassage.com and *Heartful Erotic Practice*: www.orgasmicyoga.com

Laskey, Holly: https://www.facebook.com/AncestralHighlands/

Mendiburu, Miguel: www.allpamamajourney.com

Regueiro, Javier: www.ayaruna.com

RECOMMENDED READING

Davis, Wade. *One River*. New York, Touchstone, 1997. **Print**.

Dunn, Diane. *Cusco II – The Magic of the Munay-Ki*. Charlestone, CreateSpace, 2012. **Print**.

Fromm, Erich. *The Art of Loving*. New York, HarperCollins, 2000. **Print**.

Huxley, Aldous. *The Doors of Perception* and *Heaven and Hell*. New York, HarperCollins,1954. **Print**.

Jaxon-Bear, Eli. *From Fixation to Freedom: The Enneagram of Liberation*. 3rd Printing. Ashland, Leela Foundation, 2006. **Print**.

McKenna, Terence. *Food of The Gods*. New York, Bantam Books, 1992. **Print**.

--. *The Archaic Revival*. New York, HarperSanFrancisco, 1991. **Print**.

Watts, Alan. *The Joyous Cosmology*. New York, Vintage Books, 1965. **Print**.

ABOUT THE AUTHOR AND THE COVER ARTIST

Javier Regueiro is a Spanish national, born and raised in Lugano, Switzerland. He is a certified Massage Therapist, Rebirther, and Avatar© Master.

He moved to Peru in 2004 to study Amazonian plant medicine and shamanism, and has apprenticed with various teachers in the Iquitos and Pucallpa areas. He has undergone several months of shamanic diets, learning the use and healing properties of plant teachers such as Ayahuasca, Tobacco and Datura among others, and has become a full-time plant medicine person since. His commitment is to make San Pedro and Ayahuasca available to all people who feel called to respectfully use these medicines for personal healing, spiritual guidance, and the evolution of consciousness, He lives in Pisac, Peru, where he has created the Ayaruna Center, and conducts his healing work with traditional Peruvian plant medicines. He can be contacted through the website www.ayaruna.com

Harry Chavez (Lima, 1978) is a graduate of the Pontificia Universidad Catolica of Peru, and has studied Korean art and culture at Dankook University, South Korea. His work integrates the wisdom and iconography of ancient cultures, with particular emphasis on the Peruvian Andean and Amazonian worldview. Making a powerful synthesis of this knowledge with a unique technique, he proposes a lively, contemporary mythology.

He has had solo exhibitions in Lima, Iquitos and Cusco and participated in various group exhibitions in Peru, Argentina, Chile, Bolivia and Spain.

He can be contacted at https://www.facebook.com/harry.chavez.

298

Printed in Great Britain
by Amazon

25387638R00175